Africa in the Iron Age

Africa in the Iron Age

c. 500 B.C. to A.D. 1400

ROLAND OLIVER
Professor of African History in the University of London

BRIAN M. FAGAN
Professor of Anthropology, University of California, Santa Barbara

CAMBRIDGE UNIVERSITY PRESS

CAMBRIDGE
LONDON · NEW YORK · MELBOURNE

Published by the Syndics of the Cambridge University Press
The Pitt Building, Trumpington Street, Cambridge CB2 1RP
Bentley House, 200 Euston Road, London NW1 2DB
32 East 57th Street, New York, NY 10022, USA
296 Beaconsfield Parade, Middle Park, Melbourne 3206, Australia

© Cambridge University Press 1975

First published 1975

Photoset and printed in Malta by St Paul's Press Ltd

Library of Congress Cataloguing in Publication Data

Oliver, Roland Anthony.
   Africa in the Iron Age, c. 500 B.C. to A.D. 1400

   Bibliography: p. 215.
   Includes index.
   1. Iron age – Africa.   2. Africa – Antiquities.   3. Africa – History.
   I. Fagan, Brian M., joint author.   II. Title.
GN780.4.A1044   960   74-25639
ISBN 0 521 20598 0 hard covers
ISBN 0 521 09900 5 paperback

Contents

List of figures

Preface

This book is first of all the fruit of a good friendship, which began within sound of the Victoria Falls in July 1960. In that year the *Journal of African History* was founded, as a vehicle for the publication of new research in African history and archaeology from the beginning of the Iron Age until the present day. One of us was for fourteen years an editor of the journal. The other was a frequent contributor and a constant advisor. Since then, we have maintained a regular correspondence, and we have met not only after the fashion of the wandering scholars of the twentieth century, at conferences in Europe and Africa and North America, but at archaeological sites and in each other's homes. We are acutely conscious of the vast dimensions in time and space of the subject we have tried to tackle, as well as of the necessarily narrow limits of our own first-hand experience of the evidence. For all that, our mutual understanding has given us courage, if not confidence. Every chapter, every paragraph, and almost every sentence in this book has been written twice, if not more often. We have at least tried each to meet the scruples of the other, and we hope that the result will reflect in some measure a real encounter of two disciplines in their approach to the African past.

We wish to express our thanks to Dr Michael Bisson, Dr Michael Brett, Dr Humphrey Fisher, Dr John Sutton and Professor Jan Vansina, all of whom have read parts of this book in manuscript and have made valuable suggestions for its improvement.

1 Northern Africa at the end of the Bronze Age

In Africa the Iron Age has a special significance. Over most of the continent there was no preceding Age of Bronze. In most of Africa iron was the first metal to be worked into tools by man. In most of Africa iron tools replaced tools of stone, and in much of the continent these stone tools were not even those of the more advanced, ground and polished kind made by Stone Age farmers. In nearly half of Africa iron tools and weapons replaced stone tools of the kind used by men who were still hunters, gatherers and fishermen rather than farmers and stock-breeders. In most of Africa south of the Equator the coming of the Iron Age marked also the beginning of deliberate food production. In much of Sudanic Africa, between the Sahara and the Equator, Stone Age food production was, so far as we know, a sparse and fragile development, spanning little more than a thousand years before the coming of iron. Only in the northern third of Africa, in Saharan and Mediterranean latitudes, did cereal production and stock-raising spread in the fifth and fourth millennia B.C., at a period comparable with their dispersal through western Asia and southern Europe. And only in these latitudes was a period of Stone Age agriculture succeeded by a well-defined Age of Bronze. Taking the continent as a whole, the ten thousand years before Christ were those in which Africa slept. In the Iron Age it began to re-awake, although the process took a thousand years to spread from one end of Africa to the other.

Though taking its title from the Iron Age, this book is not so much concerned with a particular technological revolution as with a period in African history – a period which runs from about 500 B.C. until about A.D. 1400. Although literary sources are not wanting, particularly for the northern third of the continent, this is a period the evidence for which is dominated by what is usually called Iron Age archaeology. This is not a separate science, but a field of specialisation. The techniques of archaeological excavation and analysis are basically the same for the Iron Age as for any other period. The Iron Age archaeologist is simply one who concentrates his energies on the more recent end of the time spectrum, giving the detailed attention to the comparatively small chronological differences which that involves. For Iron Age archaeology in Africa the crucial development has been the technique of radiocarbon analysis, which enables even simple, unstratified sites to be dated, with a high probability of success, within the margin of error of about 200 years. At a distance of 2500 years from the present, such a standard of measurement is good enough for most purposes. At a distance of 1000 years it is by no means valueless. At a distance of 600 years one is approaching the threshold where, in most parts of Africa, other kinds of evidence become more useful. By A.D. 1400 literacy had crossed the Sahara to the Sudanic belt, and had crept down the East Coast to the Zambezi. By 1500 it had encircled the remaining coasts of Africa, and much of the information then recorded has some backward reference. The first whispers of the oral traditions of African peoples, recorded in more recent times, stretch back to about the same period.

By 500 B.C., when our story begins, the climate of Africa had assumed something like its modern pattern. First and foremost this

FIG. 1.   Language families of Africa (simplified).

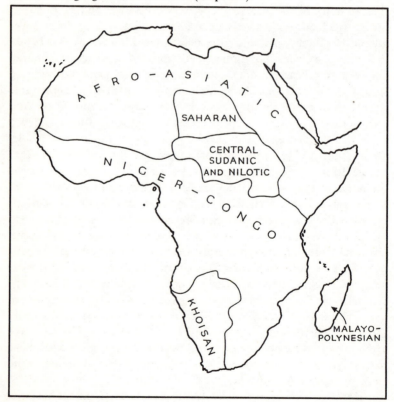

2

meant that the Sahara, much of which from about 5500 B.C. till about 2500 B.C. had been open parkland, readily inhabitable by hunters and stock-breeders, and even in part by cultivators, was now once more a desert, almost devoid of game and fish, affording only seasonal pasture to the transhumants who moved in and out of it from bases along its edges, and dividing absolutely the settled populations to the north and the south. In general, the settled peoples to the north and east of the desert were of Afro-Mediterranean or Caucasian stock, speaking languages of the Afro-Asiatic family – ancient Egyptian, Berber, Chadic, Cushitic. Those to the south were Negroes, speaking languages of the Niger–Congo, Saharan, Central Sudanic and Nilotic (including Paranilotic) families. For most of its course, the frontier between Afro-Asiatic and Negro languages followed the southern edge of the desert; but east of the Nile Afro-Asiatic languages made a great loop to the southward, encompassing much of the Ethiopian and East African highlands. It was in the lands of the Afro-Asiatic speakers that the history of food production was the longest. It was among them that the later stone industries could most generally be described as neolithic. It was among some of these peoples that copper and bronze had come to the aid of stone.

The most important and the most numerous of the Afro-Asiatic speaking peoples were, of course, those who lived in the Nile delta and along the thin green ribbon, seldom more than ten miles wide, of the great river valley. By 500 B.C. the glory of ancient Egypt had long departed. The proud kingdom of the Pharoahs, which had dominated the Near East for more than two thousand years, was now a Persian satrapy. Its agricultural surplus supported a foreign army of occupation, and its manufactures were sold to enrich an Asian capital. Egyptian youths were drafted to serve on distant frontiers, and to dig the great canal from the Nile to the Gulf of Suez, intended to carry the intercontinental trade of the Persian overlord. Nevertheless, even a subjugated Egypt was by far the most significant corner of Africa. To Herodotus, surveying the known world from the vantage-point of mid-fifth-century Athens, there was nowhere with 'so many marvellous things, nor in the whole world beside are there to be seen so many works of unspeakable greatness'. About the main reason for this greatness, Herodotus was in no doubt:

Now, indeed, there are no men, neither in the rest of Egypt, nor in the whole world, who get in their produce with so little labour; they have not the toil of ploughing up their land into furrows, nor of hoeing, nor of any other work which other men do to get them a crop; the river rises of itself, waters the 3 fields, and then sinks back again; thereupon each man sows his field and sends swine into it to tread down the seed, and waits for the harvest; then he makes the swine to thresh his grain, and so garners it.[1]

Though the whole of habitable Egypt could be traversed from end to end in little more than fifteen days of river travel, Herodotus was told that on the eve of the Persian conquest in 525 B.C., when Egypt 'attained to its greatest prosperity, in respect of what the river did for the land and the land for its people', there were twenty thousand inhabited towns in the delta and strung out along the valley's edge. It is obvious that Herodotus looked up to the Egyptians, even under Persian rule, as the most civilised and cleanly, and certainly as the most religious of mankind. He reported that seven hundred thousand people gathered annually at Busiris in the delta for the great festival of Osiris. No doubt this was an exaggeration; but with a population of perhaps five million crowded into a habitable area the size of Belgium, it is clear that the Egypt of 2500 years ago was as urbanised as most modern industrial societies.

Even granting the unique opportunities offered to Egypt by the Nile flood, it is at first sight astonishing that one small corner of Africa should have progressed so immeasurably beyond the rest. There is no doubt that, physically, the Egyptians were Africans, in the sense that their Afro-Asiatic stock had been present in Africa for at least ten thousand years before Christ. And certainly to comparative students of the Bronze Age it is clear that dynastic Egypt had an African culture and a sense of values quite different from anything found in the eastern European and western Asian Bronze Age world to the north. Yet the predominant factor was the ecological one, that to the east and the west Egypt was surrounded by deserts habitable only very sparsely by hunters and pastoralists, whereas to the south lay a frontier hardly less formidable, in the climate of the Sudanic belt, with its uniform hours of daylight and its pattern of summer rainfall. Wheat and barley, the staples of the food-producing revolution in Egypt, could not grow in the Sudan. Therefore, although Egyptian miners, hunters and traders had been penetrating the Sudan since the earliest dynastic times, the growth of a significant agricultural population there was necessarily delayed until the successful ennoblement of cereals such as the millets and sorghums from the wild ancestral grasses that grew in these latitudes.

Thus, although the Egyptians had been pushing their religious and political influence southwards into the cataract region of Nubia from

[1] Herodotus, *History*, Book II, Ch. 14. Tr. A. D. Godley, Loeb Classical Library.

the early second millennium onwards, it was not until a thousand years later that there emerged a culturally Egyptianised kingdom of Kush, with its capital at Napata near the fourth cataract, of the size and strength to be independent of even a decadent Egypt. For a brief period, from 750 until 664 B.C., the kings of Kush conquered and ruled Egypt as the XXV Dynasty of Pharoahs. Driven out by the Assyrians under Ashurbannipal, the dynasty retreated to Napata, where neither the Assyrians nor the Persians ever followed them. By the middle of the sixth century they had shifted their headquarters still further southwards to Meroe, situated in the well-watered triangle above the confluence of the Nile and the Atbara. Here at last was a growing-

FIG. 2.   The Nile valley: localities and sites mentioned in the text.

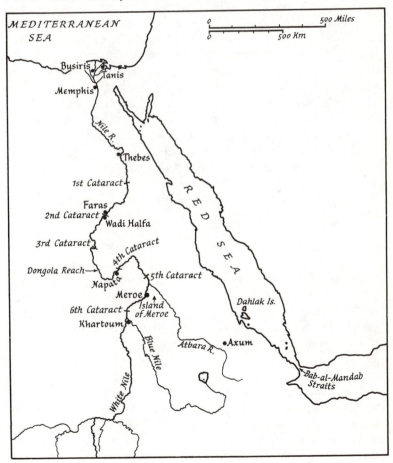

5

point of Egypt-inspired civilisation, statecraft and religion, which had emerged to the south of the ecological barrier, in the land of the summer rains. We do not yet know exactly what languages were spoken in the Meroitic kingdom, nor even how the central Meroitic tongue itself should be classified; but it seems likely that the population was composed at least as much of Negro elements as of Afro-Asiatic ones.

The Meroitic state was based, like that of Egypt, on the Nile. The central population of Meroe consisted of the settled, farming and fishing communities of the more open stretches of the river valley, such as the Dongola reach between the third and fourth cataracts, the island of Meroe between the fifth and sixth cataracts, and the lower valley of the Blue Nile. Here, and especially in the central 'island', the narrow strip of alluvial flood-plain was backed by wooded savanna with plentiful grass, watered by occasional floods as well as by annual rains. Cattle and other stock were relatively more important than in Egypt, and in the rainy season herders no doubt wandered far from their riverine bases. Where the Egyptians grew wheat and barley, the Meroites grew millet. Where the Egyptians grew flax and wove linen, the Meroites used cotton. Like the Egyptians, their nobles bred horses and used them both for riding and for driving in light, swift chariots. Unlike the Egyptians, who had little iron ore and even less fuel with which to smelt it, the island of Meroe was rich in both commodities, and the arts of iron-working, stimulated no doubt by the victories of the Assyrians with their iron weapons, were practised to some extent from the occupation of Meroe onwards.

It is abundantly clear that both the international standing and the urban wealth of Meroe came from its hunting, mining and trading activities in connection with the traditional luxury commodities of inner Africa, ivory, slaves, rare skins, ostrich feathers, gold, copper and ebony. Throughout early African history, the hunting of elephants for their ivory was apt to be an almost military operation, involving not merely the slaughter of large and dangerous animals but the protection of rich caravans travelling through alien country. Slave-catching, too, is a military activity, the success of which depends on removing the victims to a distance from which escape is a hopeless risk. We may suppose, therefore, that the armed hunters and horsemen of Meroe ranged even further afield than her transhumant pastoralists, and that they contacted barter networks extending deep into the Ethiopian highlands on one side and far across the sub-Saharan savanna on the other. Both the Nile and the Red Sea provided routes for Meroe's trade with the civilised world, which now included not only the Mediterranean lands but, increasingly, eastern countries, the south Arabian states, Persia and India.

Indeed, it was developments in Mesopotamia and Persia, even more than those in Egypt, which were ultimately responsible for awakening the Horn of Africa and bringing it into the age of metals. The main Stone Age populations of all this region, stretching from the Red Sea far down into East Africa, had been Afro-Asiatics speaking languages of the southernmost Afro-Asiatic sub-family called Cushitic. Some of them, at least, had become Stone Age food producers by the early part of the first millennium B.C. The introduction of metals, however, came only in the fifth century B.C., with the migration across the Red Sea of Bronze Age settlers from southern Arabia. These people are known to us from the inscriptions written in the Sabaean language found at sites on the Red Sea coast between the Dahlak Islands and the Bab-al-Mandab straits. The pioneers were hunters and traders, seeking ivory and slaves for the great intercontinental trade route then being developed by the Persians in the Red Sea and the Indian Ocean. Soon, however, Bronze Age agricultural colonists were pressing into the delectable highlands of Tigre and Amhara, bringing with them the Semitic speech of south-west Arabia, and building up on the Ethiopian plateau a pocket of dense population, from which the powerful state of Axum would one day emerge to conquer and supersede the kingdom of Meroe.

West of the Nile, in North African and Saharan latitudes, the main indigenous populations of neolithic and Bronze Age times were the Berbers, their languages representing the western sub-family of Afro-Asiatic. These are the Libyans of classical literature, and from the time of Herodotus onwards references to them are frequent. From the edge of the Nile valley to the western corner of the Gulf of Sirte nearly all of them were still at this time pastoralists, moving between the coastlands and the edges of the desert according to the seasons. In the Tunisian plains, however, and between the Atlas and the sea, there were already in Herodotus' time some settled communities of agricultural Berbers tilling the fertile soils of the river valleys and the coastal plain, and looking with the wary eye of the possessor at the warlike propensities of the nomads to the south of them.

The other inhabitants of North Africa were, as Herodotus remarked, the newcomers, the Phoenicians and the Greeks. The Egyptians, lacking any large timber for shipbuilding, had always been indifferent mariners. For their trading contacts across the Mediterranean they had relied much upon the coastal peoples of the Lebanon, Syria and Palestine. The Phoenicians were the most active merchants of the Bronze Age Mediterranean. From prosperous homelands in Syria, they dominated the trade of the Levant and the Red Sea. With the decline of the Minoans and the Mycenaeans late in the second

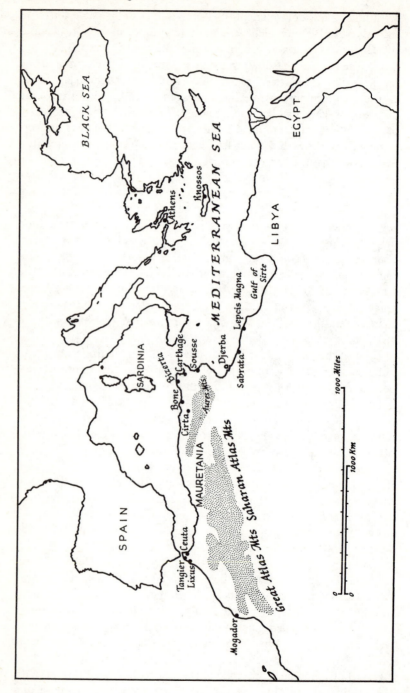

millennium, the Phoenicians began to venture into the western Mediterranean in search of the copper, silver, lead and iron of Spain and southern Sardinia. By the middle of the first millennium B.C., when the eastern Mediterranean was passing into the power of the Persians and the Greeks, the Phoenician trading posts in the west, especially Carthage on the site of modern Tunis, were growing into true colonies, based around manufacturing cities and surrounded each by its own agricultural territory under Phoenician rule. On the Tripolitanian coast were Sabrata and Lepcis Magna; in Tunisia, besides Carthage, there were cities at Djerba, Sousse and Bizerta; in Algeria were Bone and Cirta; in Morocco, Ceuta, Tangier, Lixus and Mogador. From Carthage and from Spain, further maritime networks extended into the Atlantic, northwards to reach the tin of Brittany and Cornwall, and southwards down the coast of Morocco in search of West African gold. A trading-post at Mogador is archaeologically attested. The invariable pattern of strong north-easterly winds blowing from the Sahara makes it almost certain that no ancient voyages passed beyond Cape Juby.

The influence of the Carthaginians touched the Berber populations of north-west Africa in many ways, and indirectly it reached across the desert into the heart of black Africa. Carthage itself had a profound effect on its own surrounding territory. Bronze Age agricultural techniques turned north-eastern Tunisia into a fertile granary, worked by large labour forces of Berber tribesmen. Independent Berber nomads settled near the Phoenician colonies, acquiring new agricultural methods and assimilating some of the benefits of the new culture. By the time of Carthage's decline some Berber chieftains had founded settled agricultural kingdoms around the edges of the Tunisian plain. The Phoenician language, Punic, became the common language of trade, administration and urban life. Its alphabetic script was even applied to writing Berber languages, and still survives in the Tifinag script of the Tuareg of the central Sahara. By the time of Herodotus, the Phoenician cities were trading extensively with the Berbers of the Sahara, bartering cloth and beads and metal goods for ivory, gold and slaves from south of the desert. The Berbers brought black African commodities across the Sahara, no doubt using Carthaginian beads and trinkets to augment an already existing trade in Saharan salt for West African gold. Herodotus reports that the Berber Garamantes of the Fezzan had four-horse chariots 'in which they chase the troglodite Ethiopians'. This is presumably an early reference to slave-raiding practised by the Berbers against the Negroes then living in the Hoggar and Tibesti massifs of the central Sahara. The horse is well authenticated in Bronze Age Libya, and the chariots were of a light two-wheeled variety, well known in Asia Minor during the first millennium B.C. Again, Herodotus tells of a journey made by some young Libyans, who had crossed the desert to a wooded country on its southern side, where they had been captured by small black men, by whose town there flowed a great river, running from west to east and full of crocodiles. This suggests the Niger, and this supposition has been confirmed by the discovery of numerous rock drawings of horse-drawn chariots in the Sahara. These are clustered along two main routes, still used by desert caravans and motor traffic, one passing over the Hoggar and along the ridge of the Adrar of the Ifoghas running south-west-wards to the Niger bend, and the other passing to the west of the main desert area, through inland Mauritania towards the upper Senegal. It is known that wheeled vehicles were superseded by camels in the central and western Sahara during the early centuries A.D., so that the rock drawings are probably old enough to support the travellers' tales told to Herodotus.

It is clear, then, that by the middle of the first millennium B.C. northern Africa, from Mauritania in the west to Ethiopia in the east, was at the threshold of a new age. Food production had been practised in a few favoured areas for nearly five thousand years. Copper and gold had been worked for three thousand years, bronze and all that went with it for at least a thousand. Iron-working had been discovered in Asia Minor, but it was as yet a very minor element in the African scene. In politics and civilisation Egypt had lost its long and unique predominance. The brilliant art and culture of earlier millennia had faded to a dull stereotype. Nevertheless, a living offshoot of Egyptian civilisation had, at long last, sprung up in the Meroitic Sudan, among people of predominantly Negro stock and in a region where iron was plentiful. Through Meroe, Egypt was able to influence profoundly, though often at tens and hundreds of removes, nearly all the African peoples to the west and the south. Finally, the world to the north and the east of Egypt had matured into the fullness of Bronze Age life, and was making demands upon a far wider stretch of Africa than Egypt had ever contacted during the times of her greatness. Ships were plying the Indian Ocean and the Red Sea, the Mediterranean and even the wild Atlantic. Caravans were crossing the Sahara. Semitic-speaking Bronze Age farmers were irrigating the Tunisian plain and terracing the hillsides of the Ethiopian highlands. Here and there around the fringes of the continent smiths and armourers were experimenting with the new metal which was to revolutionise the life of Africa. The continent was about to join the Iron Age.

FIG. 4.   Limestone stele dedicated to Persephone by Milkyaton the suffete, son of Maharbaal the suffete. From Carthage. Third or second century B.C.

2   Early food production in middle Africa

As we explained in the last chapter, what was the Bronze Age in most of northern Africa corresponded with what was still only the pioneer stage of Stone Age farming in most of middle Africa between the Sahara and the Equator. And the reason for this, as we saw in connection with Egypt and Meroe, was not mainly the difficulty of communication between one side of the Sahara and the other. It was, rather, the ecological barrier that coincided with the region of summer rainfall, which required that tropical substitutes should be found and developed for the staple food plants of the early Eurasian farmers. Even assuming that the *idea* of domestication spread fairly rapidly from north to south, there remained a long process of observation, experiment, selective breeding and local diffusion before the idea could be translated into practice. To a very large extent, the food-producing revolution in the Sudanic belt of Africa was a separate development from its Near Eastern counterpart.

In fact, according to one very well-known hypothesis, that of the American anthropologist G. P. Murdock, the food-producing revolution of the Sudanic belt was not only separate from, but contemporary with, that of the Near East. Murdock's argument is that if the Sudanic cereals, the millets and the sorghums, had not been in course of domestication by about 4500 B.C., they would have been forestalled by wheat and barley coming up the Nile from Egypt. This argument, as we have seen, is based upon a botanical fallacy. Moreover, it is not supported by such evidence as we have from archaeology, all of which at present suggests that hunting, gathering and fishing continued for nearly three thousand years longer than the date postulated by Murdock, and that it was only towards the middle of the second millennium B.C. that food production and the stone tool-kits of early farmers reached the Sudanic belt.

The nearest ancient food-producing sites to the Sudanic belt are those of the Saharan pastoralists, more than a dozen of which have been dated by radiocarbon analysis to the fourth and third millennia B.C., while one or two sites in the western Fezzan have produced even older dates. Most of these sites were discovered by the French archaeologist Henri Lhote, some of them associated with rock paintings, drawings and engravings. They have yielded plentiful bones of domestic cattle and small stock, along with pottery sherds and farming tools, including ground and polished axes, adzes, and stone dishes and platters. The dated sites are mostly from the Tassili-n-Ajjer, the northern foothills of the Hoggar massif, but the tools and the pottery, much of it incised with a characteristic decorative motif called Dotted Wavy Line, have been found at many sites in the Tibesti massif, and also in the sites of settled fishing communities living at a comparable period in the Nile valley at Early Khartoum and in the East African Rift valley.

The rock art of the Saharan pastoralists provides a much fuller

FIG. 5.   Rock painting of a group of cattle, Sefar, Sahara.

picture of their way of life than could be reconstructed by archaeological methods alone. Battle scenes and religious friezes depict elaborate ornaments and weapons, some of which must have been of metal. They show both long- and short-horned cattle, also sheep and goats. There are many hunting scenes, which show that the Sahara was still at this time inhabited by many wild animals, including elephant, hippopotamus, buffalo and many kinds of antelope. It is significant that while some of the hunters and warriors are of Afro-Mediterranean build and colouring, others are black and negroid, suggesting that at this period populations from both sides of the Sahara were meeting and mingling in these latitudes. However, apart from the fishing practised near lakes and perennial streams, it is clear that the way of life depicted by the rock artists was essentially nomadic. At none of the fourth- and third-millennia sites is there any indication that food plants were being deliberately cultivated. There is nothing suggestive of agriculture in the paintings. No carbonised seeds have yet been found, nor any pottery bearing grain impressions.

On present evidence, it is not in fact until the late second millennium B.C. that we have any archaeological proof of cereal cultivation from the southern half of the Sahara. This is from the Dar Tichitt in southern Mauritania, where careful excavations by an American archaeologist, Patrick Munson, have revealed eight separate phases of hunting and farming cultures spanning the thousand years from 1500 to 500 B.C. Cattle and goats occur throughout the cultural sequence. Fish, shellfish and other aquatic resources were collected by the inhabitants of the earlier Tichitt sites, which were associated with lakeshore deposits at the foot of an escarpment. There is also evidence that wild cereals were gathered from the earliest phase onwards.

The villages of the Naghez phase, dating to around 1200 B.C., were located just behind the beaches of the small lakes which still existed at the base of the escarpment. The villages were composed of circular compounds, from 60 to 120 feet in diameter, which were connected with one another by wide paths. Cattle and goats were herded. Gazelle, topi and hares were occasionally taken in the chase. Fishing and plant gathering were important. Grains of wild grasses were found both as plant remains and as impressions on pottery. There may have been some limited cultivation of bulrush millet (*Pennisetum*). Pottery, ground stone axes and gouges were all in use, along with stone arrowheads and grinders. The Naghez villages were fairly large, but were separated from each other by an average distance of twelve miles. The rainfall is estimated to have been about three times the present, permitting the survival of permanent lakes with relatively dense vegetation around their margins.

Sites of the following, Chebka, phase date to about 1000 B.C., and they are found in easily defensible positions at the top of the 900-foot escarpment. While still laid out in compounds, the villages were surrounded by protective walls with fortified entrance gates. Although subsistence was still oriented towards the herding of cattle and goats, fishing was no longer practised, presumably because the lakes in the valley had now dried up. On the other hand, *Pennisetum* was now deliberately cultivated. About half of the total grain consumption now consisted of domesticated varieties, the remainder coming still from wild plants. As time went on, cultivated millet became more and more important, although by the latest, Akanjeir, phase, radiocarbon-dated to between 700 and 300 B.C., there is strong evidence for futher climatic deterioration.

The Tichitt sites thus give us a clear picture of the development of Stone Age farming on the fringes of the desert, where it seems that a fairly dense population once flourished, before increasing desiccation forced people either to modify their economy or else to move on southwards into better-watered country. Although no skeletal remains were discovered, Munson is strongly of opinion that the Tichitt people were negroes. He points out that the villages, though built of masonry, were remarkably similar in layout to the brush and wattle compounds of the northern Mande peoples, such as the Soninke and the Bambara, who now inhabit the savanna country three or four hundred miles to the south. Moreover, the economy and material culture of the Tichitt farmers clearly resembles that of modern West African savanna peoples much more than that of the desert Berbers. These last are indeed most likely to have been those responsible for the preoccupation with defence shown by the later villagers. The Tichitt valley has always been one of the natural lines of communication in the western Sahara, connecting the salt mines of Idjil and the copper mines of Akjoujt in western Mauritania with Walata and the Niger bend. The western line of rock engravings depicting the horse-drawn vehicles of pre-cameline days passes right down the Tichitt valley. It is therefore very probable indeed that the latter days of the Stone Age villages were often disturbed by well-armed caravans from the already copper-using Berber country to the north-west. We do not know when iron first reached this part of West Africa, but certainly no traces of iron-working were found at Tichitt, and it must be assumed that the neolithic farming tradition there had come to an end before iron made its appearance.

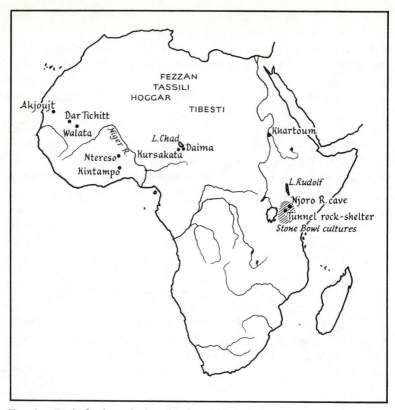

Fig. 6.   Early food-producing sites in middle Africa.

Four hundred miles to the south of Tichitt, and two thousand miles to the east of it, the flood-plain around the southern perimeter of Lake Chad has revealed a number of early farming sites, in the shape of artificial mounds deliberately raised by the inhabitants of the area to protect their villages from the annual inundations. The flood-plain is thought to have been deposited under lagoon conditions around the fifth to the third millennium B.C., when Lake Chad was in the course of shrinking to its present dimensions. The region therefore offers an excellent prospect for obtaining a fairly precisely dated sequence for the emergence of food production in a latitude still well to the north of the West African forest zone. So far only one of these great mounds, that at Daima in the Bornu province of Nigeria, has been thoroughly excavated, by Graham Connah. Another mound settlement, at Kursakata, twenty miles to the west of Daima, has been dug on a small scale, and deserves mention because it has yielded a radiocarbon date around the tenth century B.C. from the bottom of the test cutting. This is some four hundred years earlier than the lowest levels of the Daima mound, and may indicate that occupation of the area by food producers stretches back at least to the late second millennium B.C.

The Daima people built their first village around 600 B.C., first laying down thick deposits of clay in order to raise their huts above flood level. To avoid repeating this preliminary exertion, their successors built and rebuilt on the same site, so that by the time the mound was finally abandoned in the eleventh century A.D. it had risen to a height of thirty-five feet above the surrounding plain. For five or six centuries at least, and perhaps for much longer, the Daima people had no iron tools. They used polished stone axes, stone grinders and querns, as well as a range of tools and projectile-heads of polished bone. Pottery was in use from the first, some of it a fine, red burnished ware with comb or roulette decoration. The dead were buried, in a crouched position, within the settlement. As at Tichitt, the economy seems to have been based on the herding of cattle and small stock. To judge from the querns and grinders, cereal crops were probably cultivated, although archaeologists are generally reluctant to accept these alone as proof positive that edible grain, rather than wild vegetable foods, was being ground.

Pending the accumulation of more evidence, it would seem likely that the people of the Chad flood-plain were, like those of Tichitt, in origin pastoralists, retreating from conditions of increasing desiccation in the desert latitudes into a limited area of better-watered country, where they had to practice more intensive methods of food production. Modern Saharan nomads still collect wild sorghum and other grasses in season, timing their movements so as to harvest suitable tracts of wild grasses when they are ripe. In the same way, peoples of the sub-Saharan savanna in Stone Age times were presumably in origin pastoralists who were accustomed to harvesting a whole range of seed-bearing grasses. As progressive desiccation forced them closer to river lines and standing water, the deliberate sowing of seed in alluvial soils would have been a natural development, which would have given rise in turn to the long process of domestication by selective breeding. Despite the present paucity of evidence as compared with regions like the Near East and Mesoamerica, where intensive excavations have actually demonstrated the gradual emergence of domesticated crops like barley and maize, it is clear that the cultivated forms of the Sudanic belt must have been evolved by a similar process of trial and error. Whatever the precise causes, a variety of cultigens were domesticated, most of which are still confined to their regions of origin. Only sorghum and some millets have been diffused widely over sub-Saharan Africa. Guinea rice and *fonio* have remained concentrated in the western half of West Africa, where they are indigenous. Bulrush millet is characteristic of the Sudanic belt immediately to the south of the desert. Finger millet (*eleusine*), teff and *ensete* are characteristically Ethiopian domesticates, although the first has spread widely in eastern Africa.

To the south of the Sudanic belt, where the light woodlands merged into the forest, there occurred a second ecological frontier, no less marked than that between the lands of the winter and the summer rains. In the moist conditions of the forest and its fringes the tsetse-fly, spreading trypanosomiasis, is a major hazard to domestic animals. Again, the millets and the sorghums of the savanna do not flourish in the conditions of tree-shade and cloud-cover prevailing in the forest. Here, therefore, the trend to deliberate food production took a very different course. Here farming took the form of planting rather than sowing, of clearing and weeding rather than digging. Fruit- and root-crops were more important than cereals. In the absence of domestic animals, protein was scarce and was more likely to come from fishing than from hunting. The Stone Age peoples who lived on the fringes of the forest had a long history of gathering behind them. Wild yams, for example, must certainly have been collected long before they were deliberately planted, the transition between gathering and planting being almost undetectable. As Oliver Davies has written,

> The heads would fall, either into the holes where there had been digging for wild tubers, or onto the partly eroded ground round a camp enriched by human rubbish; they would take root, and if men continued to occupy the same site, as concentrations of implements suggest that they did, they would have a crop ready to hand.[1]

The earliest attempts at gardening may thus have been little more than the intentional protection of plants and trees known to be useful, and the propagation of root-crops by replanting the tops. In these circumstances it was not the domestication of animals or plants so much as the introduction of tools suitable for effective forest clearance and garden cultivation which provoked a more intensive food-producing occupation of the forest regions.

The forest belt of West Africa is archaeologically even more sparsely documented than the Sudanic belt to the north of it; but the forest

[1] *West Africa before the Europeans*, 1967, p. 151.

margins of west-central Ghana have yielded evidence for one extensive early farming population practising the culture known as Kintampo. These people lived in the lower valley of the Black Volta, but also on the Accra plain. Their material culture is best known from the Kintampo rock shelters and the Ntereso site, where a Late Stone Age culture using microlithic tools and pottery underlies a food-producing occupation layer. The earlier, Punpun, phase is characterised by the gathering of wild fruit, the trapping of small game and the collecting of snails. There are no traces of domestic animals or of cultivation in the Punpun horizons, which were abandoned around 1400 B.C. An abrupt break in the cultural tradition follows. The people of the succeeding, Kintampo, culture probably kept domestic cattle and goats, and certainly cultivated the oil-palm and the cow-pea (*vigna*). Polished axes, cigar-shaped terracotta graters, stone bracelets and grooved stones for grinding were all in common use. Microlithic tools continue to abound. The Kintampo people, unlike their predecessors, lived in mud huts and occupied permanent settlements. Although existing radiocarbon dates for the Kintampo culture fall in the late second millennium B.C., it is likely that it continued to flourish until the coming of iron. Although two second-millennium dates for iron-working have been claimed from Ntereso, these are both so eccentrically early that they cannot be accepted without much more confirmatory evidence. Meantime, it must be considered much more likely that the Iron Age began sometime in the second half of the first millennium B.C.

It is a striking fact that at the present time the excavations at Tichitt, Daima and Kintampo are the only ones, out of many hundreds of Stone Age sites in the savanna and forest belts of West Africa, to have yielded firm chronological evidence about the origins and development of food production. No doubt, as the range of evidence grows, the sequence of events will prove to be more complex than it now appears. But, for the time being, the conclusions to be drawn seem clear. First, there was a time-lag of about three thousand years between the domestication of the Middle Eastern and the Sudanic cereals. During these three thousand years the only kind of food production to establish itself anywhere to the south of Egypt was pastoralism. South of the Sahara, two kinds of agriculture developed side by side, at about the same time, and linked, at least in West Africa, by the use of similar neolithic tools. One kind was based on cereal cultivation in the open savanna, the other on the roots and fruits of the forest. In both the savanna and the forest, the period of Stone Age food production lasted for about a thousand years before the coming of iron.

Over most of the width of the continent, equatorial forest provided an effective barrier to the southward transmission of cereal agriculture and stock-raising. The main exception was in the eastern sector, where the Ethiopian and East African highlands provided a southward projection of savanna conditions. Here developments probably followed a pattern similar to those in the West African savanna belt. That is to say, pastoralism established itself in the Libyan desert between the Tibesti massif and the Nile, and east of the Nile in the Red Sea hills and the Ethiopian borderlands. Indeed, though excavation in these regions lags behind the Sahara, rock-paintings have been reported from eastern Ethiopia and Somalia, depicting long-horned cattle which strongly recall those of the Sahara. As desiccation increased in the northern part of the region during the late third and the whole of the second millennium, pastoral populations would have retreated southwards, and the Ethiopian and Sudan borderlands would have become an obvious area for experimentation with food crops. Finger millet (*eleusine*) occurs wild in south-west Ethiopia, and may well have been domesticated there, while in the moist, forested valleys of Kaffa, to the north of Lake Rudolf, the false banana (*ensete edule*) has a long history as a staple food-plant, which might well go back to the third millennium or even further.

At least by the end of the second millennium B.C., cattle must have reached the northern borders of East Africa, for the Rift Valley and adjoining plateau lands of Kenya and northern Tanzania have provided ample evidence of Stone Age pastoralists. Throughout the first millennium B.C. the Stone Bowl people, so called from their characteristic stone vessels, pestles and mortars, ranged widely over the grasslands. Cattle bones have been found at several sites, including the Tunnel rock-shelter and Narosura in western Kenya. So far no conclusive evidence exists for agriculture, although some planting of *eleusine* and sorghum seems not unlikely. The burial customs of the Stone Bowl people are well documented; cairn burials were usual, but there is one site, the Njoro River cave, where a series of cremated burials were associated with stone pestles and mortars. Fine pottery, basketry and beads of semi-precious stone came from the same site. While many of these traits suggest links with the neolithic pastoralists of the eastern Sahara and the Ethiopian region, the Stone Bowl people still made many of their tools in forms typical of the Late Stone Age hunter-gatherers and fishers who preceded them. It is as if new economic and cultural traits had been grafted onto indigenous Late Stone Age cultural traditions.

What is clear is that the East African pastoralists of the first millennium B.C. formed, at best, an enclave in the midst of populations in eastern Africa who were in general still hunters and gatherers and remained so until the start of the next millennium. Outside East Africa, their links were with the farming peoples of the Sudanic savanna rather than with those of the equatorial forest belt. Ethnically and linguistically, the eastern pastoralists were Afro-Mediterraneans or Caucasians, who almost certainly spoke some kind of Cushitic language of the Afro-Asiatic family. To the west of them, the pioneer food producers of the Congo forest and its fringes were Negroes, originating in the equatorial zone, whose development south of the Equator we shall follow in another chapter.

3 Late Stone Age hunter-gatherers in Africa south of the Equator

We have seen that the Bronze Age in northern Africa corresponded to the period of Stone Age farming in middle Africa. In most of Africa south of the equator this period was still one of Late Stone Age hunting and gathering. Towards the end of the period, almost certainly within the first millennium B.C., in a few exceptional areas Stone Age peoples became farmers and herders. But these developments were sparse and late. They affected only the northern parts of East Africa and the fringes of the Congo forest. In at least three-quarters of the subcontinent men continued to live by hunting and gathering until the coming of the Iron Age little more than two thousand years ago.

The essential reason for the conservatism of sub-equatorial Africa may well be that the climatic changes, so drastic in Saharan latitudes, were here much more marginal in their effects. In the southern hemisphere as in the northern, the climate began to get markedly drier from about 2500 B.C. onwards. In the southern hemisphere as in the northern, the change was most critical in those areas already tending to aridity, which here ran not in a lateral zone corresponding to the Sahara and Sudan, but in a diagonal line from north-east to south-west, from the deserts of Somalia and north-eastern Kenya, across the central plateau of Tanzania and Zambia to the Kalahari desert of Botswana and South West Africa. However it was only at the two extreme ends of this dry zone that any large areas became uninhabitable. In general, hunting and gathering populations survived quite easily by adapting to larger territories with sparser food resources and by learning to use smaller and lighter tools and weapons. The microlithic Late Stone Age industries show a general similarity all the way down the eastern side of Africa from Ethiopia to the Cape, and are collectively known as Wilton, after a rock shelter near Grahamstown in South Africa, where such tools were first found.

All the indications are that the great majority of the Wilton toolmakers were of Bush stock, small remnants of which survive today in the south-western corner of Africa, speaking very distinctive clicking languages called Khoikhoi (Hottentot) and San (Bushman) or, collectively, Khoisan. Even as recently as the eighteenth century A.D., the area occupied by the Khoisan peoples covered the whole of South

West Africa, Botswana and the Cape Province of South Africa, and many of them were still practising industries of the Wilton type. Bush skeletal material has been recovered by archaeologists from all over South Africa, Rhodesia, Zambia, Tanzania, Uganda, the southern Sudan, Ethiopia and Somalia. Throughout much of this area a common tradition of rock art depicts a common mode of Late Stone Age hunting and gathering existence. A Khoikhoi language still survives among the Sandawe people of north-eastern Tanzania. Physically, the Bush type was yellowish rather than black. The hair grew in separate ringlets rather than in a woolly mat. The skull was broad at the forehead and narrow at the jaw, giving a characteristically triangular appearance to the face. Though modern Bushmen are short in stature, archaeology shows that in former times part of the stock was larger. Dwarfing changes began around ten thousand years ago, but larger individuals occur in sites as recent as the third and second millennium B.C.

The Bush hunter-gatherers of the savanna regions of eastern and southern Africa could draw for their meat supplies on a rich and varied fauna. Their prey is often depicted in rock-paintings, which show eland and kudu, impala and bushbuck, and other fauna as large

F IG. 7.   A running hunter from a rock shelter at Ho Khotso, Lesotho, southern Africa.

23

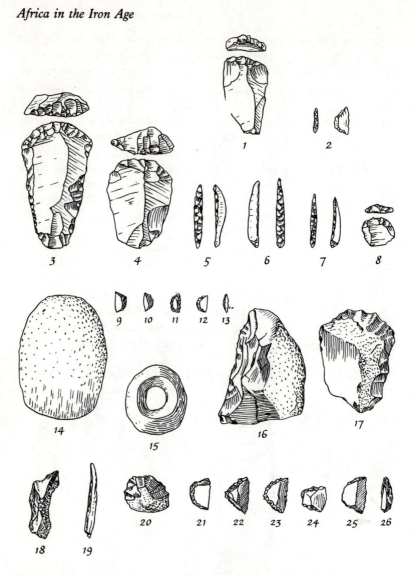

Fig. 8. Typical Wilton stone tools (1–8), including small and medium-sized scrapers (1, 3, 4, 8) as well as arrowbarbs (microliths) (2, 5–7); ×$\frac{4}{5}$. Nachikufan bored stones, microliths, scrapers and a ground axe are illustrated in 9–26; ×$\frac{2}{5}$.

as the rhinoceros and as small as the duiker. The fragmentary bones of these animals litter their abandoned camp-sites, together with a few fish bones and the remains of birds snared for the pot. Weapons were

24

light, consisting of bows and arrows and light spears. Arrowheads were of wood and bone, often poisoned. Small crescent-shaped flakes of stone were inserted as barbs in the shafts of spears and arrows. Clothing was of skin, which was scraped with stone fragments set in wooden handles. Wilton tool-kits show considerable variation from one local environment to another, and a higher degree of specialisation than had been evident in earlier times.

A remarkably complete picture of Late Stone Age life came from a series of Wilton camp sites at the Gwisho hot springs in central Zambia. The lower levels of these settlements, dating to the third and second millennia B.C., were waterlogged, and consequently many wooden tools, vegetal remains and fragments of animal bones were preserved. Gwisho springs lie at the edge of the Kafue flood-plain. They are bounded by savanna woodland rich in vegetable foods. The hunters killed rhinoceros and hippopotamus from the flood-plain, and warthog and antelope from the woodland. Some fish were also taken from the river. However, vegetable foods were much used, and the remains of several wooden digging-sticks were recovered, which might have been used for unearthing roots and tubers. Nearly all the seeds found at the site came from a half-dozen species, all of them edible and still widely collected by modern populations. Significantly, only a small proportion of the available vegetable foods were used by the Gwisho hunters, who were evidently in no danger of starving. Traces of temporary windbreaks, hearths and butchery areas were found at one of the Gwisho sites. Numerous burials were deposited in shallow graves dug into the occupation levels of the camps. The remains show that the population was of large Bush stock.

In the more thickly wooded savanna areas it is clear that the Late Stone Age hunting and gathering populations placed more emphasis on food-gathering than their contemporaries who lived in more open country. In north-eastern Zambia and northern Malawi, for example, a distinctive tool-kit occurs, known as the Nachikufan, which includes many stone artifacts heavier than those normally found in Wilton sites. These people used round, bored stones as weights for digging-sticks, and a kind of axe with a ground edge which was perhaps used for stripping bark as well as for collecting vegetable foods. Large numbers of upper and lower grinding stones come from Nachikufan sites. These were undoubtedly used for grinding vegetable foods, among them the *musuku* nut, which is still commonly eaten in the region today. Scraping tools are here far more numerous than in the more open Wilton sites.

It is not yet known how far the Nachikufan tool-kit spread into the thickly wooded savanna of the Katanga region, but it is probable

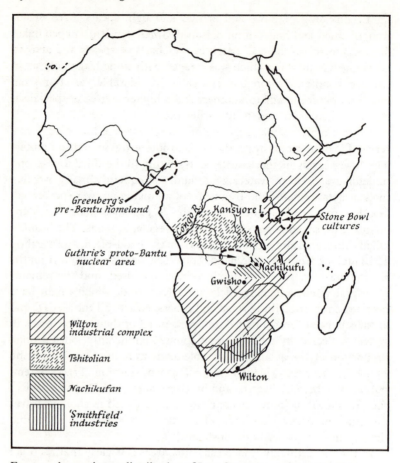

FIG. 9. Approximate distribution of Late Stone Age cultures in sub-equatorial Africa.

that it will be found to spread up to the fringes of the rain-forest, where it will be found to give way to yet another Late Stone Age tool-kit, known as the Tshitolian, after its type-site on the Bena Tshitoli plateau of the Kasai province. The Tshitolian is usually described as a forest culture, and indeed sites have been found in the central lowlands of the Congo basin, where they apparently represent the earliest human colonisation of this densely forested, swampy region. But in fact Tshitolian sites are best known in the forest fringes in the southern and western parts of the Congo basin, where hunter-gatherers could make use of the whole mosaic of open grassland interfluves seamed with gallery forest in the river valleys.

26

Unfortunately, the archaeology of the forest margins has been little studied, but we do have from surface finds evidence of a comparatively dense and widespread Tshitolian population to the south and west of the forest, where, in the Zaïre–Angola borderlands, there is evidence of man-made savanna corresponding to that found along the northern edges of the Guinea forests. Most of the sites consist of unstratified scatters of artifacts, but even in their present undated form they provide evidence of the artificial restriction of the forest by a population much denser than had existed before. Some bands, encamped near rivers, may have been comparatively sedentary and permanent. Others may have ranged widely over the interfluves, relying mostly on game. Some bands may have lived within the forest, gathering vegetable foods. Whatever their economic bias, however, it is clear that the Late Stone Age peoples who lived near the southern edges of the forest were exploiting their environment intensively. And certainly the gatherers among them must have had abundant opportunities to learn and practise simple vegecultural techniques, even if they did not yet grow vegetable foods as a deliberate act.

There are many reasons why we know less about the archaeology of the forested regions of Africa than about any others. Movement there is more difficult. Land surfaces are obscured by vegetation. Air photography becomes quite useless as a means of site detection. But, above all, even when the sites have been found and excavated, forest soils are acid and destructive. Metal corrodes. Bone dissolves. In the absence of skeletal evidence, archaeology cannot help us to establish whether the makers of Tshitolian artifacts were predominantly of Bush or Negro stock. Certainly Tshitolian industries lasted for a very long time – from the fourteenth or thirteenth millennium B.C. until shortly before the coming of iron. As we shall presently see, this makes it impossible that the early Tshitolians should have spoken Bantu, since, on linguistic evidence, even the parent language of Bantu would have emerged more recently. Khoikhoi, which is still spoken by surviving groups of hunter-gatherers in south-eastern Angola, would seem a much more likely candidate, though one should recognise the limitations of this term. Strictly, it means a family of clicking languages still spoken by some remnant peoples in the Cape Province, South West Africa, southern Angola and north-central Tanzania. The Bush physical type was much widely spread, and the varieties of 'Khoisan' speech were doubtless correspondingly wide and deep.

We come, now, to the evidences of food production which began to appear in some northerly parts of sub-equatorial Africa before the $\qquad$ 27 beginning of the Iron Age. One such manifestation was, of course, the Stone Bowl culture of central Kenya and northern Tanzania, which we described in the last chapter. This was certainly a cattle-keeping culture, if not also a cereal-growing one, which was in existence through most of the first millennium B.C., and it might on the face of it seem surprising that it did not in all this period spread further to the south. Yet the characteristic stone bowls and platters of this culture have not as yet been found in stratigraphical contexts to the south of central Tanzania. A few stone mortars have been found in northern Zambia, but their dates and cultural associations are doubtful. No stone vessels have been found in the rest of Zambia, Rhodesia or South Africa, although a few have been found in South West Africa, but not associated with other cultural material. Above all, no traces of Stone Age agriculture or domestic animals have been found in any of the many Late Stone Age sites examined in the region between central Tanzania and the Cape, except in a few obviously recent settlement sites associated with Stone Age cultures which survived into the Iron Age. All in all, therefore, it looks as though the Stone Bowl sites represent the southern tip of a culture which had its main base further north, among the Cushitic-speaking peoples of north-east Africa. For whatever reason, it does not seem that the Stone Bowl people either themselves penetrated further than about latitude 4°S., or that they passed on their stock to the hunting peoples to the south of them.

Apart from the Stone Bowl culture, there is the possibility, which has not yet been adequately explored, that there was a brief period in the history of Uganda and north-western Tanzania when pottery was in use, but not yet iron. This is the pottery called Kansyore ware, after the island of that name in the Kagera River, which flows into Lake Victoria from the west. Kansyore ware has also been found, apparently in a pre-Iron Age context, at a number of rock-shelter sites all around Lake Victoria. Pottery in sub-Saharan Africa normally betokens some kind of food production, but the existing sites appear to be those of Late Stone Age hunters, who may have acquired their pottery from food-producing neighbours as yet unknown in the archaeological record. Should such a Stone Age food-producing culture be discovered in the well-watered savanna country around Lake Victoria, it might explain many present problems about the southward transmission of cattle and cereals.

Meanwhile, the region which seems to have played the most crucial part in the movement towards food production in sub-equatorial Africa is the Congo basin. Once again, the evidence is full of problems, and the archaeological data taken by themselves would certainly not lead to any decisive conclusion. Nevertheless, the peripheries of the Congo basin have yielded a good many stone tools which can almost be called 'neolithic'. True, nearly all of them have come from surface finds by amateurs, who have collected only the polished and easily recognisable tools from assemblages which may have included more primitive elements. True, all these finds are still undated, and there is the possibility that some of them could have been made in Iron Age times. Still, from the Uele basin in the north-east, from the lower Congo between Kinshasa and Thysville, and from the Katanga in the south have come not only ground and polished axes and adzes, but artifacts that are reminiscent of hoes, together with grooved grinding stones, which suggest that deliberate vegeculture preceded the Iron Age in all these areas.

There the matter might have been allowed to rest but for the findings of linguistic classification, which show strong reasons for supposing that, on the eve of the Iron Age, the Congo basin in general, and perhaps more particularly its southern forest fringes, became the cradleland of a language that was destined to spread its progeny over virtually the whole of sub-equatorial Africa. This language was Bantu, of which the hypothetical parent language can be distinguished from its offspring as proto-Bantu. Proto-Bantu can be partially reconstructed from the common elements among its surviving offspring, and the parent language can itself be seen to be descended from one branch of the Niger–Congo languages family briefly described in Chapter 1. What linguistic classification essentially tells us is that the whole Bantu sub-family is a *new* sub-family, the members of which, though they have spread far across the map, have still had so little time in which to grow apart from each other that they still resemble each other as much as, say, the Germanic languages of western Europe. It would be entirely reasonable to suppose that between two and three thousand years ago proto-Bantu was being spoken in a small nuclear area somewhere at the heart of the vast sphere now occupied by its descendants.

There is not as yet complete agreement among the relevant experts about the precise geographical location of this nucleus. The American linguist and anthropologist Joseph Greenberg, whose concern is with the general problems of African linguistic classification, places it in the Cameroun grasslands, on the northern fringes of the equatorial forest. Malcolm Guthrie, the most recent and the most thorough British classifier of the Bantu languages themselves, finds that the modern languages which have retained the highest proportion of common Bantu roots inherited from the parent language are those spoken just to the south of the forest, in the Katanga and the Kasai.

Recently, Alick Henrici, using statistical methods based on the size of common vocabulary for measuring the relative distances of individual languages from one another, has shown that on the basis of Guthrie's own data the Bantu languages of the north-western sector are far more distant from each other than those of the rest of the Bantu sphere, which he describes collectively as 'Central Bantu'. 'The general picture suggested is thus of a phase in which some North-western languages split off followed, possibly after a considerable interval in view of the overall similarity of Central Bantu, by a quite rapid break-up of these central languages into at least half a dozen different groups, which have since spread to cover between them nearly all of southern Africa.'[1] Henrici in effect sees the nuclear area to the south of the Congo forest, favoured by Guthrie, as the possible home of the parent language of his 'Central Bantu' languages spoken in the east and the south. But he thinks that the north-western Bantu languages had already diverged from proto-Bantu by the time this area was reached. Without entering into technical linguistic controversies, the historian is today justified in accepting two conclusions. First, that the ultimate origin of Bantu lies to the north-west of its present sphere, in the West African heartland of the Niger–Congo language family. Second, that the Congo basin, whether the northern, forested half or the southern, savanna half, included the cradleland in which proto-Bantu or 'proto-Central Bantu' was spoken by a single coherent population, whose descendants later carried it far and wide across the subcontinent.

It is a fact of the greatest historical interest that proto-Bantu, before its dispersion from the cradleland, was already quite clearly a language of food producers. Among domestic animals, it included words for dog, goat, pig, chicken, and probably also a word for cow, although there were no special words either for cow's milk or for the act of milking. Among useful flora, proto-Bantu had two words for palm-tree, and one for fig-tree. Among cultivated plants, it included a general word for vegetables, and also words for bananas, beans, mushrooms, oil and probably for some kind of yam; but significantly it did not include words for *eleusine*, sorghum or any other cereal plant. Again, while there are several terms connected with boats and fishing, the hunting vocabulary seems to have been poor. None

[1] Alick Henrici, 'Numerical Classification of Bantu Languages', *African Language Studies*, XIV (1973), p. 100.

of these items taken in isolation would have any significance at all; but, taken together, they make it clear enough that the food production of the Bantu ancestors was of the planting kind rather than the sowing kind. Cattle apart, the list could indicate either a full forest environment or one situated in the woodland savanna mosaic of the forest margin. What it could *not* indicate is any large stretch of country to the east of the great lakes or to the south of the Congo–Zambezi watershed.

It does, therefore, look very much as though, within the Congo basin, the Bantu established themselves as the pioneers of vege-cultural food production, accompanied by the keeping of domestic animals, in territory where the earlier inhabitants had been limited to hunting and gathering. These techniques of food production could in theory have spread across the Congo basin without any significant change in the population. However, the fact that these innovations are detected within the context of a language which is agreed on all sides to be of West African origin surely suggests that the spread of this kind of food production was the result of an expansion of West African, that is to say, Negro, people. There is no need to postulate great migrations with tens of thousands or even thousands of people on the march. The pioneers may have been few in number. They may have achieved their success partly by the faster natural reproduction of people with wider food resources, and partly by living in denser communities than their hunting predecessors, who would thus have been attracted into their orbit as clients. The example of such relationships can still be seen in the symbiosis of pygmy hunting bands with agricultural tribes in the Ituri forest today. The hunters learn the language of the cultivators, never the reverse, and where individuals cross from one culture to the other, it is always a one-way traffic. As we have said, we do not know what languages were spoken by the hunter-gatherers of the Congo basin in Late Stone Age times; but it is likely that somewhere across this region, and more likely towards the north of it than the south, there ran the linguistic frontier between Niger–Congo and Khoisan. This frontier probably moved southwards with the introduction of food production. Certainly, when it came to the expansion of the Bantu sphere beyond the boundaries of the Congo basin, it was the expansion of Bantu languages at the expense of Khoisan that was in question.

If there are linguistic reasons for concluding that proto-Bantu emerged as the language of a food-producing population, there are also linguistic reasons for supposing that during the formative period of the language this population was using stone and not iron. The 31 evidence is of a highly technical kind, and should be studied by the curious in Guthrie's own words.[1] However, the essence of the matter is that a part of the vocabulary of proto-Bantu can be assigned with fair confidence to a later stage of the development of the proto-language than the rest. And it would seem that most of the proto-Bantu words connected with iron and metallurgy fall into this later part. In other words, the evidence suggests that the knowledge of iron-working reached the speakers of proto-Bantu as an innovation, though at a period when they still formed a single, coherent speech community, confined more or less to the small nuclear area in which their language evolved its distinctive character. When they later expanded east and west, south and north, they carried with them common words for 'iron' and 'to forge', 'bellows' and 'to blow bellows', 'hammer' and 'to hit with a hammer', 'axe', 'knife' and 'wire'. The expansion of the Bantu from their nuclear area, therefore, took place within the Iron Age, and, as we shall see, this means within the A.D. period, or nearly. But their establishment as a food-producing population, practising deliberate vegeculture and stock-raising somewhere within the forest or the forest margins of the Congo basin looks like a development of the first millennium B.C.

---

[1] Malcolm Guthrie, *Comparative Bantu*, vol. IV, 82.11 and 84.22–4.

4 North-east Africa and the Greek-speaking world

We saw in Chapter I that by the middle of the first millennium B.C. the leading position in the trade of the eastern Mediterranean had passed from the Phoenicians to the Greeks. Already by the end of the seventh century the Ionian Greeks had driven the Phoenicians from the Aegean and were beginning to plant their own colonies around the coasts of Asia Minor, Libya, Italy and Sicily. Egypt was too densely populated to offer any scope for colonisation in this sense; but at Naukratis in the delta Greek merchants established a trading settlement which enjoyed extra-territorial rights of self-government from successive rulers of Egypt, and which survived through the period of Persian rule as a steadily growing focus for Greek trade and Greek culture. In the early fifth century the mainland Greeks halted the Persian advance into Europe at the great battles of Marathon, Salamis and Plataea. In the second half of the fourth century, under Alexander the Great of Macedon, the Greeks assumed the offensive, driving the Persians out of Asia Minor, Syria and Phoenicia, and conquering Egypt in 332 B.C. From this date until the Arab conquest of A.D. 639, for a period of all but a thousand years therefore, Greek-speaking people were the dominant outsiders in north-east Africa. The Greek dynasty of the Ptolemies ruled Egypt from 323 until 30 B.C., making their capital at Alexandria into the foremost city of the Greek-speaking world, and extending their commercial hegemony from the Mediterranean to the Red Sea and the Indian Ocean. When the Romans put an end to the Ptolemies with the defeat and suicide of Cleopatra, Egypt remained, commercially and culturally, in the Greek-speaking half of the Roman Empire. The Red Sea trade, in particular, continued to be managed by Greek-speaking merchants and sailors. By the fourth century A.D. Alexandria, traditionally the see of St Mark, had become the intellectual capital of the Christian Church, the seat of the Patriarch Athanasius, the centre of a Greek-speaking Christianity that was spreading through Egypt into Nubia and the Sudan and down the Red Sea to Ethiopia and southern Arabia. With the division of the Roman Empire into its eastern and western halves during the same fourth century, Egypt and north-east Africa passed into the Byzantine sphere of empire and influence, and so remained until the rise of Islam.

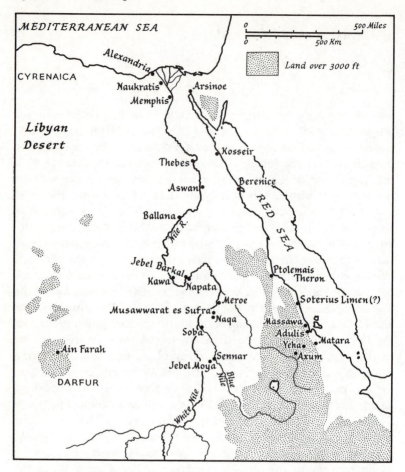

FIG. 10.   North-east Africa from the Ptolemies to the Byzantines.

For much of the first half of the period, therefore, the dominant power in the whole region was the independent kingdom of the Ptolemies, which at first included not only Egypt, but Cyrenaica and Phoenicia, Syria and Cyprus. In area this equalled the greatest extent of dynastic Egypt, and the volume of trade controlled by it was certainly much greater. The founder of the dynasty, Ptolemy Soter (the Saviour) was in origin a Macedonian general, who at Alexander's death secured the satrapy of Egypt, and arrived there as a military conqueror in 323 B.C. Transferring the capital from Memphis to Alexandria, he concentrated on control of the eastern Mediterranean,

34

building a great fleet to secure his independence from his rivals in Macedon and in Seleucid Persia. From the first it was a part of his strategy to attract Greek-speaking immigrants – soldiers, scholars and skilled men of all sorts – for whom a privileged, urban existence was provided by engaging the seven millions or so of native Egyptians in a more centralised and disciplined economic system than had ever been attempted anywhere in the world. With the aid of a vast bureaucracy literate in Greek, the cultivable land was re-surveyed and re-allocated on a competitive basis to those who undertook to pay the largest taxes in corn and coin. Military governors and garrisons were placed in each of the thirty-six traditional units of Egyptian administration, the nomes, together with supporting civil, legal and, above all, fiscal officials. All the way up the river, from the delta to Thebes and beyond, tax-gatherers probed and ships stood waiting to load the king's corn and carry it down to Alexandria, for sale to the citizens of the metropolis and for export to the growing cities of the Mediterranean. State monopolies in oil-pressing and textile-weaving, in brewing and banking, in paper-making and timber-cutting, and in the mining of salt and gold, ensured a large government stake in industry, while much of the internal and external commerce of the country passed through government hands and was carried in government shipping. From the Mediterranean world Egypt imported timber, copper, purple dye, marble and wine, which she paid for on the one hand with Egyptian corn, on the other hand with urban manufactures, gold and jewellery, unguents and perfumes, ivories and objets d'art, the raw materials of which were obtained either from the African interior or from further east, in exchange for Egyptian textiles, oil, glass and metal goods especially manufactured for the barbarian trade.

The second Ptolemy, Philadelphus (285-247 B.C.), is said to have owned four thousand ships. He extended the maritime supremacy of Egypt from the Mediterranean to the Red Sea, completing the canal from the Nile to the Gulf of Suez begun two centuries before by the Persians, and opening ports and trading settlements at Arsinoe (Suez), Kosseir (the port for Thebes), Berenice (the port for Aswan), Soterius Limen (the port for Meroe) and Ptolemais Theron, a port and hunting station situated below the northern tip of the Ethiopian plateau. The Indian campaigns of Alexander had roused the interest of the Greeks in the military uses of elephants, and Ptolemy II was concerned not merely with the ivory trade, but in capturing young elephants and shipping them to Egypt for training. His successor, Ptolemy III Euergetes, founded the trading settlement at Adulis, 35 just to the south of the modern Massawa, which was to become the main port for the kingdom of Axum. The Indian trade, particularly in silks and spices, was a major preoccupation of all the Ptolemies, but until late in the second century B.C. Egyptian ships sailed no further than the Yemen, where Mocha was the main port of transhipment for the Asian trade. From the reign of the second Euergetes (145-116 B.C.), however, Egyptian Greeks began to pass the Straits of Bab-al-Mandab, and sometime in the first century they discovered the regular alternation of the monsoon winds, which enabled them to sail boldly across the Indian Ocean instead of coasting northwards past the Persian Gulf.

This commercial outreach of Ptolemaic Egypt is something that needs to be remembered as we consider the development of the Meroitic kingdom, the origins of which were described in Chapter 1. For it can be seriously argued that the flowering of Meroitic, as opposed to Napatan, civilisation was at least partly a response to the stimulus of the Ptolemaic expansion. Much of the argument turns upon Meroitic chronology, our existing knowledge of which still depends mainly on the excavations of Reisner and Dows Dunham at the royal cemeteries of Napata and Meroe. These yielded an approximate sequence of rulers, whose dates could only be roughly estimated by averaging reign lengths around a handful of known dates. They established that, following the southward retreat from Egypt of the XXV Dynasty, there was a period of about 115 years, from 653 until about 530 B.C., when all the kings and queens were buried at the northern capital at Napata. Next came a period of about 230 years, from about 530 till about 300 B.C., when, although the kings continued to be buried at Napata, an increasing proportion of their queens was buried at Meroe, suggesting that the southern capital was now the normal seat of government, the pyramids of kings continuing to be built at the obsolete centre for antiquarian and traditional reasons. From about 300 B.C., for about 600 years more, kings as well as queens were buried at Meroe in three successive royal cemeteries, of which the first two gave evidence of considerable prosperity, while the third and latest clearly indicated a period of severe decline.

Archaeology has made it clear that, for three and a half centuries following the retreat from Egypt, the kingdom continued to be entirely Egyptian in religion and culture. Although the writ of the kings already ran from Aswan as far as the lower Blue Nile, public building was concentrated in the northern half of the region, and it was fully Egyptian in inspiration. Temples were dedicated to the

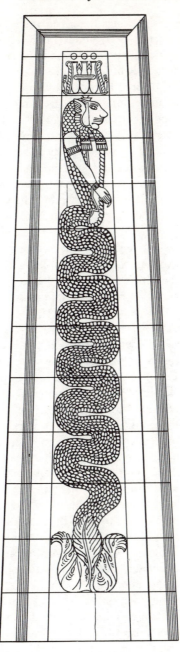

FIG. 11. Meroitic Lion God with the body of a snake, from Naqa.

37

Theban god Amun. The kings described themselves as Pharoahs of Egypt, and were buried in pyramids inscribed with religious texts carved in Egyptian hieroglyphics. At the same time trade with Egypt was declining, and there is little evidence of any regular contact with the outside world. The rare historical inscriptions refer to the ritual visits of newly ascended kings to the great temples of Jebel Barkal, Kawa and Pnubs, and otherwise merely mention punitive expeditions undertaken against the Beja and other pastoral nomads of the surrounding deserts. Though iron occurs sporadically in the royal tombs of Napata from the sixth century B.C., the general run of grave goods continues to be of copper or bronze until that of Harsiyotef, whose death occurred sometime in the late fourth century. However, it was not until the third century B.C., when the southern capital had finally achieved the ascendancy, that there emerged a culture which could be called distinctively Meroitic. Although we know that the site of Meroe had been regularly occupied since the sixth century B.C., and that by the fifth century some palace- and temple-building had been undertaken, it would appear that most of the urban development of Meroe, and all that at the other two major cities of the south at Naqa and Musarawwat-es-Sufra, dates from the third to the first century, at a period contemporary with the Ptolemaic ascendancy in Egypt and the Red Sea. Probably it was at this stage that the great hills of iron slag began to arise around the outskirts of the capital, the size of which caused the archaeologist Sayce to dub Meroe 'the Birmingham of central Africa'. Certainly at this stage Egyptian hieroglyphics disappeared in favour of a cursive script which has not yet been deciphered. At this stage, too, Meroitic sculptors began to portray new subjects, especially elephants and lions, which had featured very little in Egyptian art. The lion was the emblem of a local god, Apedemek, and it would seem that tame lions were bred and kept at his temples. The elephant, too, seems to have had a ritual significance. There is some reason to think that it was used by the Meroites in warfare, and it is even possible that some of the elephants imported into Egypt by the Ptolemies had been captured and trained in Meroe. This in turn would probably presuppose some contact between Meroe and India, which is suggested also by the Meroitic use of cotton, and by the construction of stone reservoirs, tanks and dams.

Thus, the commercial activity generated by Ptolemaic Egypt, and in particular the development of the Red Sea trade, must have played a considerable part in the second period of Meroitic prosperity and in the renascence of Meroitic culture. Archaeological finds in the island of Meroe indicate a cosmopolitan material culture, which included

Greek and Roman luxuries as well as eastern artifacts. Exports were doubtless the traditional products of the African interior – gold, ivory, skins and feathers, ebony, slaves. At the same time, it must be admitted that the political and religious organisation of the Meroitic kingdom showed little if any sign of Hellenistic influence, and even the innovations like the lion and elephant cults seem to have been of Sudanese rather than Ptolemaic Egyptian inspiration. It would seem that, for the most part, the Meroitic kings still modelled their lives on those of the Dynastic Pharoahs, surrounding themselves with ritual pomp and mystery, committing royal incest with their sisters, building ever more temples to the Egyptian gods.

As for the customs of the Ethiopians [wrote Diodorus Siculus in the first century B.C.], not a few of them are thought to differ greatly from the rest of mankind, this being especially true of those which concern the selection of their kings. The priests first choose out the noblest men, and whichever from this group the god may select, as he is borne about in a procession in accordance with their practice, him the multitude take for their king, and straightway it both worships and honours him like a god, believing that the sovereignty has been entrusted to him by the divine providence. And the king who has been thus chosen both follows a regimen which has been fixed in accordance with the laws, and performs all his other deeds in accordance with the ancestral customs ... They also say that it is customary for the comrades of the kings to die with them of their own accord ... And it is for this reason that a conspiracy against the king is not easily raised among the Ethiopians, all his friends being equally concerned both for his safety and their own.[1]

Even today the ruins of Meroe make an impressive sight. Six low hills of iron slag mark the southern and western perimeters of the town, bearing witness to what must surely have been the main industry of its inhabitants. To the east of the main housing areas are the ruins of a whole series of temples and cemeteries, while the burial pyramids of the royal family crown the summit of a low ridge overlooking the site. Only a small part of the town has so far been cleared and excavated – the royal cemeteries, some scattered temples, and the so-called Royal City, which extends along the banks of the Nile near the main landing stage. Here, the Temple of Amun was found to be 450 feet long, built of brick and sandstone blocks, and forming a series of courts and halls enclosing a small central shrine. Few of the buildings are firmly dated, but most of them bear some marks of Greek or Roman influence, and should thus have been built during the last two or three centuries B.C. or the first century A.D.

[1] Diodorus Siculus, *Bibliotheca Historica*, Book III, Ch. 5.

Domestic architecture is so far little known. Much of the population probably lived in typical African houses of mud and thatch, although some examples of brick-built houses have been uncovered, mostly comprising sets of two-roomed dwelling units set around central compounds which may have housed extended families or other social groupings. Household possessions were simple, including cooking pots and beer pots of African hand-made form, grindstones and iron tools, baskets and bedsteads.

It is clear from the archaeological record that from about the middle of the first century A.D. Meroe was in a state of rapidly accelerating decline. About 25 B.C., shortly after the Roman conquest of Egypt, the Meroites invaded upper Egypt and burnt Aswan. This provoked a reprisal raid by the Roman general Petronius, who marched all the way to the fourth cataract and sacked Napata. King Natakamani, who reigned from about 15 B.C. until about A.D. 15, was the last great builder of the dynasty, restoring the huge Temple of Amun at Meroe and rebuilding the one razed by the Romans at Napata. The Lion Temple, as well as the Temple of Amun at Naqa, were built by him, and also, significantly, the artificial reservoirs which indicate that the island of Meroe, like Napata five hundred years earlier, was running short of water. When the Emperor Nero (A.D. 54–68) sent two centurians to spy out the whole length of the land, they reported on their return that it was too poor to be worth conquering. Although twenty-two rulers followed Natakamani before the kingdom broke up, their grave goods included none of the imports from the Hellenistic world which had been so common before. Their pyramids were of steadily diminishing size and workmanship. The decline in stone carving, perhaps also in literacy, was such that only

FIG. 12.   Tombs of the rulers of Meroitic Kush, on a ridge overlooking Meroe.

half of their names have come down to posterity. It looks as if the fortunes of Meroe preceded rather than followed the decline of Roman Egypt from the second century A.D. onwards. One factor may have been the deterioration of the environment. Another may have been the rise of Axum as a trade rival. Certainly what remained of the state was impoverished and isolated from the outside world, a prey for nomadic invaders from the hinterland long before its final overthrow by the Axumites.

For the history of Africa, the most important question that has to be asked about Meroe is how far afield its influence spread, whether in the technological sphere of iron metallurgy or in the institutional sphere of Pharaonic kingship. One highly respected scholar, A. J. Arkell, has popularised the hypothesis that, when the Meroitic kingdom came to an end in the fourth century A.D., its royal family and its ruling class retreated westwards to Darfur, propagating both their material and their political culture as they went. This theory was always suspect for the reason that, in history as a whole, civilisations have tended to spread when at their most powerful rather than when at their weakest. It is in every way more likely, as we suggested in Chapter I, that slave-raiding and ivory-hunting expeditions, accompanied by soldiers and armourers, travelled great distances from Meroe when at the height of its power, and that frequently they deposited colonies of settlers, who used their superior knowledge to build up little states among the local inhabitants of the hunting terrain. This is certainly a process of which there are many amply documented examples in later African history; but in relation to Meroe it must be said that no tell-tale scatters of Meroitic manufactures have as yet been found outside the Nile valley. Structures in sun-dried brick, containing sherds of painted pottery, at Jebel Moya and Ain Farah in Darfur, formerly claimed by Arkell as examples of Meroitic culture contact, are now known to belong to the Christian period in the Sudan. As to iron-working, recent archaeological researches have tended to bring forward the chronology for the Nile valley and to push back the dates for West Africa, so that a diffusion of the relevant knowledge across the Sahara from Libya or Carthage now seems at least as likely as a westward diffusion from Meroe. There remains, therefore, the question of Pharaonic kingship and the political culture traits which go with it. Here the claims of Meroe look stronger. It is indisputable that by the time of the first expansion of Islam across the Sahara the northernmost Negro communities of the Sudanic belt had already been organised into kingdoms reminiscent of the Pharaonic model. A direct diffusion from Egypt seems to be precluded by the fact that, even by the end of the Egyptian

New Kingdom, Africa south of the Sahara had hardly embarked upon food production. The high Meroitic period was probably the earliest at which Sudanic Africa would have been capable of using Egyptian political ideas. However, it would seem more likely that these ideas passed, in many degrees of attenuation, through communities of caravan traders, perhaps even of nomadic pastoral conquerors of agricultural communities near the desert's edge, than that they were carried by a Meroitic family on the run.

The state which succeeded Meroe as the main trading kingdom of north-east Africa was that of Axum, the ancestor state of modern Ethiopia, which had its capital situated high on the northern edge of the Ethiopian plateau, and its main seaport at Adulis. The process of its emergence is quite unknown, except for the fact that it came to command the area colonised since the sixth or seventh century B.C. by Semitic-speaking settlers from southern Arabia. Archaeological excavations at pre-Axumite centres such as Yeha and Matara have yielded Bronze Age artifacts dated by inscriptions to the fifth and fourth centuries B.C. By the late fourth or early third century, the people of Yeha were being buried with iron weapons. Their agricultural methods included terracing and irrigation, and perhaps also the plough – the same farming methods as those practised across the Red Sea in the Yemen. About the beginning of the Christian era a new political power began to emerge, based on new cities and almost independent of south Arabian influences. This was the kingdom of Axum, first described in writing in an Alexandrian commercial handbook called the *Periplus of the Erythraean Sea*, written in the early second century A.D. The *Periplus* tells us that the road to Axum started from Adulis, and that it was an eight days' journey up and over the 8000-foot escarpment of the northern highlands. Probably the author had never made the journey, for there is no description of the capital city. However, the *Periplus* leaves no doubt at all that the commercial significance of Axum was that it was at this time the most important ivory market in north-east Africa. 'To that place', the author says, 'all the ivory is brought from the country beyond the Nile, through the district called Cyeneum.' Cyeneum is usually interpreted as Sennar, the district on the Blue Nile near Khartoum, and the implication is that Axum now monopolised the ivory trade of southern Meroe and of further large areas to the south and west. The king of Axum, Zoscales, is described as 'miserly in his ways and always striving for more, but otherwise upright and literate in Greek'. Imports into the kingdom included undressed cloth made in Egypt for the barbarian trade, robes and cheap cloaks dyed in colours, cotton cloth and muslins from India, many articles of flint glass made in Thebes, brass and copper sheets, which were made up locally into ornaments and cooking pots, and Indian iron and steel which were made into spears for hunting and warfare. Swords and axes were also imported, copper drinking cups, a little coin, a little wine, a little olive oil, and, for the royal household, gold and silver plate.

It is clear that, by the early second century A.D., Axum had overtaken Meroe as the first city in north-east Africa outside Egypt; and from inscriptions and coinage, as well as from the comments of outside observers, we know that this ascendancy was maintained through most of the first millennium A.D. The public buildings of Axum, which have attracted three major archaeological expeditions since 1906, are at least as impressive, and much more original, than those of Meroe. Unfortunately, they have not as yet yielded much chronological evidence. The best-known examples are the great stelae, thought to be the funerary monuments of the kings. Only one of the elaborately carved examples now stands erect, but formerly there were many, and some of them were as much as a hundred feet in height. All of them, though quite solid, represent many-storied towers with scrupulously repeated external features. The fact that all are surmounted by the crescent and disc of the south Arabian goddess Ashtar has usually been taken to suggest that they belong to the pre-Christian period, that is to say, before the fourth century A.D.; but the latest excavations by Neville Chittick suggest that in fact many of them were erected in Christian times. The palace and temple architecture of Axum has suffered grave damage through time, and it was only in 1966–7 that the Ethiopian Institute of Archaeology, starting from a shapeless mound of fallen masonry, managed to clear the remains of one fine example dating to the sixth or seventh century. The earlier description by Kammerer, working from the German report of 1910, of 'an almost Assyrian assemblage of towers and terraces, with surrounding walls and a keep of many storeys' is certainly exaggerated. The Axumites built without mortar; arches and domes were unknown to them; and the highest wall uncovered so far is only about eighteen feet high. Nevertheless, some imposing mansions were constructed as the focal points of extensive complexes of minor dwellings. Many houses had two storeys. After the fourth century, Christian models were increasingly followed, owing much to the basilican form of early churches in the east.

It is generally accepted that the Axumite court was converted to Christianity during the reign of a king called Ezana, who ruled through the middle part of the fourth century A.D. The orthodox   43

FIG. 13. The only standing Axum monolith, which is 70 feet (21 m) high.

tradition recorded by Rufinus in his sixth-century *Ecclesiastical History* tells how a Syrian Christian travelling to India with his two sons, Aedesius and Frumentius, was shipwrecked on the coast of Axum during the reign of Ella Amida, the father of Ezana. Ella Amida adopted the two young Syrians and placed them in the service of his son Ezana. When Ezana at length succeeded his father, Frumentius became a power in the land, using his influence to spread Christianity, and eventually travelling to Alexandria to be consecrated bishop by the Patriarch Athanasius. Ezana, meantime, was engaged in a career of military conquests, which culminated in a great expedition to the island of Meroe, now overrun by two groups of nomadic invaders known from an Axumite inscription as the Red and Black Noba. In this inscription Ezana tells how 'the Blacks waged war upon the Red Peoples, and a second and a third time broke their oath, and without cause slew their neighbours and plundered our envoys'. And he boasts that he burnt their towns, 'those of masonry and those of straw, and my people seized their iron and their bronze, and the dried meat and the images in their temples, and destroyed their stocks of corn and cotton'. But, what is more significant, Ezana, who had dedicated three earlier inscriptions to the Sabean god of war, Mahrem, addressed this one to 'the Lord of Heaven, the Perfect One, who reigns to all Eternity'. And at the same period the crescent and disc of Ashtar were replaced on the coinage by the Christian cross.

We know very little indeed about the state of affairs in the Meroitic kingdom during and immediately after the period of the Axumite incursion. It seems that the northern province of Nubia, between the first and third cataracts, had fallen into the hands of one group of people called by the Byzantine sources Nobatians, and by archaeologists the X Group. These were in origin nomads from the western deserts, pastoralists and horsemen, and they set up a kingdom in lower Nubia, of which the capital, Ballana, has been excavated and has revealed a curious amalgam of Byzantine, Meroitic and Sabean culture. Most probably there was another Nobatian group, which had created a kingdom in the central, Napatan region of old Meroe. This kingdom, with its capital at Old Dongola, became un-known as Makurra. The area conquered by Ezana was therefore just the southern half of the Meroitic kingdom, and what happened there after the conquest is the greatest mystery of all. What we do know is that by the sixth century a third Nobatian state, called Alodia or Alwa, had come into existence there, with its capital at Soba, some ten miles up the Blue Nile from modern Khartoum. During the fifth and sixth centuries A.D. all three of these kingdoms were 45 converted by Christian missionaries working southwards from Byzantine Egypt. At the same period Christian Axum was attempting, with Byzantine help, to introduce Christianity by force into the Sabean kingdoms of southern Arabia. The Greek monk Cosmas, who was at Adulis in 528, witnessed the preparations for the Axumite invasion, which was transported across the Red Sea in Byzantine ships. For half a century, from 528 until 575, Axumite viceroys ruled in the Yemen. Arabian Christianity was supported both against Judaism and the older Sabean cults. It seemed as though not only Egypt, but Nubia, Ethiopia and Arabia were destined for the Christian fold. But nationalist opposition to the Axumites provoked exactly the reaction that Byzantium most feared. The people of southern Arabia appealed for help to the Sassanid kings of Persia. Two Persian expeditions arrived by sea in 575, and the Axumites were driven back to the African shore, leaving Arabia open for the conquests of Muhammad and his successors early in the following century. One important characteristic of this north-east African Christendom in the face of Muslim expansion was, as we shall see in Chapter 11, that most if it had originated from missionaries holding to the Monophysite doctrine about the nature of Christ. During the sixth and early seventh centuries monks and clergy were progressively driven out of the main centres of Byzantine Orthodoxy. This weakened the political link with Byzantium, with the result that the conquering Arabs saw African Christianity as an indigenous institution to be conciliated, rather than as an enemy to be crushed. The Coptic Church survived in Egypt as the religion of the conservative Egyptians. In the Sudan and Ethiopia it continued as the religion of the state.

5 North Africa and its invaders from 500 B.C. till the Arab conquests

The greatest problem of North African history is to learn to look at it from the point of view of its main indigenous population, the Afro-Asiatic-speaking Berbers. More than any other part of the continent, ancient North Africa is known by its invaders – the Phoenicians, the Greeks, the Romans, the Vandals, the Byzantines and finally the Arabs. Yet these invaders never constituted more than a fraction of the population of North Africa. Each layer was more or less assimilated before the next arrived. Moreover the area actually settled by them scarcely extended beyond the coastal plain. Broadly speaking, the invaders built the towns and farmed the market-gardening areas necessary to feed the urban populations. Beyond these towns and suburbs lived a steadily growing population of Berbers who had become sedentary farmers. When the invaders were strong, most of the sedentaries would obey their rule; but when they grew weak, they would organise a rule of their own. Beyond these again, in the mountains and the deserts, lived those usually described as nomads – the hunters and the pastoralists and the marginal cultivators of the oases. These were most of the people, occupying most of the land. They never recognised the rule of the invaders unless temporarily, at the point of the sword. Mostly they kept the military initiative, swooping upon the sedentaries, who had wealth to steal.

The Berbers, so-called by the Arabs, were known to the Greeks as Libyans and to the Romans as Moors. As we first meet them in literature in the works of Herodotus, the Libyans living to the south of the Gulf of Sirte in the country still called Libya are already clearly recognisable. In eastern Tripolitania there were the Nasamonians, who spent the winter months as pastoralists in the coastal belt, and in the summer left their flocks and herds by the seashore and trekked inland to the oasis of Augila to gather the dates from the palms. Ten days' journey to the west of Augila was the great oasis region of Garama (the modern Jerma), the home of the Garamantes, who were the most powerful group among the Libyan Berbers. In this part of the Fezzan mixed farming was possible, and there is abundant archaeological evidence of dense population along the lines of seasonal watercourses flowing north-westwards from the Hoggar massif. At 47

Garama itself the Italian expedition of Caputo, Pace and Sergi in 1933–4 discovered a cemetery estimated to contain some 45 000 burials, the earliest of them dating from the fifth century B.C. and continuing through the Carthaginian and Roman periods. As we saw in Chapter 1, Herodotus reported that the Garamantes used chariots to raid for slaves among the black 'Ethiopians' who lived in caves in the Hoggar and Tibesti massifs. The distribution of the rock paintings of chariots, mostly established by Henri Lhote, extends right across the Hoggar to Adrar of the Ifoghas, and suggests that, here at least, the Berbers were in regular touch with the Negro peoples of the western Sudan for a considerable period before the horse gave way to the camel.

North and west of the Fezzan, the Berbers largely escaped the notice of Herodotus, and first appear only in the writings of later historians who chronicled the victories of Carthage and of Rome. The picture, however, is similar. For so long as they were left to themselves, the Tunisian and Algerian Berbers remained primarily pastoralists, breeding cattle, sheep and goats for their milk and wool, meat and skins. They rode and fought bareback and with great skill on their big Barbary horses, using mules as beasts of burden, to which camels were only added during the first few centuries A.D. Before the imperial expansion of Carthage in the late fifth century B.C., pastoral Berbers of the same general character as the Nasamonians occupied the coastlands of western Tripolitania, most of the Tunisian plain, and the coastal belt of Algeria and Morocco. The mountains, from the Aures right across the Saharan Atlas to the High Atlas, and the great desert area lying between the Hoggar and the Mauritanian steppe, were still full of wild animals, including the lion, the leopard, the elephant and the rhinoceros, all of which were hunted by the Berbers, who traded ivory, skins and feathers with the Carthaginians and later exported great numbers of wild animals for the circuses of imperial Rome. Finally, just as we know from the rock paintings of the Hoggar that the Libyans crossed the central Sahara during the period of horse-drawn chariots, so we know that the western Berbers were driving horse-drawn vehicles southwards across the Mauritanian steppe to the latitudes of Timbuktu and ancient Ghana. These rock drawings of the western Sahara are both cruder and more weather-beaten than those of the Hoggar, and their interpretation is correspondingly more uncertain. It would appear, however, that in this area many of the wheeled vehicles are to be described as carts for carrying goods rather than as chariots for slave-raiding and warfare. If so, it becomes probable that the exchange of Saharan salt for the copper of southern Mauritania and the gold of the western Sudan was already being practised by the Berbers during the first millennium B.C. If we remember that the final Stone Age settlements at Tichitt date to around the third century B.C., and that the camel was first reported in Algeria and Morocco in the fourth century A.D., we can set approximate limits to the period of the horse-drawn trade.

Such then was the indigenous Berber population of North Africa, among whom the maritime peoples of the Mediterranean began to settle during the course of the first millennium B.C. By 500 B.C. the process was not very far advanced. A series of Greek colonies spanned the coast of Cyrenaica and sent trading expeditions down the eastern side of the Gulf of Sirte. On the western side of the gulf, Phoenician territory was still confined to the north-eastern corner of modern Tunisia, and virtually to the suburbs of Carthage and Utica. During the course of the fifth century, however, Carthage conquered the Tunisian plain and the coastal belt of Tripolitania. There thus began the process which was to continue through more than two thousand years, whereby the coast-based conqueror sought to divide the sedentary people from the nomads, absorbing the first into his own system of government and driving out the second into the deserts and the hills. It never worked oµt as it was intended to, because there was in fact no clear distinction between one way of life and the other. However far outwards the frontier was pushed, the dissidents re-grouped themselves behind it, and the main concentrations of resistant power were found along the edges of the colony or province. From the fifth-century expansion of Carthage three types of situation resulted. There was first of all the *chora*, the nodal territory farmed by Carthaginian proprietors using Berber slaves acquired by trade or captured in the wars of conquest. Next there was the dependent territory, farmed by tax-paying Berbers, who would revolt whenever they saw a chance of success. Finally there was the independent periphery, where resisting nomads regrouped and became sedentary, imitating the ways of the conqueror, planting his crops, copying his weapons, learning his literacy, adopting and adapting his religion and his political ideas, supplying his trade needs and making alliances with his imperial rivals.

In Tripolitania the *chora* consisted of the narrow coastal plain with its three great trading and manufacturing cities of Sabratha, Oea and Lepcis Magna. Around and between the cities Carthaginian proprietors established their farms and olive groves worked by slave labour, while inland on the broken plateau north of the desert 49

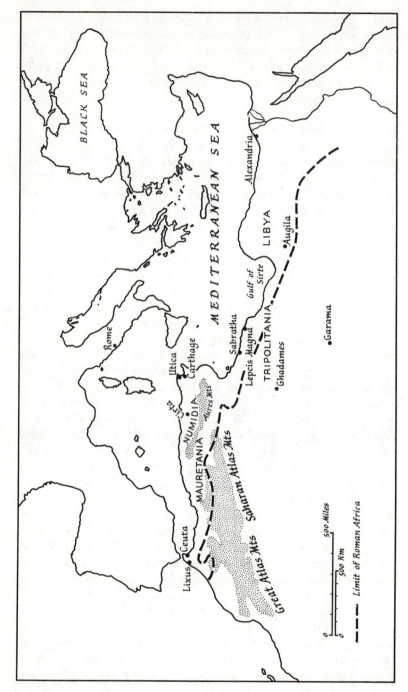

sedentary, tax-paying Berbers took to growing corn and olives while continuing to graze their flocks. The main regroupment area for the independent Berbers was four hundred miles to the south, in the Fezzan, where the Garamantes bestrode the caravan routes leading across the Hoggar to the south. So far as we know, no Carthaginian force ever reached this area, and in Roman times only two or three major punitive expeditions went so far. Yet archaeology in the Fezzan has shown a steady growth of Carthaginian and Roman influences, starting with the import of pottery and glass, cloth and metal goods, and leading on to the adoption of sophisticated irrigation works, fortifications and funerary monuments with inscriptions based on Punic characters but adapted to a Berber tongue.

In relation to Carthage itself, the *chora* was confined to north-eastern Tunisia, while the area farmed by tax-paying though potentially rebellious Berbers extended over the rest of the Tunisian plain. The regroupment area lay to the west, in the foothills of the Aures mountains in eastern Algeria. Here, where events from the third century B.C. onwards were extensively reported by Greek and Latin writers, it is possible to form some impression not only of developments in material culture but also of the way in which the Berbers adapted their social and political organisation in response to the frontier situation. Basically, Berber society, as still exemplified by the Berbers of the High Atlas and those of the Sahara, is designed for the pastoral life, in which groups of five or six families with their dependents and slaves move seasonally over a grazing area. Even this grouping is no more than a temporary alliance between families, and above it there is only a system of equally loose federations organised for the purposes of defence and diplomacy around the person of an *aguellid*, or war-leader. Nevertheless, in the circumstances of the Carthaginian frontier, the nucleus of the extruded Berbers became sedentary, and the most successful of the *aguellids* became kings. The foundations of this process were no doubt laid in the fourth century B.C. By the third century two main kingdoms had emerged in eastern Algeria, and a third in western Algeria and Morocco. This was the situation when Carthage entered upon its century-long struggle with the Roman Republic, and it is hardly surprising that the Roman tactic was to make friends with the Berbers. Thanks to this alliance, we have particularly good information about an *aguellid* called

◀ Fig. 14. Roman North Africa.

Massinissa, whose career spanned the late third and early second centuries B.C., who became the ally of Scipio Africanus in his victories over Carthage in 204, and who went on to unite the two Berber kingdoms in eastern Algeria, making his capital at Cirta (the modern Constantine), and carrying his western frontier almost to the border of Morocco. Following his conquests, Massinissa became a civilised ruler, keeping the friendship of Rome, patronising Greek and Latin scholars at his court, indulging in monumental building. More important, he devoted himself to the spread of agriculture, and it was under his rule that the largest number of the Algerian Berbers living to the north of the Atlas became sedentary farmers, many of them living in towns for protection and going out by day to work the surrounding countryside.

During a reign of more than fifty years (201–148 B.C.) Massinissa annexed first one slice and then another of a Carthage gravely weakened by its wars with Rome. From the Aures foothills his armies descended upon the Tunisian plain and pressed steadily to the sea. Turning southwards, in 162 B.C., he conquered the Tripolitanian coastlands and occupied the three cities. In the last years of his reign he was closing in upon Carthage itself. In the event, he died just before the final and decisive Roman attack on the city in 146 B.C., but it could well be that the Roman annexation of Carthage was primarily designed to forestall Rome's Berber allies of the previous century. Certainly, from this time onwards, Roman policy was to divide the

FIG. 15.   Roman Carthage.

Numidian Berbers, so that they should not threaten the new Province of *Africa*, which was destined to give its name to the whole continent.

However, it was another two hundred years before Roman North Africa became anything more than a small strategic foothold on the southern shore of the Mediterranean, and during all this time it was in the successor states to Massinissa's Numidia, and in the neighbouring kingdom known to the Romans as 'Mauretania', that the greatest number of Berbers were converted to a civilised way of life on the Roman pattern. Roman ships frequented the ports of North Africa. Roman merchants established themselves in the Berber towns in order to buy the wheat and the olives of the Berber farmers of the coastal plain, the wool and the leather goods of the Berber pastoralists of the Atlas, the wild animals, the ivory and skins of the Berber hunters of the desert frontier, and here and there – especially at Lepcis in Tripolitania and at Lixus on the Atlantic coast of Morocco – to deal in the gold and slaves brought across the Sahara by Berber caravan-traders.

From time to time the authorities of the Roman province intervened in the affairs of their Numidian neighbours, as for example in 111–105 B.C., when Jugurtha, a great-nephew of Massinissa, came near to re-creating his ancestor's great kingdom. The Tripolitanian cities at this stage declared themselves the allies of the Roman Republic, and Bocchus, king of eastern 'Mauretania', gained the western half of Numidia on Jugurtha's defeat. However, it was not until 46 B.C. that Roman territory was formally extended by Julius Caesar beyond the confines of modern Tunisia, by the annexation of the Numidian kingdom of Juba I, which still at that time stretched across the whole south-western frontier of Roman Africa, from eastern Algeria to the Gulf of Sirte. 'Mauretania' was annexed to the empire by Caligula in A.D. 40, after the two highly Romanised successors of Bocchus had had to call in the aid of the legions to defend them from the Getuli and the Musalames, pastoral Berbers of the Saharan Atlas, which was to be the main area of Berber regroupment and resistance during the first three centuries A.D.

Roman North Africa had now reached almost its widest extent. It stretched from the Atlantic coast of Morocco, in the neighbourhood of modern Rabat, eastwards to Tripolitania, including the whole of the coastal plain, but keeping to the north of all the main mountain ranges. Later extensions were to carry it a little further south, to include most of the high plateaux between the Atlas and the coast, but never into the Atlas itself. Within this narrow corridor the first three centuries A.D. saw great developments in agriculture, and above

53

all in urbanisation. Roman North Africa was not, in the modern sense, a colony of settlement. The colonisers consisted mainly of soldiers, administrators, merchants and tax-farmers. They came from all over the empire. They made common cause with the ruling class of town-dwelling, propertied Berbers which had emerged in the pre-colonial kingdoms. They took Berber wives, and had children and grandchildren who spoke Latin, but were increasingly Berbers by race. The army especially tended to be a hereditary occupation, and the half-Berber children of the military camps, destined to form the next generation of legionaries, typified the process of cultural assimilation. The camps grew into garrison towns, which, being new foundations, were planned from the first on Roman lines. The older towns, centring on ports and markets, were enlarged and adapted by the addition of forums, baths, schools and temples.

As in so much of the ancient world, townsmen were the privileged class, largely exempt from taxation, the main weight of which was borne by 'pagan' country-dwellers, hounded on by tax-gatherers who had bought their practices at auction and could make their profit only by exercising the utmost rigour. Many countryfolk who had no land of their own were forced to take holdings as crop-sharers on the imperial domains or those belonging to municipalities and large

FIG. 16.   Ruins of the Roman town of Dougga, Tunisia.

proprietors. Still, even in the countryside there were some success stories, such as that of the worthy citizen of Mactaris, who recorded:

I was born of a poor family. My father had neither revenues nor a house of his own. From the day of my birth I always cultivated my field. Neither my land nor I ever took any repose. When it came towards harvest time, I was always the first to reap my grain... Then, leaving my own district, for twelve years running I reaped for others under a sun of fire. For eleven years I commanded a team of harvesters and reaped corn in the fields of the Numidians. By hard work and by consuming little, I at last became the owner of a house and farm. Now I live at ease. I have even attained to some honour. I was called to sit in the senate of my town, and from a small farmer I became at last a censor. I have lived to see my children and grandchildren grow up around me. My life has been peaceful and respected by all.[1]

In general, however, it would seem that the rural population of North Africa was more exploited than benefited by Roman rule. The area under wheat grew greatly, but the tax gatherer took most of the produce and exported it down the new Roman roads to the ports, whence it was shipped for free distribution to the citizens of the metropolis. In a very real sense, North Africa was 'the granary of Rome'. But the rural producer enjoyed none of the privileges of the townsman. In default of education and the wider contacts of urban life, he remained Berber-speaking and nursed the memory of his pre-colonial freedom. When he saw a chance of success, he revolted. When he became a Christian, he had a bias towards heresy, in order to defy the urban establishment. When his descendants at last became Muslims, it was to be the same.

Christianity came early to North Africa, entering through the Jewish communities of the ports, and spreading rapidly to the towns of the interior. By A.D. 180 the North African Church had produced its first twelve martyrs, who were beheaded in the little town of Scilli. In 203 Perpetua, a young noblewoman of Carthage with a child at the breast, was thrown to the lions during the persecution of Septimius Severus. Tertullian, who lived at Carthage from about 160 till about 240, was a great apologist of the faith, and the first of the Church Fathers to write in Latin rather than Greek. In 212 he wrote: 'We are an immense multitude, nearly the majority in every city.' The Council of Carthage, held about 225, was attended by seventy bishops of the North African dioceses. From 249 the great Cyprian, Bishop of Carthage, led the Church through the persecution of Decius

---

[1] *Corpus Inscriptionum Latinarum*, vol. VIII, 11814, cited in C.-A. Julien, *Histoire de L'Afrique du Nord*, vol. I, p. 163.

until his own martyrdom in 258. Throughout the fourth century North African Christianity was preoccupied with Donatism, originally a barren doctrine of rigorism against Christians who had lapsed under persecution. But it resulted in the ordination of a rival clergy and persisted for nearly three centuries. The hero of the orthodox side in this struggle was St Augustine (356–430), who was probably the greatest African of all time, whose *City of God* is still studied by political scientists, and whose *Confessions* have retained their appeal to the human heart through sixteen centuries. Ironically, however, St Augustine was triumphant over Donatism only in branding it officially a heresy and in driving out its clergy, the survivors of whom took to the countryside and became the leaders of the underprivileged Berber-speaking peasantry in their grievances against the urban establishment. Driven thence by further persecution, they retreated into the mountains and across the frontiers and helped to nourish the spirit of Berber independence.

Already by the late third century Roman power in North Africa was declining. Serious Berber risings burst out from the mountain enclaves of Kabylia and the Aures. In the fourth century 'Mauretania' was largely abandoned, and all around the edges of the reduced colony Berber *aguellids* began to rebuild their strength. In the fifth century the whole structure of Roman rule crumbled before the Vandals, predatory migrants from the Baltic regions of Europe, who swept across Poland, Germany, France and Spain and, in 429, crossed the Straits of Gibraltar 80 000 strong under their young king Genseric. The first concern of the Vandals was with plunder, and, their ancestors having been converted by Arian missionaries, they had ever since made free with the accumulating treasures of the Catholic churches. Once landed in North Africa, they moved swiftly eastwards across the coastal plain of Morocco and Algeria, taking Carthage in 435, and distributing among themselves the rich villas and the great estates of the Tunisian plain. Here at last they settled, and for just a century they took the places of the Romano-Berber aristocracy, while their leaders preoccupied themselves with the building of a fleet and with organised piracy throughout the western Mediterranean; the city of Rome itself was plundered by them in 455.

On land, however, the Vandals were never numerous enough to hold more than the Tunisian plain and a small part of eastern Algeria. Their period of rule saw a great strengthening of the Berber kingdoms all the way from the Tripolitanian border to the Atlantic. The mountain Berbers descended in all directions from the Aures, and laid waste the garrison towns of the old Roman frontier. One of their *aguellids* called Masties even proclaimed himself Emperor, and exercised the title unchallenged through forty years. In 'Mauretania' too, independent kingdoms developed, especially that of a ruler called Masuna, who described himself as 'King of the Moors and the Romans', and whose dynasty was probably responsible for the thirteen remarkable pyramids inscribed with Christian symbols at Djedar in the Oranian Tell. Developments like these have traditionally been described by historians of the classical period as part of the regrettable breakdown of Roman civilisation. In fact they were probably much less regrettable than the coming of the Vandals, for they showed that both Christianity and civilised political ideas had spread beyond the Roman frontier to a wide population of sedentary Berbers. When the Vandal state was conquered in 533 by Belisarius, the general of the Byzantine emperor Justinian, the Vandal population simply disappeared without trace. The Byzantines found themselves dealing on the one hand with the Romano-Berbers of the coastal cities and the Tunisian plain, and on the other hand with a whole series of half-civilised, half-Christianised federations of half-sedentary Berbers, with whose *aguellids*, now turned princes, they established a patron and client relationship, conferring recognition and regalia in exchange for hostages, tribute, nominal adherence to Christianity and freedom for missionary work.

It may be that the Byzantine formula for dealing with frontier peoples was a good one, which might in more favourable circumstances have enabled Christianity, and the Byzantine idea of the Christian state, to penetrate across the Sahara into West Africa in much the same way as Islam was later to do. Already during the reign of Justinian, the Tripolitanians living in the oases of Augila and Ghadames were converted to Christianity, and in 569 the Garamantes of the Fezzan signed a treaty of peace and of conversion. The Fezzan was on the edge of West Africa, and it is most likely that the Christian symbols still surviving among the Tuareg of the central Sahara derive, directly or indirectly, from the brief episode of Byzantine influence in the Fezzan during the half-century preceding the Arab conquests. But the impediments to culture contact across the desert were not only geographical but human. Between the sedentary peoples of North Africa and the sedentary peoples of West Africa lay a vast region in which the only possible way of life was specialised pastoralism. And the evidence is that, precisely during the period of the Vandal and Byzantine ascendancy in North Africa, the pastoral life of the desert margins was undergoing a revolution through the appearance of the camel. There has been much confused and contradictory writing on   57 this subject. According to Charles-André Julien, the author of the best-known history of North Africa, this revolution coincided with the expulsion of the pastoral Berbers from the Roman provinces. 'Camel and Berber,' he writes, 'one carrying the other, penetrated into the Sahara.' In fact, however, the camel-breeding pastoralists seem to have been a largely new element in the population of western North Africa. Though Berbers, they seem to have come from the eastern end of Berber country, from Cyrenaica and the Libyan desert to the south of it. Both the Vandals and the Byzantines had to fight them in the marches between eastern Tripolitania and southern Tunisia. They were *new* people, by name Zanata, who had not grown up on the Roman frontier and half-submitted to its attractions. Their camels were to provide the most efficient form of transport yet known in the central and western Sahara. It was inevitable that they would supersede the older Berber caravan-drivers with their horses and their mules. In time they would mix with the western Berbers to form the Tuareg of the Hoggar and the Sanhaja of the Mauritanian steppe. In time they would be influenced by Islam, which would soften their relationships both to the north and the south of the desert. But in the circumstances of the fifth and sixth centuries they were the outlaws of the desert marches. Their hand was against every man's, and every man's hand was against them. They were the barrier through which every influence passing from North Africa to West Africa had to find its way.

6   Sub-Saharan West Africa in the
Early Iron Age – 500 B.C. to A.D. 1000

In Chapter 2 we saw that food production in West Africa was a process which began in Saharan latitudes with the pastoralism depicted in rock art and attested to by associated sites dating from the sixth millennium B.C. onwards. However, it was apparently not until the second millennium B.C. that cereals suited to the sub-Saharan tropics were developed from the wild grasses ancestral to millet and sorghum, thus permitting the start of sedentary agricultural life. If the cultural sequence of the Tichitt valley and escarpment can be taken as typical, it would seem that little more than a thousand years of Stone Age agriculture separated the period of specialised pastoralism from the beginning of the Iron Age, which is probably to be placed around the third or second century B.C. And yet, only about a thousand years on from there, in the eighth century A.D., we find the Arab conquerors of North Africa making contact with a fully fledged Soninke (Mande) kingdom of Ghana, situated between the Senegal and the upper Niger. Down the eastern side of the Niger bend there was certainly in existence by the same period the nucleus of a Songhay kingdom, commanding both the river traffic and the land route through Adrar of the Ifoghas to the Hoggar and North Africa. Eastwards again, the Hausa of Niger and northern Nigeria were already developing the density of population that within two or three more centuries would permit the emergence of urban life. And beyond Lake Chad the agricultural Sao peoples of Kanem were shortly to become aware of a conquering polity of horsemen and camel-drivers expanding systematically from the north, which would shortly incorporate most of them within the great state of Kanem-Bornu. Ill-documented though it still is, the Early Iron Age of the West African Sudanic belt must clearly have been a period of very rapid progress in human control of the environment.

In West Africa the Early Iron Age, like the preceding period of Stone Age agriculture, is to be seen in the context of the progressive desiccation of Saharan latitudes, causing a southward drift of the early food-producing populations and their concentration in the Sudanic belt. Whereas most evidence of Stone Age agriculture has been found between latitudes 15° and 20° N., by the time of the first   59

Arab contacts the belt of cereal cultivation had shifted three or four degrees to the south, and it has since moved about two or three degrees further. This is a change which would correspond with the shift in the population centre of the Nilotic Sudan from the latitude of Dongola and Napata southwards to Meroe during the second half of the first millennium B.C., and from there southwards to the Khartoum region during the first millennium A.D. And, as in the Nilotic Sudan, the main significance of the shift in terms of human geography was to transfer the centre of population increase ever more surely from the Afro-Asiatic into the Negro sphere. The rock art of the pastoral period of the central Sahara shows that Negroes were then living alongside Afro-Mediterranean or Caucasian peoles as far north as latitude 25°. Skeletal evidence from about thirty neolithic sites lying between latitudes 15° and 21° shows a considerable preponderance of Negroes. The southward drift of mixed farmers was therefore a movement by people who were already mainly Negro into wholly Negro country. Behind them, from the Hoggar west to the Senegal, the deteriorating Sahara remained fit only for the most specialised pastoralists, and it was the Berbers from the north who sparsely filled the vacuum.

There is no real doubt that the Iron Age must have spread to West Africa from the outside, from the north or the east, or, more probably, from both. At present, the main clues to the process lie in the equine phase of Saharan rock art. Chariots do not of themselves provide evidence for the use of metals, for it has been demonstrated that a light chariot, suitable for hunting or slave-raiding, could be made entirely of wood and leather and by using only stone tools for carpentry and tanning. However, the strong likelihood is that these vehicles appeared in the Sahara only during the Iron Age period of North Africa. Moreover, the western line of chariot drawings passes close to the important copper deposits of Akjoujt in southern Mauritania, where excavations by Madame Lambert in an ancient mining gallery at Guelb Moghrein in 1968 have produced four carbon dates, all in the fifth century B.C. The associated artifacts were all of copper, and the fact that they are the most southerly examples of copper artifacts yet found in western West Africa suggests that the miners were Berbers from the north rather than Negroes from the south. Nevertheless, this mining and metallurgical centre must have been almost at the frontier of the Berber and Negro spheres, and there is the further consideration that at Akjoujt copper and iron ores are so intermixed that it would have been impossible to smelt one without the other. It would in fact have been the ignorance of the techniques of hardening iron by hammering that would have caused the copper to be worked before the iron, and we do not yet know how long the interval may have been. But with iron-working techniques already known to the Carthaginians on the Atlantic coast of Morocco by the fifth century B.C., the line of approach through Mauritania has to be judged a strong possibility, at least for the western part of West Africa.

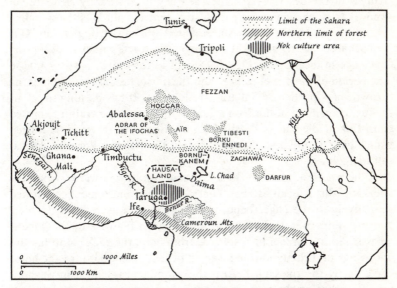

FIG. 17.   The Sahara and western Sudan in the Early Iron Age.

At least two other lines of approach have to be considered, however, one being the line of communications passing from Tripolitania through the Fezzan and across the Hoggar massif, and the other being a line passing to the south of the Libyan desert from the Nile valley. Once again, dated sites are still lacking, and the main source of evidence is the rock art of the Hoggar and Tibesti massifs and of the belt of hilly country to the south of them in Aïr, Borku and Ennedi. We have already looked at the distribution of chariot drawings across the Hoggar and Adrar of the Ifoghas. There is no doubt that these charioteers were of northern origin. The rock art, wherever it is sufficiently detailed, shows them wearing the characteristic Libyan plume, and carrying the round shield typical of the Libyan Berbers. Besides the charioteers there are horsemen, similarly accoutred, and armed with a sheathed dagger bound to the forearm and with two or three javelins for throwing, which were also typical of the northern 61

Libyans. In what must be the later pictures, the horsemen are joined by cameleers, their beasts saddled in Libyan fashion, and with the camels there appear inscriptions in a Libyan Berber script ancestral to that of the Tuareg. Throughout the whole of this sequence the element of metallurgy is minimal. So far as we know, there was no central Saharan equivalent of the Mauritanian copper mines, with their implication that smiths were living and working on the southern fringes of the desert by the fifth century B.C. The only rich site yet known from the southern part of the central Sahara is the so-called 'tomb of Tin Hinan', near Abalessa in Adrar of the Ifoghas, and it is remarkable for the range of its imported objects rather than for any evidence of local production. It belongs to the fourth century A.D., to the period of the camel rather than the horse. Probably it signifies the growth of a particular Saharan trade-route. It has nothing to tell us about the coming of the Iron Age to West Africa. If metallurgy passed into the middle part of West Africa by this route, it would have been much earlier, and one can only say that the evidence does not seem at all compelling.

Whereas the rock-art tells us that, south-westwards from the Fezzan, the Libyan Berber charioteers and horsemen penetrated effectively to the Niger bend, it tells us that, south-eastwards, their normal limit was the northern and western foothills of the Tibesti massif. Southwards and eastwards from here, the rock paintings and drawings of Tchad indicate a very different origin both for the horse and, later, for the camel. Also the prominence of iron in weapons suggests that smiths accompanied the horsemen from the time of their first appearance in these regions. Throughout southern Tibesti, Borku and Ennedi, the bows and arrows and the wooden staves of Late Stone Age times are succeeded by spears with large blades, clearly of iron, and these weapons are used as lances by horsemen. The horses are the small horses of Nubia, very different from the large Libyan barbs. They are always ridden, never driven, and when they are joined by camels, these are saddled in the Nubian fashion with a square pack encompassing the hump. The mounted lancers carry large oval or violin-shaped shields very different from the round ones of Libya. Some of them wear leather bonnets, like those of the Beja living between the Nile and the Red Sea, and their horses are portrayed in the 'flying gallop' of Meroitic as well as Mycenaean art. Although we have as yet no radiocarbon dates from this area, the evidence of ancient iron-working in sites long abandoned to the desert is very plentiful. It certainly looks as though iron-working accompanied the horse, and as if both came from the east. We do not yet know the dates, but Meroitic evidence would suggest that, while the fifth century B.C. is not impossible, the fourth or the third century would be more likely. And on the other hand any date much later than the third or second century B.C. would hardly allow a sufficient time for the horse to have manifested itself in advance of the camel, as it clearly did.

Moreover, whether the Iron Age spread into West Africa from the north-west or the north-east, or from both, it now seems certain that in one very typical region of Sudanic orchard-bush country, only about ten degrees north of the Equator and far from the terminus of any obvious trans-Saharan trade route, iron was in regular use by at least the third century B.C., and perhaps by a century or so earlier. This is the region on and immediately to the south of the Jos plateau in northern Nigeria, where modern tin-mining has resulted in the recovery of some hundreds of examples of terracotta figurines known, rightly or wrongly, as the 'Nok culture'. Strictly speaking, the word

FIG. 18.   Terracotta head from a tin mine in the Nok Hills, Nigeria, about 8 inches (20 cm) high.

'culture' is at the very least premature, since most of the figurines have come not from scientifically controlled excavations, but as the by-products of rough mining operations, which have followed the lines of ancient and now deeply buried river beds. For all we know, the sculptures may not have come from any single consistent material culture, and they may have been produced over a long period of time. It may be that some of them were fashioned during the Stone Age. However, iron slag has been found in association with many terra-cottas, and at Taruga, just to the south of the main mining area, Bernard Fagg was able to carry out one controlled excavation of a site containing both figurines and iron slag, which has produced several radiocarbon dates around the fourth and third centuries B.C. There is certainly a grave discrepancy between these dates and those for the coming of iron at the Daima mound in Bornu (see Chapter 2), where the earliest Iron Age levels have been radiocarbon dated to between the fifth and the seventh century A.D. On the other hand, it would appear that similar mound sites investigated by J.-P. Lebeuf to the north of Fort Lamy have Iron Age levels (Sao I and II) approximately as early as Taruga.

As we have suggested, there is nothing freakish about the geo-graphical environment of the 'Nok culture'. It is typical of the Nigerian 'middle belt', of northern Cameroun and Tchad to the eastwards, and of much of Dahomey, the southern part of northern Ghana, and the northern Ivory Coast to the westwards. Two thousand years ago this belt was probably a little moister and somewhat more thickly wooded than it is today. But it was still to the north of the high forest. It was cereal country, suited to millet and sorghum, though yams might also have been grown there. It was the latitude where the life of settled agriculture, as distinct from that of mixed farming and cattle-keeping, must have taken shape. It is most unlikely that any one part of this zone passed into the Iron Age much earlier than the rest. At the same time, we need not think that the artists of the Nok tradition were necessarily the ancestors of the 'middle belt' peoples of modern Nigeria. Everything points to there having been a southward drift of climate, of culture, of people. Art historians are of opinion that the Nok tradition of plastic art is, in a loose way, ancestral to the medieval sculpture tradition of Igala and Nupe, Yoruba and Ibo. Probably, therefore, it is sensible to think in terms of people, as well as culture, moving southwards with the climate – the belt of densest population keeping just to the north of the retreating forest, and only the pioneers pressing forward into the land of the oil-palm and the kola-nut. West of Nigeria and Dahomey, this is a pattern that would accommodate equally the historical traditions of the Akan peoples of Ghana and the Ivory Coast, most of whom would seem to have drifted from the orchard bush to the forest only in medieval times. It is in fact significant that several major languages and language groupings – the Mande languages in the west, the Akan languages in the middle, the Yoruba and Ibo languages in the east – all straddle the forest line. Different as the forest environment undoubtedly is from that of the orchard bush, the same groups of people now occupy both zones. The most likely inference is that they developed in one and spread to the other, and the indications are that the spread was from north to south.

Thus, during the early Iron Age period, roughly between 500 B.C. and A.D. 1000, the most actively developing zone of West Africa was probably that between about 11° and 16° N. and the peoples who became the first Iron Age farmers probably included, among many others, the ancestors of the Mande and the Akan, the Hausa, the Yoruba and the Ibo. That is not, of course, to say that the social institutions characterising these peoples in recent times would, by the beginning of the period, have reached more than a very rudimentary stage. Nevertheless, we know that by the end of the period there were to be found kingdoms and armies, towns and industries, and cultures capable of producing great works of art. It is certain that the foundations of all these achievements must be sought far back in the Iron Age, even the early stages of which must have involved more dynamic changes than they did elsewhere in Africa south of the Sahara. Poor though the archaeological evidence may be, some discussion of the main elements of the problem cannot be avoided.

First and foremost, it must be that, even during the early part of the Iron Age, there developed in the Sudanic belt of West Africa a density of population much greater than that existing in any other part of Africa, saving only the Nile valley. Without such a population density there could not have been the widespread urbanisation that was already manifest, particularly at the Nigerian end of West Africa, by the end of the first millennium A.D. If we are to place the Nok sculptures in a social context which makes any sense, we must imagine a rural society aggregated enough and stable enough to be commemorating its ancestors and tribal heroes in a highly permanent medium, and one demanding both artistic genius and technical skill. If we are to judge from later Nigerian societies, we may be fairly sure that the figurines were made to rest in the family shrines of large and permanent compounds, each housing three or four generations of an extended family, and forming in itself a kind of compact village. These compounds would probably have been set down, as they still are, within hailing distance of each other, so as to form a wider community, in which all farmed, but in which different families specialised in the various arts and crafts. This is a pattern still familiar from end to end of the West African savanna, and it is a pattern recognisable in the first chapter of the Kano Chronicle, which embodies the traditions concerning the rural origins of the city in the late first millennium A.D.

The greatest of the chiefs of the country was Mazauda, the grandfather of Sarkin Makafi. Gijigiji was the blacksmith. Bugazau was the brewer. Hanburki doctored every sickness ... Besides these there was Maguji, who begot the Maguzawa, and was the miner and smelter among them. Again there was Asanni, the forefather of the minstrels and chief of the dancers. Bakonyaki was the hunter with bow and arrow. Awar, grandfather of the Awrawa, worked salt of Awar ... In all there were eleven of these pagan chiefs, and each was head of a large clan. They were the original stock of Kano.[1]

Ile Ife, the religious centre of Yorubaland and the traditional dispersal point of the Yoruba city-builders, does not have genealogically articulated traditions like those of Kano; but its exquisite terracotta figurines and its unparalleled sculptured heads in cast brass have come from levels dated by radiocarbon to around the eleventh century, while the burial pits of the Orun Oba Ada grove in the centre of the town have yielded dates from the sixth century to the tenth. Ife today stands just inside the forest margin, and it is clear that in this latitude, just as six or seven hundred miles further north in Hausaland, semi-urban conditions must have existed by the end of the first millennium A.D.

Obviously, in such societies there must from a very early stage have been some political leadership wider than that of lineage heads, and one may suppose that in many cases this was not merely buttressed by ritual and magic but actually coincident with ritual and magic powers. In the Kano Chronicle, for example, we read of one Barbushe, who during the pagan period at the end of the first millennium succeeded his forefathers as chief, through the magic which he exercised as the priest of a tree-spirit called Tchunburburai.

The tree was surrounded by a wall, and no man could come within it save Barbushe. Whoever else entered, he entered but to die. Barbushe never descended from his house on Dala hill except on the two days of Idi. When the days drew near, the people came in from east and west and south and north, men and women alike. Some brought a black dog, some a black fowl, others a black he-goat, when they met together on the day of Jajibere at the

[1] The translation is from H. R. Palmer, *Sudanese Memoirs*, vol. III, p. 99.

foot of Dala hill at eve. When darkness came, Barbushe went forth from his house with his drummers. He cried aloud and said 'Great Father of us all, we have come nigh to thy dwelling in supplication, Tchunburburai.' And the people said 'Look on Tchunburburai ye men of Kano. Look toward Dala.' Then Barbushe descended and the people went with him to the god. And when they drew near, they sacrificed that which they had brought with them. Barbushe entered the sacred place – he alone – and said 'I am the heir of Dala. Like it or no, follow me ye must, perforce.' And all the people said 'Dweller on the rock, our Lord Amane, we follow thee perforce.'[1]

The variations on this theme were no doubt almost infinite, although neighbouring communities speaking a common language probably tended to develop a family likeness in their political and ritual systems also. The question which has to be asked, however, even if it can never be fully answered, is how far all the small-town chieftaincies of West Africa – the *sarkis* of Hausaland, the *obas* of the Yoruba, the *oman-henes* of the Akan, the *mansas* of the Mande – emerged from the grass-roots of local communities, and how far they tended to be local reflections of larger kingships, whether imposed by conquest or copied from afar. It is here that we have to remember the mounted horsemen with their spears, who had been present in parts of the region since the beginning of the Iron Age. Whereas the horse was eliminated from the Sahara by the camel, in the open country to the south of the desert all the indications are that it lived on and multiplied, becoming first the instrument and then the symbol of political dominion. As Jack Goody has written,

With technologies of the bow and the stone-tipped arrow, any kind of centralisation is almost impossible. But with the introduction of metals kingdoms are on the cards ... Iron weapons became of much greater importance when they were combined with a method of delivery that harnessed the power of the horse ... In West Africa, as in medieval Europe and most other parts of the globe, horses were the possessions of a politically dominant estate that was usually of immigrant origin and had established its domination over a land of peasant farmers.[2]

Most of Africa south of the Sahara was protected from the horseman by the tsetse-fly, but in the belt of open country to the south of the desert, from the Red Sea to the mouth of the Senegal, conditions for the horse-borne warrior were almost ideal. In open country, without natural cover, the horse was the most effective means both of raiding for slaves and of controlling subject populations. Given plenty of

[1] *Ibid.* pp. 97–8.
[2] *Technology, Tradition and the State in Africa*, 1971, pp. 46–9.

slave labour, a group of knights could establish a comfortable head-quarters in a mud-built, mud-walled camp, which would soon grow into the nucleus of a town. Servants and artisans would be housed within the walls. Servile agriculturalists would be quartered in villages close enough for a substantial share of the produce to be seized for the town's consumption. The most significant sites would be those chosen for their command of natural resources or natural highways – places where it was convenient for the camel caravans of the desert crossings to rest and turn round, intersections of land and water transport systems, places from which the output of dispersed copper-mining or gold-digging could be controlled. Here, customs duties could be added to tribute and a share taken in the profits of long-distance luxury trades. Here the needs of security would act as a constant goad to political expansion. Here empires, as opposed to city-states, would be born.

We do not know precisely when or from where the horse-borne conquerors came. It could be that in some sense they were the descendants of the Saharan charioteers. It could be that they came from the kingdom of Meroe, or from the savannas to the east. It could be that some of the later and more powerful waves of migrants were in origin connected with the X-Group horsemen of post-Meroitic Nubia, whose capital at Ballana revealed a curious mixture of Meroitic and Sassanian Persian influences, and also the earliest iron bits and bridles found in any African archaeological site. Such a suggestion does not, of course, mean that the whole of the western Sudan was at any time flooded with migrant conquerors from Nubia. Conquering groups always assimilate local people, and only when the first stage of conquest has thrown up a larger elite than the conquered territory can support do subsidiary groups break off and try to repeat the process elsewhere. At every such stage there is a fresh dilution of the elite and a fresh compromise with the institutions of the conquered. If this is diffusion, it is not so in the crude sense which has rightly incurred the suspicion of social scientists during the past thirty or forty years. The result of such a process shows some common features spread over very wide areas, but also differences which make close comparisons impossible.

What we do know for sure is that the prototypes of these Sudanic states antedated the expansion of Islam. When the Muslims first crossed the Sahara in 753, the kingdom of Ghana was already a going concern. According to the oral traditions current in the western Sudan in medieval times, there had been twenty-two kings of Ghana before the coming of Islam. This is not to be taken literally, but equally it is not to be ignored. Certainly, the type of state described by the early Arab geographers who had their information from living witnesses was not one which owed anything to Islamic influence. 'The religion of the kingdom of Ghana is paganism and the worship of idols', wrote al-Bakri of Cordoba in the eleventh century. While the king lived, his pavilion was surrounded by horses in golden trappings; his subjects fell on their knees before him and sprinkled their heads with dust. When the king died, he was buried with his regalia and his weapons, his plate and his drinking vessels, and with those who had served him his meals in life. Two thousand miles to the east of Ghana, the king of the Zaghawa in northern Kanem was of the same kind. 'Him they respect and worship to the neglect of Allah the most high ... Their religion is the worship of their kings, for they believe that it is they who bring life and death and sickness and health', wrote al-Muhallabi in the tenth century. The king was a god; therefore he must not be seen to eat or drink, or to have to perform any other natural function. If he fell off his horse, or if he sneezed, he must have done so on purpose, and everyone else in sight or hearing had to do the same. The king was a god; therefore he could not die a natural death, but must be killed, supposedly at his own command.

Horses apart, therefore, West African kingship seems too stereo-typed to be wholly the product of local evolution. The ideas behind the big states must have come, one feels, from a common source, probably outside the region. And, if so, then the small indigenous village chiefs, the *sarkis* and the *obas*, the *mansas* and the *henes*, must frequently have been more than clan heads who had grown into kings. Their eyes would have been partly on their own ancestors, but partly also upon the example and prestige of the horse-borne immigrants who had triumphed in their midst, or nearby. A chief would try to keep up with the most advanced ideas, whether in the possession of a horse, or, in tsetse-fly country, by riding in a litter, with parasols bobbing overhead, with the royal stool carried in front and the royal drum thumping in the rear.

7   West-central Africa around
the first millennium A.D.

We have seen that in most of Africa south of the Equator the period of food production coincided with the Iron Age. The Kenya highlands had a well-marked period of Stone Age food production, but, so far as we know at present, this was more pastoral than agricultural. In southern Uganda and north-west Tanzania there may have been a brief period, marked by Kansyore ware pottery, of food production without an accompanying iron industry. The only other area where food production may have been practised extensively during the Stone Age is the Congo basin, and here the evidence is unusually hard to interpret. Collections of stone hoes and of ground stone axes, usually associated with food production, have been found both in the forest and on its margins; but none has as yet been dated. There is also the linguistic evidence, cited in Chapter 3, that iron-working terminology was a late introduction into a proto-Bantu language that already included a large food-producing vocabulary; but this is only significant if Guthrie is right in concluding that the nuclear area of proto-Bantu lay to the south of the Equator. The opposite conclusion, popularised by Greenberg and Murdock, would maintain that Bantu expanded to the south of the Equator only during the Iron Age.

Murdock, indeed, propounded the arresting theory that since none of the important forest food crops was indigenous to Africa, the forest country both of Guinea and the Congo must have been uninhabitable by food producers until after the introduction of the South-East Asian food plants, such as the banana, the Asian yam and the cocoa-yam, with the start of Indian Ocean navigation. He therefore postulated a long interval between the coming of food production to the northern savannas and the penetration of the forests by the ancestors of the Bantu and others to the west of them, following their adoption of the South-East Asian plants. The most obvious weakness in the theory was the assumption that the South-East Asian crops would have worked their way along the northern edge of the forest as far west as Cameroun before entering it with the Bantu. In fact, however, Murdock's main premise, that Africa was devoid of indigenous forest food-plants, is now regarded by botanists as an exaggeration. There is the oil-plam. There are several African varieties of yams.

There is the so-called 'kaffir potato', and there are several kinds of beans and peas which grow quite well in forest conditions.

But perhaps the main sense in which Murdock's theory was inadequate was in its view of the equatorial forest as a single, consistent block of vegetation, without variation, without relief, without corridors. It is true that the greatest part of any area of high forest is useless to food producers until it has been cut down. This is because forest soils are acid and because insufficient sunlight penetrates the treecover. But even the densest stands of forest are broken by streams and rivers, with fish and aquatic mammals in their waters, and with sunlight and alluvial soil along their banks. Here fisherman-farmers could make their clearings, stringing out their villages in long lines by the waterside, and moving them every two or three years in order to allow the vegetation to grow back and regenerate the fragile humic layers overlying hard laterite soils. In terms of men to the square mile, the early farmer-fishermen of the Congo forest would have been a population almost negligibly sparse – even today, populations of one person to the square mile are normal in forested regions. But the main river lines could nevertheless have been permanently occupied. Communications could have been open from one side of the forest to the other. If this was how the first Stone Age food producers moved from the northern woodlands to the southern woodlands, this should not be seen as an isolated, accidental migration, but as the establishment of a series of permanent routes by which other innovations would automatically follow. Archaeologists have not so far investigated the forest flood plains of the Congo basin, but there is no reason at all why Stone Age peoples could not have developed flourishing agricultural economies along the banks of the major rivers before the advent of iron. Judging by the work of American archaeologists in the analogous circumstances of the upper Amazon basin, it would seem highly likely that sites and stratigraphical evidence both for early agriculture and for the arrival of metallurgy must exist in the Congo basin also.

Indeed, one discovery of great potential importance for the vital period of transition from the Stone to the Iron Age has come from a layer of humic deposit at the source of the Funa River near Kinshasa, where a collection of potsherds, as yet, alas, unpublished, has been excavated from a depth of forty-two inches by a Belgian geologist. Charcoal fragments found in the same layer have since been radiocarbon dated to around the third century B.C. Unfortunately, the circumstances of this most interesting find remain obscure. We do not yet know if iron slag or the remains of iron tools were found with

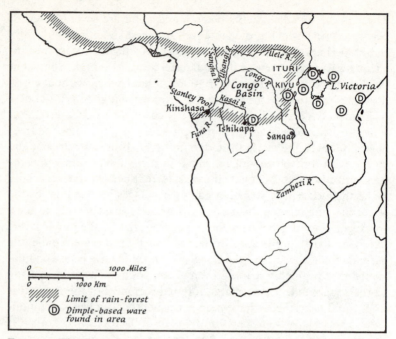

FIG. 19. The Congo basin, showing forest and waterways, with sites
mentioned in Chapter 7.

the potsherds. But, whether this proves on further investigation to be
a Late Stone Age site or an Early Iron Age one, the outcome will be
highly significant. If the former, it will be evidence of a pottery-using,
and therefore almost certainly food-producing, phase of the Stone Age
at the heart of the Congo basin. If the latter, it will be an Iron Age site
some two or three centuries earlier than any other yet known in Africa
south of the Equator, with the possible exception of the Katuruka
site, near Bukoba, Tanzania (Chapter 8). And yet it would still be later
by a century or more than the Iron Age readings from Taruga in
Nigeria. Either way, it is the more significant in that Kinshasa lies at
the meeting-point of the rivers which flow through the forest from the
north with the savanna woodlands of north-east Angola, which form
the south-western rim of the Congo basin. A glance at the map will
show how all the waterways flowing southwards into the Congo river
system converge inexorably upon the Stanley Pool, the southern
shores of which rise into the lightly wooded hills of the southern
savanna. It may well be that intensive investigation of the Kinshasa
region could resolve many of the questions surrounding the Bantu
72 penetration of the Congo forest.

Meantime, the most significant evidence relating to the Early Iron Age from the regions immediately to the south and the east of the Congo forest have been the sites containing the pottery known as Dimple-based. This is a very characteristic style of pottery, first identified around the north-eastern shores of Lake Victoria and subsequently found at all the earliest Iron Age sites in southern Uganda, north-western Tanzania, Rwanda, Burundi and the Kivu province of Zaïre. In addition to the thumb impression at the bottom of the pot from which it derives its name, Dimple-based pottery is decorated with striking bands of grooved ornamentation, arranged in scrolls, circles and triangles around the upper walls of the vessels, while their rims are almost invariably bevelled and their necks incised with two or three grooved lines. As will be seen in later chapters, Dimple-based pottery bears an ultimate relationship with other Early Iron Age pottery styles in eastern, central and southern Africa. However tantalisingly unsatisfactory the evidence, it is therefore a fact of the utmost importance that several complete and entirely characteristic Dimple-based pots were recovered during mining operations at Tshikapa on the upper Kasai, in the woodland savanna country immediately to the south of the Congo forest, a thousand miles to the south-west of the other main areas of Dimple-based discoveries, and well within the nuclear area postulated by Guthrie for the emergence of proto-Bantu. The Tshikapa pots were recovered accidentally, without their cultural context. We do not know whether or not they were associated, here as everywhere else, with the earliest phase of the Iron Age. And we have no radiocarbon date by which to compare them with the other Dimple-based wares. It therefore remains wide open whether the Dimple-based style and decorative motifs were developed in the forest, or north of the forest, and spread by the waterways to its eastern and southern peripheries – or whether they were developed to the south or the east of the forest and spread either clockwise or anti-clockwise round its margins.

It should certainly not be assumed from the distribution of present finds that the eastern area was the main centre of Dimple-based pottery manufacture, for this could be a simple reflection of the distribution of archaeological work so far. The fact is that we have at the present absolutely no scientifically controlled evidence for the Early Iron Age anywhere between the northern margins of the Congo forest and the Congo–Zambezi watershed. All we do have is one major site from the Later Iron Age, namely the extensive cemetery site at Sanga, by the shores of Lake Kisale on the upper Lualaba. Here in 1957 and 1958 two Belgian archaeologists, Jean Hiernaux and

Fig. 20.   Top: Kisalian pottery from Sanga. Bottom: Partial view of Burial no. 53.

Jacques Nenquin, excavated sixty burials, chosen at random among tens or hundreds of thousands which extend for mile upon mile by the shores of the lake. On the basis of pottery and other grave goods, the

74

burials are now divided into two cultural groups, which are called Kisalian and Red Slip, and which are known to have been contemporary. The Kisalian burials were richly accompanied with pottery specially made for funerary purposes, with iron and ivory ornaments and iron weapons. The burials accompanied by Red Slip ware appear to have been those of an intrusive group of merchants and miners, and they contain jewellery and ingots of copper. The radiocarbon dates for both groups gave readings around the eighth and ninth centuries A.D. The Kisalian pots have rounded bases, contracted shoulders and flaring necks with in-turned rims. The shoulders are decorated with incised half-moon motifs, and the inverted rims are often bevelled, incised or comb-stamped. The Red Slip ware vessels are covered with a shiny red finish and have only simple ornamentation. The general characteristics of the Kisalian pots strongly recall Early Iron Age pottery traditions in eastern and south-central Africa, both in the forms of some of the vessels and in the bevelled rims and grooved decoration. There is every reason to think that they must descend from an Early Iron Age pottery of the Katanga similar to the Dimple-based or the other Early Iron Age forms.

The dominant metal of the objects of the Red Slip culture is copper, which is found in the form of croisettes, or miniature cruciform ingots suggesting a use as currency, and also in the form of jewellery, especially necklaces and ornamental chains of copper wire. A few iron implements were found, including an axe. A handful of glass beads and a single, perforated cowrie shell were the only imported trade objects. The Lake Kisale region was an important centre for trade in both copper and salt in later times, and it is evident from the Sanga excavations that the roots of this later commerce were already planted in the late first millennium. The exceptional richness of the Sanga graves reflects what must have been an already flourishing copper and iron industry in the Katanga, which is in the strongest contrast with the poverty-striken character of contemporary sites elsewhere in eastern and southern Africa.

In other words, despite the deplorable paucity of archaeological work in the western half of Bantu Africa, there do seem to be some good archaeological reasons for thinking that both some kinds of food production and, at a somewhat later date, the techniques of metallurgy passed into sub-equatorial Africa through this side of the sub-continent. This is the message of the linguistic evidence also. We have seen in Chapter 3 that proto-Bantu was the language of a food-producing people living in a land of rivers and forest patches, in which boats and fishing were more prominent than hunting, and in which most of

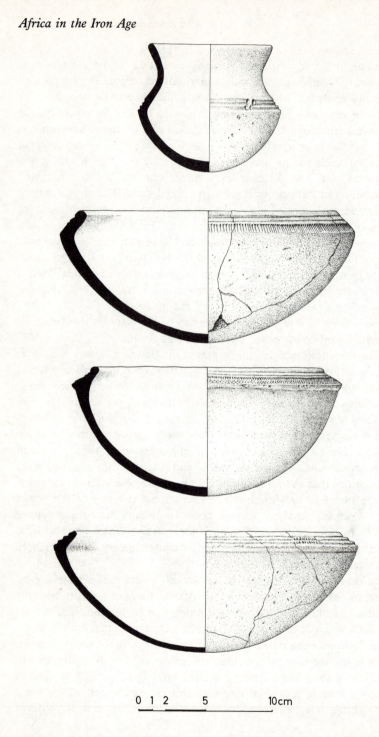

0 1 2　　5　　　　10cm

FIG. 21. Left: Pottery from Burial no. 34 at Sanga; Kisalian ware.
Above: Copper chain made of single and multiple copper rings from
Burial no. 34.

the large game animals of the eastern and southern savannas were
unknown. We have seen that the elements of a metallurgical terminology were added to this language at a somewhat later stage, but still
before its original unity was broken up by wide geographical dispersion.
What we have now to consider are the early stages of that dispersion.
Here, Guthrie and Greenberg are in agreement that the basic division
was into western and eastern forms. Greenberg sees the western forms
as older and the eastern forms as younger, but that may only mean
that the proto-language and its nearest ancestors were spoken entirely
within the western part of the area. Guthrie, working from much
more detailed evidence than Greenberg, sees a split of the proto-
language into an eastern and a western dialect. That is to say, in the
modern Bantu languages he finds about 500 word roots with a dis-

77

tribution wide enough to be called 'general', and these are those which are presumed to descend from the proto-language, whereas he finds some 1800 other roots, the distribution of which, though wide, tends to fall into either a western or an eastern pattern, suggesting that the languages in which they now occur must descend from one or other dialect of the proto-language. What is especially significant about the division is that, whereas in the latitude of Katanga and north-eastern Zambia western and eastern dialects form a continuum, in the northern parts of the Bantu sphere there is a sharp break between the descendants of the western and the eastern dialects, which is so marked that the only possible implication would seem to be that the languages on each side of the line must have broken away, not from each other, but from parent dialects further to the south. If the makers of Dimple-based pottery are to be equated with the Bantu, this might argue for a dispersion of iron-working and pottery techniques from the area to the south of the forest, running anti-clockwise around the margins of the forest to the east.

Linguists and anthropologists of Greenberg's persuasion see the Bantu as people whose first achievement was the mastery of the Congo forest environment, and Guthrie's picture of the dispersion of the Bantu languages from a more southerly cradleland has been criticised by them on the basis that higher percentages of common roots are only to be expected near the geographical centre of the Bantu sphere, where interaction and borrowing would have been more frequent than at the periphery. Explanations of this sort would, however, seem to break down when applied to the sharp division between western and eastern languages towards the northern centre of the Bantu sphere. If the Bantu cradleland was indeed in the forest, it would seem at the very least necessary to conclude that the expansion from the forest went southwards before it went eastwards. Another consideration favouring Guthrie's interpretation is that the dispersal of languages from a cradleland is more likely to have taken place in all directions than in only one direction, as postulated by the Greenberg school. Again, the diverse environment of the woodland savanna to the south of the forest seems a more likely one to have given birth to an adaptable and rapidly expanding population than the very specialised conditions of the forest.

The final set of considerations which seem to support Guthrie's picture of the Bantu dispersion rather than Greenberg's are those which seem to show that the main attack by food-producing populations on the Congo forest itself has come from the south rather than the north. On the one hand we see that all the large surviving areas

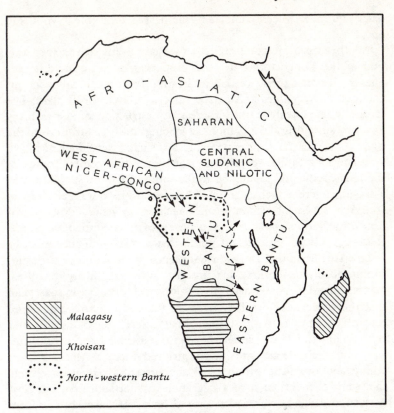

FIG. 22. Western and Eastern Bantu, according to Guthrie. North-western languages are shown as a sub-division of Western Bantu.

of primary forest are to be found to the north of the great bend of the Congo, in the Ituri forest of eastern Zaïre, and in the great forests of eastern Gabon, western Congo Republic and southern Cameroun. These are the only areas whose pygmy hunter-gatherers still survive as recognisably separate communities. In the Ituri they still equal the numbers of the agricultural Bantu in their midst. In the western forest it is clear they were still the main occupants of extensive areas until the Fang migrations of a century ago. On the other hand, to the south of the great bend of the Congo few large tracts of primary forest remain, and none of sufficient size to support specialised hunting and gathering populations. Forest growth, though often dense, is of a secondary character, having been cleared and re-cleared by cultivators. Traces of the former Stone Age hunting bands survive in the pygmoid characteristics of some of the modern populations, but otherwise the

79

older culture has been completely submerged in the food-producing one.

In other words, it would seem that we have to envisage the penetration of the Congo forest by food producers in two quite different phases. The first phase was an infiltration from north to south, but confined to river lines and narrow strips of alluvial flood-plain. The second phase involved the progressive destruction of the primary forest by agricultural populations advancing on a broad front from the south. The first phase was probably in origin a development of the very late Late Stone Age, though stone was reinforced by iron while the food-producing population to the south of the forest still formed a single, coherent speech-group. The second phase was certainly an Iron Age movement, which was just a part of the general expansion of iron-using Bantu peoples from a nuclear area to the south of the forest. It is probably in this second phase that a large influence must be assigned to the South-East Asian food plants, which Murdock attributes so improbably to the first. It is in every way more likely that these plants entered sub-equatorial Africa along its Indian Ocean coast than that they progressed overland from the Red Sea to Cameroun before turning southward to the Congo. Madagascar, we know, was first colonised by Indonesian sea-borne migrants during the early centuries A.D., and their descendants have survived there as the dominant ethnic and linguistic group until the present. It is inconceivable that some elements in such a migration did not land upon the East African mainland, where they would have been absorbed by pre-existing populations, and where the corms and tubers they brought with them would have spread wherever climate and food-producing techniques permitted. For these plants the coastal belt of East Africa offers an almost uniquely favourable climate and rainfall, and river valleys between the Rufiji and the Zambezi would have provided obvious lines of transmission to the region of the great lakes and beyond. Their arrival in the centre of the continent may well have been one of the main factors in the northward expansion of both the eastern and the western dialects, with the former colonising the northern lake region and the latter the forest to the west of it. Guthrie, unlike Greenberg, sees even the north-western Bantu languages as descendants of the western dialect. Particularly in view of Henrici's new analysis of Guthrie's data (Chapter 3, p. 30), this view is likely to prove, at the very least, an overstatement. But that there was some reflux of later Bantu colonists into the homelands of the pre-proto-Bantu in the Congo forest region would seem to be arguable on other than linguistic grounds.

8 East Africa to about the eleventh century

We have seen (Chapter 3) that the Late Stone Age population of East Africa was mainly of Bush stock, interpenetrated, especially in the highlands of Kenya and northern Tanzania, by Afro-Asiatic (Caucasian) people from the north. Judging from the surviving remnants, we can be fairly confident that most of the Bush people spoke Khoisan languages, whereas the Afro-Asiatics spoke languages of the southern sub-family of Cushitic. What we have now to examine is the evidence for the gradual encroachment upon these earlier inhabitants of people of Negro stock, speaking languages of the Bantu family, and bringing with them new cultures based upon Iron Age food production. The location of the Cushitic stronghold in the Horn of Africa makes it impossible that these Bantu newcomers should have entered East Africa from the north. They can only have come from the west or the south. The evidence from the classification of the Bantu languages themselves, which we examined in the last chapter, suggests strongly that they came from the west, though probably from the region to the south of the Congo forest rather than straight through the eastern margin of the forest itself.

Within this broader framework, derived mainly from ethnography and linguistics, the more detailed evidence, and especially the evidence of chronology, comes from Iron Age archaeology. Most of this work has been carried out during the last twenty years, since the invention of radiocarbon dating. It has been done by a handful of scholars, working with inadequate funds and therefore, often, in haste. The result is a thin scatter of radiocarbon dates and pottery collections, extending from eastern Zaïre, Rwanda and Burundi, across southern Uganda, southern Kenya and northern Tanzania. Northern Uganda and northern Kenya are as yet very little known. The southern half of Tanzania is hardly even surveyed. Nevertheless, the situation is already infinitely better than that in the western part of the Bantu sphere, which we described in the last chapter. We are beginning to have at least an outline picture of how and when Iron Age food production spread into East Africa.

As long ago as 1945, Archdeacon W. E. Owen, a missionary with archaeological interests, investigated some eroded valley slopes close 81 to the Kavirondo Gulf of Lake Victoria, and collected the first examples of the finely decorated pottery known as Dimple-based. Owen secured the interest of Louis and Mary Leakey, and together they excavated a series of sites in the Yala valley, especially one at Urewe, from which the western Kenya variety of Dimple-based pottery now takes its name. Urewe ware consists of pots, bowls and beakers, most of them decorated with striking designs of parallel grooving arranged in scrolls, circles and triangles. The rims of the

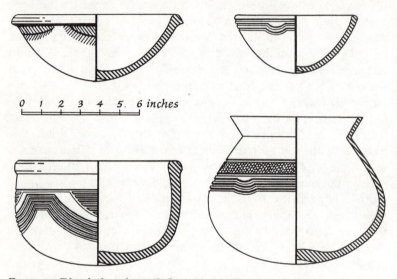

FIG. 23.   Dimple-based vessels from Urewe, Kenya.

vessels are almost invariably bevelled with two or three grooved lines, and this is a diagnostic feature of great importance. However, the most remarkable feature of the Urewe pottery is the characteristic thumb impression, or 'dimple' on the base of many of the bowls and pots. Though none of the sites was, strictly speaking, an occupation area, since all the deposits had been sorted to some extent by erosion, iron tools and slag were found in association with the pottery, and there was no doubt that the deposits belonged to the Iron Age. A closer dating was established only in the 1960s, when Robert Soper revisited Urewe and obtained charcoal samples, which yielded three dates, all ranging between the third and fifth centuries A.D.

Meanwhile, in Rwanda, Burundi and the adjoining Zaïre province of Kivu, two Belgian archaeologists, Jean Hiernaux and Emma Maquet, had been carrying out a series of small-scale excavations which had shown that, here as in western Kenya, Dimple-based pottery was the

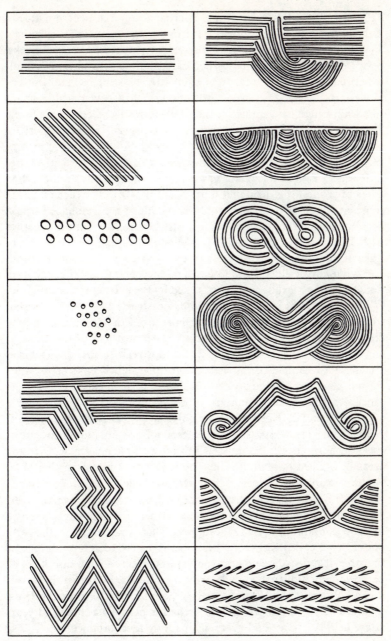

Fig. 24. Decorative motifs from Type A pottery at Nyirankuba, Rwanda. 83

hallmark of the Early Iron Age. Hiernaux and Maquet were able to identify three Iron Age pottery types in this region, which they named Types A, B and C. Type A consisted of pots with concave necks, bevelled rims and dimple bases, decorated with scroll and loop designs, which connected it beyond any doubt with the Dimple-based pottery of western Kenya. The largest collection of Type A ware came from a small hill called Nyirankuba in southern Rwanda, where a Late Stone Age occupation level, without pottery, was overlain by a later horizon which contained both potsherds and iron slag. Similar dimpled pottery was found in association with iron-smelting furnaces at two other sites in Rwanda, called Ndora and Cyamakusa, which yielded radiocarbon dates of around the third and fourth centuries A.D. The furnaces were some five feet in diameter, and were built of wedge-shaped bricks decorated with thumb impressions, which were later found, together with Dimple-based pottery, at Bishanga in Zaïre, near the shores of Lake Kivu. Altogether, more than twenty sites in Rwanda, Burundi and Kivu have yielded Dimple-based pottery, and five of them contain Late Stone Age levels, which are sealed by Early Iron Age occupation.

About ten sites yielding Dimple-based sherds have been reported from southern Uganda, and a few more from the adjoining Bukoba district in north-western Tanzania.[1] The northernmost site is at Chobi, on the banks of the Somerset Nile upstream from the Murchison Falls, where Dimple-based sherds and other debris have been radio-carbon dated to the fourth century A.D. With one exception, all the other sites known at present are within a short distance of the shores of Lake Victoria. Here, as in north-western Tanzania and western Kenya, Early Iron Age sites can reasonably be attributed to Bantu-speaking farmers who combined fishing with banana-growing in the areas of highest rainfall, on the islands and around the northern and western shores of the lake. The exceptional site is the rock shelter at Nsongezi on the Kagera River, where a Late Stone Age hearth layer, radiocarbon dated to around the eleventh century A.D., is overlain by a horizon containing both Dimple-based sherds and those of the early pottery type called Kansyore ware, mentioned in Chapter 3. It may be that the Nsongezi date comes from an imperfect sample, since the site had been much disturbed by burrowing animals. If correct, however, it can only mean that Late Stone Age populations continued to live a separate life in the drier, inland areas for perhaps a thousand years after the lake shores had been occupied by food producers.

[1] One site, at Katuruka near Bukoba, has produced one radiocarbon date as early as around the fifth century B.C., though with other datings in the early centuries A.D. One date in the third century B.C. has also been reported from Rutare in Rwanda.

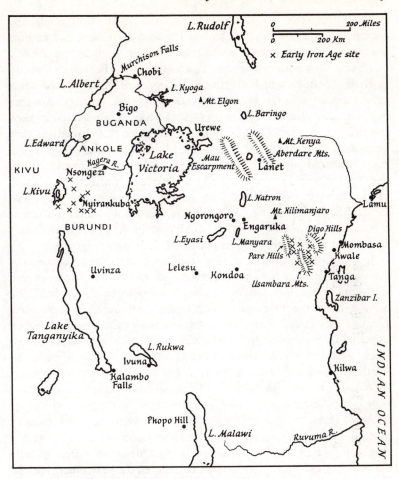

FIG. 25.   Some Early Iron Age sites in East Africa.

We do not yet know for how long the Early Iron Age, symbolised by the sites yielding Dimple-based pottery, may have lasted in the interlacustrine region. What we do know is that, all the way from Kivu province to central Kenya, the Early Iron Age wares were in time succeeded by generally coarser, roulette-decorated pottery, clearly the work of later immigrants, practising a quite different cultural tradition with a strong emphasis on cattle-keeping. These new arrivals came from the north. So far as we know, they were the first food producers to occupy the dry, grassland corridor which crosses Uganda from north-east to south-west and terminates in eastern Rwanda. Archaeologically speaking, their arrival signifies the meeting of Iron

85

Age cultures from the north and from the south. In Uganda, the rouletted wares are best attested at the vast earthwork site at Bigo (see map), but similar wares are widespread in inland Buganda, Ankole and Toro. Bigo pottery has some resemblances to Hiernaux's Type B, or Renge, pottery, which overlies Early Iron Age Dimple-based wares at a number of sites in the Rwanda gra·· ·nd country. Another roulette-decorated pottery also occurs in Kenya, where it has been labelled Lanet ware. Its distribution is confined to the relatively dry grasslands of the Rift Valley and the highlands to the west of it. All these rouletted pottery industries are probably broadly contemporary, and it is unlikely that they entered East Africa until after the beginning of the present millennium. The makers were probably peoples of Central Sudanic, Nilotic or Paranilotic speech, whose southernmost representatives interpenetrated the older established Bantu cultivators and eventually adopted the languages of their new neighbours.

It is with the situation arising from such encounters between the Bantu and their northern neighbours that the earliest layers of oral tradition in the interlacustrine region seem to be concerned. The earliest traditions of Buganda and Busoga, extending in some cases through more than thirty generations, which might amount to seven hundred or even eight hundred years, refer to clans of Bantu people living as fishermen and agriculturalists on the islands and around the northern shores of Lake Victoria, in the very areas where the Early Iron Age sites have been found. The traditional accounts next record how other Bantu clans moved into the midst of the original lineage groups. These were people who had formerly lived in the country around Mount Elgon, and they are associated in tradition with a mythical figure called Kintu, allegedly the founder of a score of little states resulting from accommodations between the newcomers and the older residents. In fact a whole series of population movements throughout the region did probably result from the meeting between the northernmost Bantu-speaking agriculturalists and non-Bantu iron-using tribesmen from further north, who, as pastoralists and mixed farmers, were probably more warlike and more mobile than the others, and who were certainly concerned to occupy the grasslands left empty by the earlier food producers. Whereas the earliest small states of Buganda and Busoga seemed to have been created through the reflux of the northernmost Bantu farmers upon the Bantu living next to them on the south, at least some of the early states of western Uganda and northern Rwanda seem to have been formed by the pastoral immigrants, who left as their monuments the series of ditched and embanked capital sites and cattle camps of which Bigo is the outstanding example.

Fifty miles to the east of Lake Victoria there rise the Mau highlands, reaching 9000 feet at Mau Summit, which form the western wall of the Rift Valley. The Nyandarua range and Mount Kenya lie to the east of the Rift. This entire highland region, from Lake Baringo in the north to Lake Manyara in the south, is still today non-Bantu country. From the first millennium B.C. onwards, it was the favoured habitat of the Stone Bowl people, described in Chapter 2. Their sites are scattered through the Rift, with no trace of iron-working identified in any settlement until well into the second millennium A.D. Dimple-based wares are absent. When iron at least appears, the pottery associated with it bears rouletted motifs, the vessel shapes and the decoration broadly similar to the contemporary wares of Uganda and Rwanda. The appearance of iron in this area can probably be associated with the southward movement of the Paranilotes ancestral to the modern Kalenjin. They probably came from the north, from the borderland between the Sudan, Ethiopia and Kenya on the western side of Lake Rudolf; and they probably settled among earlier Stone Age pastoralists of Southern Cushitic speech.

Only at the very southern end of the Rift Valley, at Engaruka, between Lake Natron and Lake Manyara, is there one, so far unique, Early Iron Age site, which is possibly to be associated with the Southern Cushites who preceded the Paranilotes in this area. At Engaruka a perennial stream, originating in the Ngorongoro hills, drops suddenly down the steep western wall of the Rift. The hillside, for nearly a mile on each side of the torrent, has been terraced with dry-stone walling, to make platforms for house sites and irrigated terraces for gardens. Paths and irrigation channels lead outwards from the stream to something like five hundred dwelling plots ranged in dense tiers along the hillside, while the flat floor of the valley below is marked out with lines of large stones in what seem to be field systems covering an area of perhaps five square miles. The flat area is dotted with stone circles, each some six feet high and thirty feet across, which were presumably pens for stock.

Engaruka is so obvious a landmark that it has aroused curiosity and speculation ever since it was first noticed by a passing expedition in 1883. Hans Reck, the German geologist who was the first to dig for fossils at Olduvai Gorge, published a description of Engaruka in 1913. Louis Leakey organised a brief expedition there in 1935. However, it was only with the excavations carried out by Hamo Sassoon in 1964 and 1966 that any clear picture emerged of the nature and chronology of the occupation. Sassoon established that the hillside terraces were used both for agriculture and for dwelling sites. He found middens with up to six feet of accumulated debris, including cattle bones and

87

grains of sorghum, as well as pottery and imported objects, such as cowrie shells and glass beads. One of the living sites on the hillside yielded traces of an iron forge and slag. Two radiocarbon samples taken from the terraces yielded dates around the fourth and the eighth centuries A.D. Unfortunately, no stratified se⌐ ⌐nces of Iron Age culture could be obtained, for the occupation apparently tended to grow outwards at the edges rather than to rebuild on the old sites. The walled enclosures on the valley floor were the latest buildings of all, yielding radiocarbon dates around the fifteenth century, and a style of pottery different from that on the hillside. Neither of the Engaruka pottery types has yet been found outside the general area of the site, which thus remains, for the time being, an isolated cultural phenomenon. The hillside village in particular, though of Early Iron Age date, is unique both in its construction and in its pottery, and provides a puzzling exception to the family likeness which marks the rest of the East African Early Iron Age sites. Here, if anywhere, it might be permissible to suspect the early infiltration of some northern Early Iron Age tradition, as yet unknown, from the Ethiopian end of the Rift Valley.

Whatever the explanation of Engaruka, it is certain that, to the east of the Rift Valley, manifestations of the Early Iron Age fall within the same broad cultural tradition as those to the west of the highlands. A hundred miles to the east of Engaruka, in the foothills of the Usambara and Pare ranges, and northwards from there in the Digo hills between Mombasa and Tanga, nearly a dozen Early Iron Age sites have been found, which are characterised by the variant of Dimple-based pottery known as Kwale ware. These sites have all been discovered within the last few years by Robert Soper. Three radio-carbon samples so far processed have given dates around the third century A.D., a period contemporary with that of the Dimple-based wares of the interlacustrine region. The distribution of Kwale ware sites suggests a pattern of Early Iron Age settlement which followed the forested margins and the deep escarpment soils at the feet of the mountain ranges. Apart from Kwale itself, which is only twenty miles from Mombasa, the most important of these eastern Early Iron Age sites is at Bombo Kaburi in the South Pare hills, radiocarbon dated to around the third century A.D. The Bombo Kaburi pottery compares closely with sherds found many years ago at Lelesu in Sandaweland, in the Kondoa district of Tanzania, to the south of Engaruka. Both the Kwale wares and those from Lelesu display the characteristic bevelled rims of all East African Early Iron Age pottery, but lack the elaborate grooved scrolls and complex looped motifs so typical of the contemporary interlacustrine Dimple-based wares. They are best thought of as the products of a neighbouring, though related, province. Lately, Keith Robinson has drawn attention to the similarities between Kwale ware and the Early Iron Age pottery of Phopo Hill in northern Malawi. When we have some more evidence from the intervening region of south-central Tanzania, this identification could prove significant.

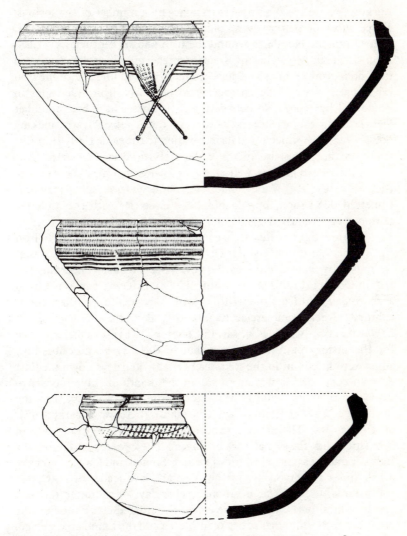

FIG. 26.   Decorated Early Iron Age bowls from Kwale, Kenya; $\times \frac{2}{5}$.

Meanwhile, the only other well-documented Early Iron Age site in Tanzania is located at the Uvinza brine springs along the Lower Malagarasi, which flows into Lake Tanganyika from the east. The salt of Uvinza was described by the explorer Richard Burton in 1858 as far superior to that from other sources, being traded 'throughout the heart of Africa, supplying the lands adjoining both the Tanganyika and Nyanza lakes'. In 1967 Andrew Roberts and John Sutton investigated the Uvinza salt pans, collecting oral traditions about salt-working, as well as digging test trenches by a number of the springs. Three types of pottery were found, of which the earliest, Class A, yielded radiocarbon dates around the fifth and six centuries A.D. Class A consists mainly of open bowls, some with bevelled rims. It is decorated with bold grooved lines and stamped motifs, including a false chevron relief pattern which is characteristic of Early Iron Ages sites in Zambia (Chapter 9). No pots with dimpled bases have been found at Uvinza, but the earliest salt-workers there were clearly making pottery of a type which owed its inspiration to the same Early Iron Age tradition that gave rise to the elaborately decorated vessels of the interlacustrine region as well as to the plainer Kwale-type wares to the east of the Rift Valley. The later pottery classes at Uvinza bear rouletted decoration, but do not have close ties with the rouletted potteries of Rwanda, Uganda and western Kenya.

It is in the light of this archaeological knowledge of the Early Iron Age in the interior of East Africa during the first millennium A.D. that we must now consider the earliest evidence we have concerning the Indian Ocean coastline of the continent. This evidence comes not from archaeology, but from the written word – above all from the second-century Greek commercial handbook called *The Periplus of the Erythraean Sea*, which as we saw in Chapter 4, was also a major source for the history of Axum. The author of the *Periplus* describes how ships were fitted out in the Red Sea ports for journeys down the East African coast, and how they set sail in the month of July, in order to catch the monsoon wind blowing across the Indian Ocean from the north-east. After rounding Cape Guardafui, there was a market-town at Opone (Ras Hafun in northern Somalia), where trade was in aromatics and 'the better sort of slaves'. These were, no doubt, the light-skinned Eastern Cushitic-speakers, Somali and Galla, who were at all times the favourites of the Arabian slave-trade. From Opone southwards, the *Periplus* mentions twelve days of sailing to the next series of local ports, which were evidently situated along the Benadir coast of southern Somalia, between Merca and the Lamu archipelago. From here it was a forty-eight-hour journey to the low, wooded island of Menouthias, which was probably Zanzibar, and the same distance again to the farthest port, called Rhapta, which would seem to have been situated somewhere near the mouth of the Rufiji River. It is clear that it was the ivory trade which brought the Red Sea ships to this section of the coast. 'Much ivory is taken away from these places, though it is inferior to that of Adulis, and also rhinoceros horn and tortoise-shell, different from that of India, and a little coconut oil.' The traders paid for their purchases with iron weapons – spears and hatchets and swords, made especially for this trade – and also 'many kinds of small glass vessels'.

It is about the inhabitants of the East African coast that the evidence of the *Periplus* is least satisfactory. 'Men of the greatest stature, who are pirates, inhabit the whole coast, and at each place have set up chiefs.' The Arab sea captains and their crews intermarried with them and knew their language. They used small boats, made of planks sewn together, for their fishing and their piracy. It does not give us much to go on. And even if we add the information from the *Geography* of Claudius Ptolemy, which in the form we have it may incorporate the results of another two or three centuries of trade and exploration, the picture does not become much clearer. In Ptolemy's text, the 'Fish-eating Ethiopians' who make sewn boats are succeeded to the south-ward by others described as 'Man-eating'. This may mean no more than that, in comparison with the Fish-eaters, they were very little known. On the other hand, the contrast could indicate a difference of race. What is more significant is that, whereas the *Periplus* says nothing about the interior, Ptolemy refers to a 'Mountain of the Moon', lying to the west of the Man-eating Ethiopians, from which 'the Lake of the Nile receives snow water'. One feels that the elephant hunters who supplied the ivory trade must have brought to the coast tales of Kilimanjaro or Mount Kenya, if not of the great lakes beyond them. Presumably these hunters were either themselves the Bantu makers of Kwale-ware pottery, who carried their tusks to the coast for sale, or else they were coastmen who carried out hunting expeditions in the country of the iron-using Bantu farmers who were beginning to occupy the foothills of the inland mountains. Either way, it is significant that the Alexandrian geographers of the third and fourth centuries A.D. apparently knew more of the East African interior than any other outsiders during our period. By the fifth century Roman trade was vanishing from the Indian Ocean. By the sixth century Cosmas Indicopleustes could achieve fame merely by sailing from Adulis to Ceylon, and without knowing anything of East Africa below Cape Guardafui. The next visitors we know of were Muslims from the

Persian Gulf, who colonised the Lamu archipelago, and probably also Zanzibar and Pemba, as early as the eighth or ninth century A.D., but whose only knowledge of the interior seems to have related to a region called Sofala, situated in all probability well to the south of the Rovuma – at least in Mozambique, if not actually beyond the Zambezi.

9   South-central Africa to the eleventh century

From East Africa we move to south-central Africa, by which we mean the region stretching from the Congo–Zambezi watershed in the north to the Limpopo valley in the south. The core of this region comprises the modern countries of Zambia, Malawi and Rhodesia, where Iron Age archaeology has gone further than in any other part of Africa. However, this core is flanked on the east by Mozambique, and on the west by southern Angola, northern South West Africa and Botswana, all of which are archaeologically very little known. The gap on the western side is perhaps not so important, since most of this is very dry and lightly inhabited country, running away to the Kalahari desert in the south. The gap in Mozambique is much more serious. It is not only that it was on this side that south-central Africa had its communications with the outside world during our period. It is even more that the lowlands of central Mozambique were very likely an important focus of the Iron Age population. When we think of Zambia and Rhodesia in isolation from Mozambique, we think of two highland plateaux divided by a short stretch of the middle Zambezi. When we include Mozambique, we think in terms of drainage rather than of elevation. The Zambezi dominates the scene, flowing itself from the borders of Lunda, and collecting in its three great tributaries – the Kafue, the Luangwa and the Shire – all the waters flowing southward from the rim of the Congo basin. If we remember that the proto-Bantu were riverine people, fishermen and vegeculturists, accustomed to a moist woodland environment, at home in boats, it would seem to follow that the river lines of south-central Africa would have been crucial for the Early Iron Age occupation. Therefore, if most of our information happens to come from the plateaux north and south of the middle Zambezi, it is an unfortunate accident for which we must make due allowance.

In south-central Africa we can be relatively sure that the coming of the Iron Age represented a wholly new way of life, introduced by a new population element expanding from the north. On the one hand, the Late Stone Age material is consistently that of hunters and gatherers. There is no Stone Age pottery and no evidence of domesticated animals or plants. Human remains, though sparse, are equally consistent, and show that the Late Stone Age population was of Bush rather than of Negro type. The surviving remnants of this population in southern Angola and northern Botswana speak Khoikhoi languages. On the other hand, the coming of iron is everywhere associated with food production and the settled life. The most striking contrast between Stone and Iron Age sites is in the size of the settlements. Early Iron Age villages often extended over an acre or more. The abandoned deposits tend to show several inches of dark midden soil, containing potsherds, bone fragments and traces of houses. Pottery is an invariable accompaniment of Iron Age sites. Bone fragments include those of domestic cattle throughout Iron Age times, though the bones of wild game are more abundant, especially at the beginning of the period. Iron Age houses seem from the first to have resembled those of modern Bantu peoples, with hardened floors, walls of mud and stick, and a thatched roof supported on a central pole. It is from the size and the siting of the settlements, rather than from carbonised seeds or surviving tools, that the practice of agriculture can be safely inferred. The density of population within these villages could not have been supported in any other way. And the siting of settlements frequently shows a skilful selection of deep soils, for example, at the edges of natural clearings in savanna woodland. Human remains, though showing negroid characteristics, are more equivocal, suggesting a slow and progressive assimilation of the earlier Bush stock by the newcomers. Since the modern practitioners of this way of life, and all those described in historical records of the present millennium, have been Bantu-speaking, and since archaeology provides no evidence of any comparable break in cultural continuity, it is only reasonable to infer that the Iron Age was brought to south-central Africa by the Bantu. The chronology of the Early Iron Age is consistent with that for East Africa. There seems to be no reason to doubt that the colonisation of both regions was part of a single process of Bantu expansion.

Research into the Iron Age archaeology of Zambia began in the early 1950s, when Desmond Clark, then Director of the Rhodes–Livingstone Museum, investigated a series of soil-pits dug by a forestry officer at Machili forest station on the borders of Barotseland. He found a series of charcoal layers in deep deposits of windblown Kalahari sand, one of which, buried some thirty-six inches below the modern gravel, yielded a scatter of pottery fragments. A simple bag-shaped pot was reconstructed, ornamented with a band of parallel grooved lines. Clark also found a few sherds of similar pottery overlying a small hearth used by Late Stone Age hunters at Lusu on the upper Zambezi. The main significance of these finds, however, was that associated charcoal samples were sent to the University of Chicago laboratory, where W. F. Libby was developing his now famous method of radiocarbon dating. The Machili and Lusu dates were among the first to come from the African continent. Moreover, the results – A.D. 96 ± 212 for Machili and 186 B.C. ± 180 for Lusu – came as a great surprise to archaeologists, most of whom had up till then assumed that the Iron Age in Bantu Africa was of much more recent origin.

Meanwhile, Clark had discovered the great prehistoric site at Kalambo Falls, near the southern extremity of Lake Tanganyika, which showed a thick layer of Iron Age occupation, yielding abundant pottery, iron slag, and the remains of pole and mud huts from several villages which had succeeded each other over a long period in the Kalambo lake basin. Radiocarbon tests eventually proved that the

FIG. 27.   Kalambo Falls near Abercorn, Zambia. The Stone and Iron Age sites are in the ancient lake basin immediately behind the falls.

occupation had lasted from about the fourth century till at least the fourteenth century A.D. The pottery from Kalambo included, on the one hand, vessels identical to that from Machili, and on the other hand a wealth of grooved and incised sherds which bore an obvious resemblance to the Dimple-based pottery which the Leakeys had recently found at Urewe and other sites in western Kenya. Two of the Kalambo sherds even had the characteristic dimples of the northern ware. Concentrating initially on the grooved decoration, Clark proposed the term 'Channelled Ware', which came into widespread use as a label describing Early Iron Age culture north of the Zambezi.

During the twenty years which have followed Clark's pioneering efforts, further work by Brian Fagan, Joseph Vogel and David Phillipson has made possible a much more sophisticated understanding of the Zambian Early Iron Age. In relation to pottery, 'channelling' is now seen as only one of several diagnostic features. As in East Africa, the bevelling of pot-rims is seen to be characteristic, while stamped decoration, especially the effect of a false relief chevron, achieved by careful placing of triangular or quadrilateral stamps, has proved to be at least as prevalent as channelling. Even in this more detailed analysis, the general features of Zambian and other south-central African pottery show similarities with the Early Iron Age wares of East Africa. Bevelled rims and grooved decoration are common in both. Globular pots and bowls are dominant. But the south-central African pottery is less elaborate. Dimples are absent, except at Kalambo. Decoration is less flamboyant. There is a definite connection between the two regions, but also difference.

Within Zambia and Malawi, as also in Rhodesia, it is now possible to make at least a tentative classification of Early Iron Age pottery traditions into local groupings. The evidence is necessarily highly technical; those who are interested can study the articles by David Phillipson and Tom Huffman cited in the suggestions for further reading at the end of this volume. The conclusion which is of general interest is that these traditions, though clearly related, were nevertheless differentiated from one another from the time of their first appearance in south-central Africa. It is as if the area of original unity was outside the region, and yet not far away. Tom Huffman has proposed a theory of radiation by small, already diverging groups from a nuclear area in the southern part of the Congo basin, and this would seem to fit the facts as we know them at present. The pity is, as we have pointed out before, that we know so little about the Early Iron Age of the Congo basin.

On this interpretation, however, we would have, to the east of

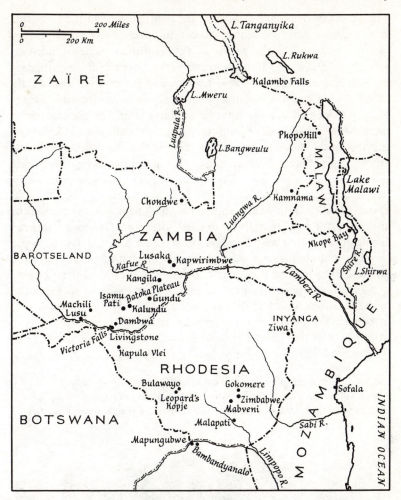

FIG. 28.   Early Iron Age sites in south-central Africa.

Huffman's nuclear area, a group of sites in north-eastern Zambia associated with the Early Iron Age levels at Kalambo Falls. This site, as we have seen, has some pots with dimple bases, and other characteristics connecting it with Uvinza in western Tanzania, and so to the interlacustrine region further to the north. Along the eastern frontier of Zambia and in northern Malawi are the sites of another group, represented at Kamnama and Phopo Hill, the more distant connections of which may prove to be with the Kwale ware sites of north-eastern Tanzania. Southern Malawi provides a third grouping,   97 with its focus at Nkope Bay, near the southern end of the lake: this is a group which we should expect to extend into Mozambique. Central Zambia, to the south of the Huffman nucleus, has two groupings, one centred on Chondwe in the Copperbelt, the other on the rich Kapwirimbwe site near Lusaka. Moving on clockwise, a little to the west of south, the Batoka plateau between Lusaka and Livingstone has yielded a large number of Early Iron Age sites, many of them lying at the base of long stratigraphical sequences of Iron Age cultures in the mounds formed where early farming peoples built and rebuilt on the best-drained ridges of a generally boggy area: this group takes its name from the mound at Kalundu, where the Early Iron Age horizon dates from the fourth century A.D. Finally, the Zambezi valley both above and below the Victoria Falls contributes another grouping, tentatively named after the Dambwa site near Livingstone, which may however prove to be a rather late example (seventh and eighth centuries) of a tradition that might stretch back far enough to include the earliest Iron Age sites of Machili and Lusu.

After twenty years of further exploration, it has to be said that the median datings for Machili and Lusu are older by some two to four hundred years than other Early Iron Age dates in south-central Africa. It may be that they should be regarded with reserve, particularly since they were obtained at an early stage of the development of the radio-

FIG. 29. A stratigraphical trench excavated through the occupation deposits at Isamu Pati mound, Zambia. The scale is in feet and the rubble lines in the trench wall are the collapsed remains of pole and mud huts.

carbon process. However, most of the groupings we have mentioned include sites dating to the third, fourth and fifth centuries A.D., and it is clear that, by this period at least, many parts of Zambia and Malawi had been infiltrated by Iron Age farming communities. There is, equally, plenty of evidence of the survival far beyond this period of hunting and gathering communities living in rock shelters and open camps and continuing to use a mainly lithic tool-kit. The Iron Age people, therefore, though living in larger settlements than the hunters, were still for a long time very thin upon the ground. The farming way of life was very different from the hunting one, but it did not at once solve all the material problems of human existence.

How slowly the Iron Age in fact developed has been shown by Brian Fagan's detailed excavations of mound sites on the Batoka plateau, at several of which the stratigraphic record runs through eight or nine hundred years, from about the fourth century till about the thirteenth. The most thoroughly investigated site is that called Isamu Pati, near Kalomo. This was not occupied during the earliest phase of the Iron Age, which is represented at Kalundu, Gundu and other sites. Isamu Pati was inhabited from the seventh century till the thirteenth, and Fagan formed the impression that, even by the end of this period, metallurgy had still had only a moderate impact on the economy and material culture. The people of Isamu Pati lived in pole and mud houses, which may have been arranged around a central cattle enclosure. They certainly grew sorghum, the carbonised remains of which have been found in the deposit. The presence of grain bins makes it likely that they also grew millet, for sorghum does not store well, whereas millet does. The implements of tillage included iron hoes and light axes, but there was a noticeable scarcity of iron tools, except for the smallest items like arrow-heads and razors. Bush clearing may have been severely restricted by the lack of really strong tools, and cultivation may have been limited to the natural clearings. Even so, gardens may have been more often cultivated with wooden digging-sticks than with iron hoes. Cattle, small stock, dogs and chickens were present from the first, but what is really striking is the persistence of hunting and gathering into the Iron Age economy. A wide range of wild vegetables and fruit was gathered. Hunting was practised throughout the occupation, the favoured game being small antelope such as the oribi and duiker. In the lowest levels of the site the bones of game animals predominate in the middens. It is only in the later stages that the bones of domestic cattle appear in large numbers.

It used to be thought that this so-called 'Kalomo culture' of the later first-millennium levels of the Batoka plateau mounds represented a change of population from that responsible for the earliest Iron Age deposits revealed in the lowest levels at Kalundu and elsewhere. The evidence turns largely on the differences in pottery decoration between the earliest levels and the later ones, and it has been convincingly argued by Vogel that these differences can be accounted for by a spread onto the Batoka plateau of influences from the neighbouring Dambwa sub-culture of the Zambezi valley. On this analysis, the Kalomo culture would be seen simply as a late manifestation of the Early Iron Age.

Recently David Phillipson, following a careful review of the Early and Late Iron Age pottery traditions throughout Zambia, has reached the conclusion that none of the developments which occurred during the first millennium A.D. need be regarded as a radical break with earlier traditions. Indeed, he believes that in the western half of the country the traditions established by the Early Iron Age potters persisted, with only local evolutionary changes, until the Kololo invasion of Barotseland in the early nineteenth century. In eastern Zambia, however, he detects one major break in tradition, which occurred early in the present millennium. This was the introduction of the Luangwa pottery tradition, which superseded the Early Iron Age forms represented by the Kalambo, Kamnama, Chondwe and Kapwirimbwe sub-cultures at a period around the twelfth century A.D. The characteristic vessels of the Luangwa tradition are necked pots and shallow bowls, which differ considerably from the globular shapes predominant earlier. The vessels have everted and tapered rims in place of the thickened rims and bevelled lips of the earlier tradition. Moreover, in contrast with western Zambia, where the Lungwebungu pottery descending from Early Iron Age traditions is invariably made by men, the pottery of the Luangwa tradition is all the work of women.

The Batoka plateau forms an intermediate area between that covered by the eastern, Luangwa tradition and that covered by the western, Lungwebungu one. Here we see the pottery tradition most characteristically revealed in the mid-second-millennium site at Kangila, near Mazabuka, the pots of which are bag-shaped and mostly undecorated. The Kangila site was clearly the work of strongly pastoral people, probably ancestral to the cattle-keeping Tonga who today occupy the whole of the Batoka plateau as far west as the Kafue. Kangila is certainly not the earliest example of this intrusive culture, the influence of which is already to be seen in the pottery of the uppermost layers of the Kalomo mounds, dating approximately from the twelfth century. From this stage onwards there appears to have been a basic cultural continuity in eastern and central Zambia, which lasted until modern times.

This relative stability of the Iron Age population of Zambia, dating from the earliest intrusive communities of Bantu farmers in the early centuries A.D., and modified by only one major infusion of people at a later date, is a picture which needs to be borne in mind when considering the Iron Age history of Rhodesia and South Africa. Here, the prime cause of confusion arises from the fact that more than sixty years of Iron Age research has been mainly concentrated on spectacular sites, such as Zimbabwe, Mapungubwe and other complexes of stone ruins dating only from the Later Iron Age. Conducted against a background of near ignorance of the Early Iron Age history of Rhodesia and the surrounding countries, these researches have given rise to speculative theories of recent, large migrations, which simply could not have happened without leaving their mark upon the archaeological record of territories further to the north. The current preoccupation of Rhodesian archaeology is therefore to reinterpret the Later Iron Age

FIG. 30. Early Iron Age pottery from south-central Africa. (a) Early Iron Age beaker from Sefula Mission, Mongu, Zambia, showing characteristic grooved and 'false relief' chevron stamped decoration. (b) Two vessels from Gokomere, Rhodesia, bearing stamped and grooved decoration; diameter of larger pot is 9 inches (22 cm).

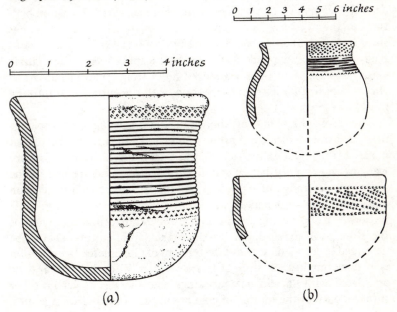

0 1 2 3 4 5 6 *inches*

0   1   2   3   4 *inches*

(a)   (b)

evidence in terms of our new knowledge of the Early Iron Age in south-central Africa as a whole.

In Rhodesia, as elsewhere, major progress in Early Iron Age archaeology had to await the invention of the radiocarbon dating process. As early as 1937 a Roman Catholic missionary, Father Gardiner, published an account of the Tunnel rock shelter at Goko-mere mission, a few miles from Zimbabwe, which had yielded a large collection of pottery quite distinct from that of the modern inhabitants of the area. The finds were examined by a South African archaeologist, John Schofield, who recognised that the stamped and grooved pottery displayed the basic features of the earliest wares found north of the Zambezi and in East Africa. However, it was only in the 1960s that Keith Robinson began a systematic exploration of the other sites of this period, notably that at Mabveni, in the Chibi Reserve west of Zimbabwe, and to send carbon samples for dating to the newly established radiocarbon laboratory at the University College at Salisbury. The dates proved strictly comparable with those that were emerging at the same time for Early Iron Age sites in Zambia. The Mabveni site produced one date in the second or third century A.D., and another in the sixth or seventh. The type-site, at Gokomere itself, was dated around the sixth century A.D. Another occurrence of Gokomere ware, from the Acropolis hill at Zimbabwe, yielded a date around the fourth century A.D. This was from the earliest Iron Age deposit (Zimbabwe I), stratified in an ochreous earth resting on bed-rock in the Western Enclosure. Pottery of the Gokomere type has since been found as far south as the Limpopo valley (at Malapati), as far west as Bulawayo, and as far north as Kapula Vlei in the Wankie Game Reserve, less than a hundred miles from Victoria Falls. The chronological span is from the second or third century A.D. until the ninth.

The eastern highlands of Rhodesia contain a group of sites belong-ing to a distinctive cultural group known as Ziwa, after a farm of that name in the Inyanga district. Ziwa pottery differs from Gokomere ware in the slightly better standard of its manufacture and in the slightly wider range of its decorative motifs. Only four radiocarbon dates have been obtained, of which one is in the fourth century, while the other three belong to the ninth and tenth centuries. There is therefore still some doubt whether the Ziwa culture should be described as a collateral or as a descendant of Gokomere. The question is of some importance, since at least two of the Ziwa sites appear to be associated with ancient gold workings, and there is as yet no other sure evidence of the mining of gold or copper in Early Iron Age sites.

A somewhat similar problem exists in relation to the cultural grouping known as Leopard's Kopje I, which succeeds the Gokomere phase in the western and south-western parts of Rhodesia. Most of the sites are found on richer soils, and many occur in the gold belts and in the vicinity of ancient mine workings. The pottery of Leopard's Kopje I, like Gokomere ware, is dominated by stamped decoration, but the forms of the vessels are slightly different. And whereas the makers of Gokomere ware preferred villages in sheltered localities, their successors built on open sites. The only two radiocarbon dates for Leopard's Kopje I lie in the eighth and ninth centuries A.D.

Whatever the status of Leopard's Kopje I, it is clear that the next phase of these rather confusingly named sites represents a sharp break with earlier traditions. Leopard's Kopje II sites are most common in the dry grassland areas of south-western Rhodesia, and occur as far south as the Limpopo valley – in fact, the best-known of all these sites is that at Bambandyanalo, just to the south of the river, in the Republic of South Africa. Most Leopard's Kopje II settlements were built within the shelter of rocky hills, and the occupants made use of rough stone walling to delineate their villages. Their pottery contains little of the Gokomere tradition, and incised, dragged and stylus impressions are the common form of decoration. Beakers, usually undecorated, represent a new pottery form, while clay figurines of women, domestic animals, and above all cattle, are very common. Although there has been one much earlier dating, the likely period for Leopard's Kopje II is the tenth and eleventh centuries.

It is clear beyond any doubt that Leopard's Kopje II represents both a largely new culture and one that was strongly pastoral. It is therefore natural to ask whether it could have been connected in any way with the new and strongly pastoral culture that affected central Zambia at about the same period. If there were such a connection, it could perhaps best be examined in relation to a southward spread of the practice of milking cattle as an addition to the human food supply, which in many parts of Africa does seem to have been a later development than the mere keeping of domestic cattle for meat and for capital accumulation. The milking complex would have led to an increase of both the human and the bovine population in the areas best suited to pastoralism. It need not necessarily have been a cause of major human migrations, though obviously it would have led to the local expansion of those societies which were successful in adopting the new means of subsistence. It is, for example, noticeable that the female human figurines which are so pronounced a feature of the Leopard's Kopje II culture clearly depict the enlarged buttocks characteristic of Bushman art, and it could well be that the pastoral population of western Rhodesia at this period included a considerable Khoikhoi element, which was only gradually absorbed by the faster-growing Bantu population of the mixed farming areas.

The cultural development in the central part of Rhodesia around the turn of the first millennium is documented by Keith Robinson's excavations on the Acropolis hill at Zimbabwe. The basal Iron Age levels, with their Gokomere pottery of about the fourth century, are overlain by a sterile deposit of earth and collapsed building materials. A new phase of occupation then appears, after what may have been a considerable interval, the upper part of which has yielded a radio-carbon date of the eleventh century. Early Iron Age vessels are now replaced by simple gourd-shaped pots, which are thought to bear some resemblance to the pottery of Leopard's Kopje II. The later stages of settlement and building at Zimbabwe are described in Chapter 18, where we deal with the period following the eleventh century. By that time it is possible to see in the archaeological record the signs of a powerful political and commercial empire centred on Zimbabwe in the central part of the Rhodesian plateau. At the period of Zimbabwe II, however, it would seem that the centre of political and economic development probably lay further to the west and the south, in the area of the Leopard's Kopje II sites. Here, a rapidly expanding pastoral and gold-mining population may already have been establishing trade connections with the Indian Ocean coast, perhaps using the Limpopo valley route. We ended our last chapter with a brief reference to a region called Sofala, known to Arab sea-farers operating from bases in the Lamu archipelago and in the islands of Zanzibar and Pemba. We end this one with a quotation from the Arabic geographer al-Masudi, who travelled around 915–16 to Pemba, and who later wrote of the population of East Africa in the following terms:

The Zanj are the only Abyssinian people to have crossed the branch which flows out of the upper stream of the Nile. They settled in that area which stretches as far as Sofala, which is the furthest limit of the land and the end of the voyages made from Oman and Siraf on the sea of Zanj. In the same way that the sea of China ends with the land of Japan, the sea of Zanj ends with the land of Sofala and the Waqwaq, which produces gold and many other wonderful things. It has a warm climate and is fertile. The Zanj capital is there and they have a king called the Mfalme. This is the ancient name of their kings, and all the other Zanj kings are subject to him. He has 300 000 riders. The Zanj use the ox as a beast of burden, for they have no horses, mules or camels in their land . . . There are many wild elephants, but no tame ones ... The Zanj rush upon them armed with very long spears, and kill them for their ivory. It is from this country that come tusks weighing fifty pounds and more. They usually go to Oman, and from there are sent to China and India ... To go back to the Zanj and their kings, these are known as Wafalme, which means the son of the Great Lord, since he is chosen to govern them justly. If he is tyrannical or strays from the truth, they kill him and exclude his seed from the throne; for they consider that in acting wrongfully he forfeits his position as the son of the Lord, the King of Heaven and Earth. They call God Mkulu Njulu, which means Great Lord.[1]

Masudi's text is clearly incapable of confident interpretation. Yet, although there is an obvious vagueness about the location of Sofala, there is no doubt that, three or four centuries after Masudi, Sofala was the name of a seaport situated between the mouth of the Zambezi and that of the Sabi, and it is on the whole unusual for place-names to shift about. Again, Masudi, having been himself to East Africa on board a trading ship, is likely to have had accurate information about trade items. If so, his reference to gold does suggest very strongly that the trade was with Rhodesia, as we know of no gold-mining further north in East Africa. Both the word for king and that for God are clearly Bantu words, the first of which might be Swahili, but the second of which suggests a more southerly Bantu language. The Waqwaq might be the Makwakwa, a Bantu people who still live around the Limpopo mouth. The apparent reference to the riding of oxen suggests either the Sotho or the Khoikhoi, who are the only peoples known to have had this custom. What is quite certain, however, is that if Masudi's information does indeed relate to Rhodesia, it is to the Rhodesia of Leopard's Kopje II and Zimbabwe II; and, if so, it means that the political structure of a kingdom ruled by a divine king was already present in the area, at least in an embryonic form, some two or three centuries before the period of large-scale stone building at Zimbabwe.

[1] The translation is from G. S. P., Freeman-Grenville, *The East African Coast: Select Documents*, pp. 15–16.

It is a strange paradox that South Africa, with its material resources and its established tradition of learning, should be among the more backward countries in Africa in the archaeological study of the local Iron Age. This is not for want of interesting problems for investigation, for as we saw in Chapter 3, South Africa was, long before the coming of its European population, an important meeting ground of races, languages and cultures. Here, the great process of Bantuisation at last ground to a halt. Here, the Khoikhoi provide the only clear example of a population which learned food production from its Bantu neighbours without losing its language and culture in the process. Here, within the period of written records, widespread groups of San-speaking hunters continued to live alongside the food producers, preparing their food and their skin clothing with stone tools, painting the walls of their caves and rock shelters with scenes of the chase.

In South Africa, the very evidence of this interaction between hunters and food producers has fostered the illusion that the Bantu, at least, were recent immigrants who had arrived in wave upon wave of massive, conquering migrations from the black north – migrations which were stopped only by the guns of the white commandoes as they approached the eastern frontiers of the Cape Colony during the eighteenth century. It comforted the white colonist of South Africa to think of the Bantu as a migrant warrior, with no more right to the land than the European who had conquered and subjugated him. This, however, is not the picture which emerges from all the careful recording of tribal traditions which has been carried out, mostly by missionaries, in different parts of South Africa during the past one hundred and fifty years. And certainly it is not the picture which is beginning to emerge from the limited use that has so far been made of the radiocarbon dating technique in relation to South African Iron Age sites.

The first lesson that we have to bring to the study of the South African Iron Age is that learned in the regions further north, namely that the beginnings of food production and metallurgy represented, in human terms, an infiltration rather than a conquest. The farmers came in search of deep, well-watered soils, which were in general not the places favoured by hunters. They established their dominance not by fighting with the hunters, but by living a more settled life in denser communities, so that in any contacts it was the hunters who came to the farmers, and not vice versa. This symbiosis lasted for centuries before the hunters were finally absorbed. The numerical expansion of the farmers was due mainly to natural increase from an original very wide, very thin dispersion of farming communities, rather than to mass migrations from one region to another. Large long-distance migrations are in fact possible only in country that has been extensively settled by food producers, country where there are crops to steal and stock to be driven off. The only large migrations we know of in southern Africa occurred during the nineteenth century, and they were snowballing movements, dependent for their momentum on the adherents recruited along the line of march.

In fact, the earliest Iron Age site so far discovered to the south of the Limpopo is in Swaziland, where two radiocarbon dates around the fourth or fifth century A.D. have been obtained from occupation debris in an artificial cave, now known as Castle Cavern, which was excavated by early miners of haematite ore. Pottery described as 'channelled', smelted iron and numerous iron-mining tools were found in the deposits from which the dates were obtained. Unfortunately, the pottery is still unpublished, so that the precise relationship with Rhodesian Early Iron Age wares cannot be assessed. But the correspondence of the dates with those from Rhodesia and Zambia is most striking, and there can be no serious doubt that some of the Early Iron Age farmers from the region north of the Limpopo must have penetrated very quickly indeed to the north-eastern part of South Africa. And if so, given the geographical location of Swaziland, there can be little doubt that the miners of Castle Cavern were, in some sense, ancestors of the Nguni people, who from the earliest historical times have been the south-easternmost of all the Bantu peoples, inhabiting the only well-watered region of South Africa, between the Drakensberg Mountains and the Indian Ocean. The leading ethnographic studies are in agreement that the Nguni are an amalgam of a formerly matrilineal stock of cultivators and fisherfolk, of a type represented today by the Tsonga of southern Mozambique, and a patrilineal and pastoral stock, with a strong aversion to fish-eating, which entered the south-eastern coastal plain from the interior plateau at a later date. The Swaziland miners could well be seen as the pioneers of the first of these two elements.

Castle Cavern apart, the only site south of the Limpopo which has yielded grooved and stamped wares demonstrably akin to the 107

Early Iron Age wares of Rhodesia is that discovered many years ago at Happy Rest farm, near Louis Trichard in the northern Transvaal. Here, numerous pot fragments were found during the construction of a school, and were published by the South African archaeologist J. B. de Vaal, who drew attention to the parallels with Father Gardiner's finds at Gokomere. The Happy Rest site is still undated, but a modern classification of its pottery would place it close to the Gokomere ware found at Malapati on the northern side of the Limpopo valley, which has been dated to the late first millennium A.D. It must be emphasised that the present sparsity of Early Iron Age evidence south of the Limpopo is to be attributed to a lack of research rather than a failure to find. The Limpopo valley is not a serious barrier to movement, and there is no reason to suppose that Bantu farming people did not cross it soon after they first settled in Botswana, Rhodesia and Mozambique. Nor need one think of the Bantu colonisation of South Africa in what are probably anachronistic 'white African' terms, of a southward progress from the Rhodesian plateau to that of the Transvaal and the Orange Free State. Once a Bantu population had been established in the lower Zambezi valley, expansion could just as well have proceeded through the Mozambique lowlands, following either the coast or the deep soils at the base of the eastern escarpment of the central plateau, and spreading *up* the river valleys from there.

It is much harder to identify in the archaeological record the later and mainly pastoral element in the Nguni ancestry. For, to the west of the Drakensberg, on most of the great interior plateau of the Transvaal and the Orange Free State, the dominant Bantu population, prior to the northward migrations of the Nguni during the last century, were the Sotho-Tswana. These people were very different from the Nguni both in language and customs. Whereas the Nguni were primarily pastoral, living in family kraals dispersed evenly over the countryside, the Sotho, though keeping cattle, lived in large settlements, often partly stone-built, and practised a way of life based essentially on agriculture and hunting, in which mining and metallurgy, trade and handicrafts, played an outstanding part. And whereas the language of the Sotho-Tswana has been most clearly influenced by the clicks of the San languages spoken by the Bush peoples of the plateau, the corresponding influence upon the Nguni language has been that of the Khoikhoi of the Cape Province and the South Atlantic coast.

Certainly, the Iron Age record of most of the central plateau seems to be the record of the Sotho. The earliest evidence has been found

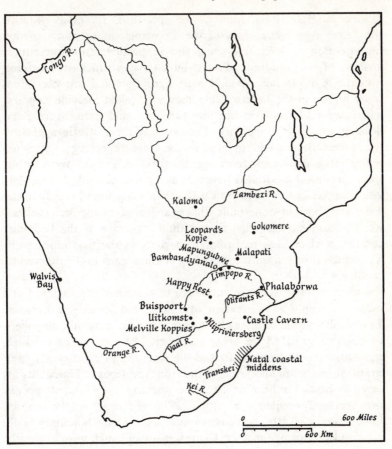

FIG. 31.   The Iron Age of southern Africa.

around Phalaborwa, in the valley of the Olifants River in the north-
eastern Transvaal. Here there are abundant traces of the ancient
mining of both iron and copper, and a series of radiocarbon dates
has been obtained by N. J. van der Merwe from occupation sites,
mining shafts and furnaces, which range from the eighth century
A.D. to the nineteenth. Unfortunately, as at Castle Cavern, detailed
publication of the pottery is still awaited, but the excavator stresses
the basic continuity of the pottery tradition from the older sites
to the more recent ones, and this would indicate a Sotho ethnic
character developing steadily throughout the period.

To the south-west of Phalaborwa, on the highest part of the South
African plateau around Johannesburg, a similar picture is beginning   109

to emerge. Here, Revil Mason, who specialised for many years in the Stone Age archaeology of the Transvaal, has recently turned his attention to Iron Age sites, and in particular to distribution analysis of the hundreds of stone-built villages which are scattered over the high plateau. Mason's most significant find was made on a small hilltop in the heart of Johannesburg, called Melville Koppies, where several early iron-smelting furnaces were found during the development of a public park. The lowest of these, stratigraphically, was radiocarbon dated to around the eleventh century A.D. Some pottery fragments came from near the furnace, and also from within the ruins of a stone-walled structure at the foot of the hill. The Melville Koppies pottery is identical to other wares found widely in the Transvaal, both in stone-built villages and in caves and rock shelters. Revil Mason has classified sites with this pottery as the Uitkomst culture, an Iron Age tradition, with roots in the first millennium A.D., which survived until the coming of Europeans in the nineteenth century.

Uitkomst itself is a cave site north of Johannesburg, where forty inches of Iron Age occupation overlie a Late Stone Age horizon. Two small circular iron-smelting furnaces with dome-like chambers were found, stratified one above the other. The upper furnace, which was radiocarbon dated to around the seventeenth century A.D., was stratified in the middle levels of the Iron Age deposit. Though using caves as bases for hunting and iron-working, the Uitkomst people were certainly builders in stone. Klipriviersberg, to the east of Johannesburg, is the best-known site, where long boundary walls surround groups of inner enclosures, many of which were obviously cattle pens. Similar sites occur widely in the Transvaal and the Orange Free State, and some had been recently in use when the pioneer missionary Robert Moffat first visited the Transvaal in 1829. The central part of the plateau between Zeerust and Pretoria was at that time in the occupation of the Ndebele, the Ngoni migrants from the south, who had scattered the indigenous Sotho and laid waste their settlements.

The plains and valleys [wrote Moffat], of the richest soil to a great depth, had once waved with native millet and been covered with pumpkins, water melons, kidney beans and sweet reed, all of which were cultivated through the interior. The ruined towns exhibited signs of immense labour and perseverance, every fence being composed of stones, averaging five or six feet high, raised apparently without either mortar, lime or hammer. Everything is circular, from the inner fences which surround each house, to the walls which sometimes encompass the town. The remains of some of the

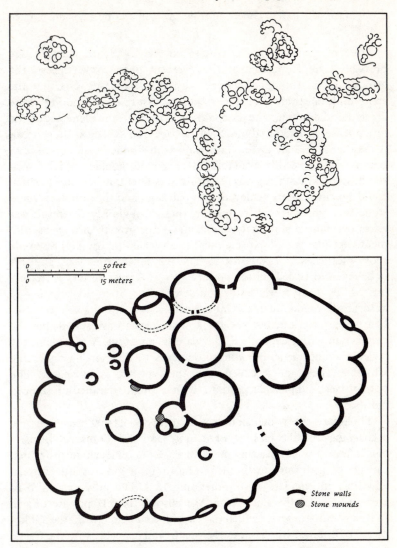

Fig. 32.   Drawing from an aerial photograph showing the network of
stone enclosures, probably hut/kraal complexes, at Klipriviersberg,
Transvaal, South Africa. The lower drawing is a detailed plan of one
complex.

houses which escaped the flames of the marauders were large ... the walls
of clay with a small mixture of cow-dung, and so well polished that they
had the appearance of being varnished. The walls and doorways were neatly
ornamented with architraves and cornices. The pillars supporting the roof,   1 1 1

in the form of pilasters projecting from the wall and fluted, showed much taste.[1]

Most of the stone enclosures to be seen in South Africa today probably date from comparatively recent times. Nevertheless, the association of Uitkomst pottery with ruin sites suggests that the stone-building tradition extends back at least to the beginning of the present millennium, and it could well be that the elements of the practice were introduced into South Africa from Rhodesia. In general, it may be said that, in the Transvaal as in Rhodesia, stone was used because it was readily available in the granite koppies which crown the hilltops in both regions. Nothing was attempted in stone which could not have been achieved with palisades and thorn fences where stone was more difficult to quarry, though obviously the result was more permanent and likely to encourage the growth of larger settlements. As one would expect, the Transvaal building styles resemble those of the early Leopard's Kopje tradition of Rhodesia, and this is believed to be true of the pottery also. Uitkomst pottery is characterised by deep bowls and shouldered pots. Stamped and incised decoration predominates. Unfortunately, we still lack a comprehensive description, but several archaeologists have stated that the connection with Leopard's Kopje wares is apparent. A related pottery style is found in stone-built settlements to the north-west of the Uitkomst sites, and is called after the type-site at Buispoort. The vessels bear simpler decoration, with a preponderance of stabbed motifs.

Thus far, the conclusion would seem to be that the Iron Age archaeology of the Orange Free State and the Transvaal forms a continuous thread, leading backwards from modern forms which can all be associated with the Sotho to an origin in south-western Rhodesia in the late first millennium A.D. The only exception to emerge so far is the Early Iron Age pottery from Happy Rest Farm in the Zoutpansberg, which is clearly connected with the Gokomere tradition of Rhodesia to the north, and probably with the Castle Cavern finds to the south. This may, as we have seen, be connected with the submerged matrilineal, agricultural strand in Nguni culture, but it does not account for the pastoral strand which has been dominant among the Nguni during historical times. Unfortunately, archaeological work in Nguni country has virtually been limited to a single pottery collection made by John Schofield from shell middens on the Natal coast. This led to the identification of four pottery types —

[1] Cited in Cecil Northcott, *Robert Moffat Pioneer in Africa* (London, 1961), p. 138.

Natal Coast 1, 2, 3 and 4. N.C.1 is thought to be the work of Khoikhoi strandloopers. N.C.3 and N.C.4 are modern wares. N.C.2 has some evident connection with both Buispoort and Uitkomst wares; but pottery from a shellfish midden cannot easily be identified with fish-avoiding pastoralists who show, in Monica Wilson's words,

marked similarities in economy, local grouping, law, ritual and symbolism with the cattle people of the Sudan, Uganda and Kenya borderlands. The identification of a man with a particular ox in his herd, the poetry in praise of cattle, the shaping of cattle horns, the association of the shades with river pools, the forms of divination and prophecy are alike. So, too, is the dispersion of homesteads, each occupied by a cattle-owner with his wives, and sons, and grandchildren, and the forms of marriage whereby cattle may even be given on behalf of a dead son so that seed may be raised in his name. Each item taken alone has little significance, but, when there are many, one begins to speculate on what ancient movements linked the Sudan with the Transkei, for it is unlikely that the whole pattern has been twice invented.[1]

There is in fact only one archaeological site so far excavated in southern Africa which could indicate the passage of a people such as Monica Wilson describes. This is the Leopard's Kopje II site at Bambandyanalo, just to the south of the Limpopo, which we mentioned in the last chapter. Bambandyanalo consists of a circular mound of occupation debris, some two hundred yards in diameter and some twenty feet deep. Captain Guy Gardner, who worked there in the 1930s, sunk large trenches into the mound, and proved that the settlement had been built around a large central cattle enclosure, which had also been used for burying the dead. Seventy-four human skeletons were recovered from the accumulated layers of cattle dung, one of which was radiocarbon dated many years later to around the eleventh century A.D. The material culture of Bambandyanalo is extremely simple. Bag-shaped pots and crude beakers are associated with very rare iron tools and some grindstones. In the early stages of the occupation the inhabitants probably lived, like the Nguni of historical times, in simple beehive huts without walls. In the later stages more permanent building methods were used.

At the time when Gardner studied the evidence he had recovered from Bambandyanalo, almost nothing was known of the contemporary sites north of the Limpopo. Also, he was deeply influenced by the findings of the physical anthropologist Alexander Galloway, to

[1] Monica Wilson and L. M. Thompson (eds.), *Oxford History of South Africa*, vol. 1 (1969), p. 130.

whom he sent his skeletal material for analysis. Galloway did not have the benefit of the large comparative collections now available for the study of human types in South Africa. Although the Bambandyanalo skeletons are now considered to be well within the range of variation of Negro skeletons in southern Africa, Galloway pronounced them to be those of a Bush rather than a Negro population. And Gardner thereupon attributed the site to Khoikhoi, accounting for the traces of iron-working, agriculture and hut-building by postulating a recent reoccupation of the site by Nguni migrants moving northwards during the nineteenth century. In fact, the Bambandyanalo pottery is quite unlike the Khoikhoi pottery with which Gardner compared it, whereas it has an obvious relationship with the Leopard's Kopje II wares of south-western Rhodesia, and also with those of the upper layers of the Kalomo mounds in Zambia. Chronologically and in other ways, it fits well enough with the intrusion into south-central Africa of distinctly pastoral peoples and cultures which seems to have occurred towards the beginning of the present millennium. Such people could well have contributed the pastoral strand of the Nguni population, and it is conceivable that the Buispoort sites of the western Transvaal might mark a further stage in their southward passage. The Leopard's Kopje III site at Mapungubwe, only a mile or two from Bambandyanalo, is at present unique in South Africa, and is probably to be thought of as part of a late medieval culture connected with the exploitation of the gold of south-

FIG. 33.   Bambandyanalo. Gardner's trench is in left centre of the site.

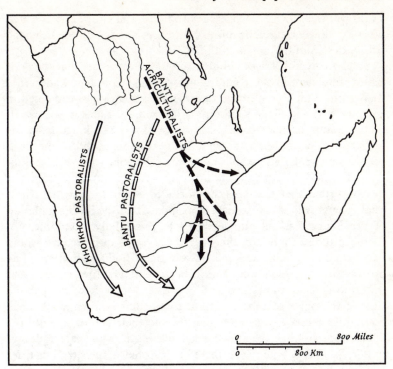

FIG. 34.   Agricultural and pastoral migration into southern Africa.

western Rhodesia and its export to the Indian Ocean by way of the Limpopo valley. We describe it, therefore, in Chapter 18, where we discuss the medieval state systems of south-central Africa.

If we are right in thinking that the Bambandyanalo site marks the settlement of the upper Limpopo valley by predominantly pastoral people, who lived to a large extent by milking their cattle, and who were connected with the Leopard's Kopje II people in Rhodesia on the one hand and with the pastoral element in the Nguni on the other, then it would seem to follow that this expansion of Bantu pastoralists would have passed to the *west* of the area of Sotho expansion in the north-eastern and central Transvaal. Such an expansion would in fact have proceeded southwards down the dry open country bordering the Kalahari desert on its eastern side, and then across the equally open plateau between the Vaal and the Orange, leading towards the Drakensberg and Natal. Such an hypothesis would accord well with the botanical researches of A. P. H. Acocks and others, which suggest that the better-watered central and eastern parts of the   115

Transvaal were formerly covered with forest and closed scrub, which was only slowly cleared by Sotho cultivators moving up the Limpopo tributaries from the north-east.

Such an hypothesis would also account for the fact that the non-Bantu influences in the Nguni language come from Khoikhoi rather than from San. For we have to remember that, as we explained in Chapter 3, the whole of southern Africa from the Kalahari westwards to the South Atlantic coast was, so far as we can judge from the distribution of its remnant populations, the homeland of the Bush people who spoke Khoikhoi. As we saw, the survival to the present day of Khoikhoi-speaking hunters in southern Angola makes it nearly certain that that area was included within the original Khoikhoi sphere. And it is reasonable to suppose that the Bush population of pre-Bantu Zambia also belonged to this family. Somewhere in these latitudes, therefore, the Early Iron Age Bantu farmers would have begun to infiltrate and absorb the Khoikhoi hunters. The process of absorption would have been most effective in the areas suited to early farming, and least effective in the arid country to the west of the upper Zambezi. Here the Khoikhoi would have retained both their Stone Age hunting culture and their language, until the appearance in their neighbourhood of Bantu who were milking-pastoralists, and who were therefore capable of penetrating drier country than the mainly agricultural Bantu of Early Iron Age times. We have seen that this important development is likely to have taken place around the turn of the present millennium.

Obviously, where the Bantu who impinged upon Khoikhoi hunters were of necessity specialised pastoralists, the pattern of interaction between the newcomers and the older inhabitants would have been very different from what it was in those areas where food production was mainly agricultural. Pastoralists would not have settled in the same dense communities as cultivators, and therefore they would not have exercised the same kind of overall cultural attraction upon the neighbouring bands of hunters. Their penetration would have been altogether thinner and more scattered. And, for their part, Khoikhoi hunting bands could have acquired domestic cattle by trading or raiding, and could have learned to pasture, breed and milk them with a much less radical change of life than that involved in the adoption of agriculture. Pastoralists, like hunters, live in temporary camps rather than fixed villages. Metallurgy has much less significance in a pastoral society than in an agricultural one. 'One does not herd cattle and blow bellows,' as a Jie informant re-marked to a recent field-worker in north-eastern Uganda. The western

Khoikhoi who adopted pastoralism also joined the age of metals, but only just. They worked copper rather than iron, and they used it for ornaments rather than for tools or weapons. Nevertheless, as stock-raisers they prospered and expanded, filling the whole of South West Africa (Namibia), and reaching and carrying the food-producing revolution into the Cape Province of South Africa before the arrival there of the Sotho or the Nguni. In this last stage of their expansion at least, they were no longer mainly converting fellow Khoikhoi from hunting to pastoralism, but invading territory previously occupied by San-speakers. A European traveller who visited the Orange River valley in the eighteenth century gave the essential picture when he wrote, 'Every tribe that owns cattle also has a number of Bushmen under its protection.' From the late fifteenth century on, Portuguese and Dutch mariners distinguished easily between the yellow-skinned herders with their outlandish, rattling speech, full of clicks and whistles, who occupied the coastlands from Walvis Bay in South West Africa to the Buffalo River in the eastern Cape Province, and the Nguni, by this time scarcely less pastoral in economy than the Khoikhoi, who lived beyond the Buffalo and the Kei and spoke the same kind of language as all the other Kaffirs on the Indian Ocean coast.

Such indeed was the pastoral ascendancy of the Khoikhoi in southern Africa that both the Nguni and the Sotho use words for 'cow', 'milk' and 'fat-tailed sheep' which appear to be derived from Khoikhoi roots. If more northerly Bantu languages had shown the same feature, it might have pointed to the conclusion that the Khoikhoi had acquired their cattle before the Bantu expansion. In fact, however, they do not, and we have seen that on other grounds it is impossible that the northern Khoikhoi could have learned specialised pastoralism from any other people than the Bantu of western Zambia or southern Angola, from the ancestors of people such as the Tonga, the Ila, the Nyaneka or the Herero. Having done so, they may well have been the first to introduce cattle and the milking complex into a wider stretch of South Africa than that in which their language survived. We have examined the indications that Bantu pastoralists may have spread down the western side of Rhodesia and the Transvaal early in the present millennium. To the west of the Kalahari, the spread of Khoikhoi pastoralism, though broadly contemporary, may have moved a little faster, so that the Bantu pastoralists, when they reached the latitude of the Vaal and the Orange, may have found the land inhabited not merely by San hunters but by Khoikhoi herders too. With these they would no doubt have fought, but also traded and intermarried, and such interaction would adequately explain the linguistic influence of Khoikhoi upon Nguni, and to a lesser degree on Sotho also. Genealogies of Nguni chiefs recorded in the mid-nineteenth century showed depths of between twelve and nineteen generations. In most cases the grave sites were known, and in all cases these were located to the east of the Drakensberg. This would indicate that the expansion of milking pastoralists reached Natal and the Transkei by the fourteenth or fifteenth century. Such a date would accord well enough with a crossing of the upper Limpopo valley around the eleventh or twelfth century.

The history of Egypt and the Sudan from the seventh century until the fourteenth is essentially that of the slow victory of Islam over the Monophysite Christianity of the Alexandrian patriarchate. Christianity had spread to Egypt during the first century, when, traditionally, Alexandria had been the see of St Mark. At first, the new religion had been espoused mainly by the Greek-speaking town-dwellers; and during the next two centuries the catechetical school of Alexandria, directed by scholars as famous as Pantaenus, Clement and Origen, was the intellectual centre of Christendom. Both Athanasius and Arius, the protagonists in the great Trinitarian controversy fought out at the Council of Nicaea in 315, were Alexandrian Greeks. Nevertheless, the indications are that Christianity spread only slowly through Egypt as a whole. Archaeologists have established that it was only in the fourth century, after the great persecutions were over, that there began to be a marked change in burial customs from the elaborate mummifications of the Osiris cult to the simpler Christian forms. Again, it was not until the fourth century that the Christian scriptures were translated from Greek into Coptic, the language of the great majority of Egyptians.

The first and greatest contribution of Coptic Christians to the Church was the idea of monasticism, the quest for spiritual perfection by retreat from the secular world, whether by individuals living as hermits or by communities of monks following a common rule and meeting together at least for worship. It could be argued that in its origins Coptic monasticism was partly a protest against imperial rule, a movement of retreat from a world that was not only sinful but dominated by a privileged urban elite speaking a foreign language. In Egypt, an imperial power could dominate irresistibly the delta and the narrow ribbon of the Nile flood-plain; but the desert was always near, where those prepared for a life of hardship could escape the attentions of the magistrate and the tax-gatherer. In pre-Christian times the word 'anchorite' meant one who withdrew his labour in protest against the conditions of life. Monasticism was in part a Christianisation of this concept. The monks, characteristically, were Coptic-speaking Egyptians, who withdrew from the world of the

Graeco-Roman establishment. They lived apart, in caves and tombs and deserted villages. But lay people came to them in their retreats, and it was they rather than the Greek-speaking clergy of the cities who carried Christianity to the Egyptian peasantry and small-town folk. As the number of Coptic Christians grew under their influence, even the Greek-speaking hierarchy of Alexandria had to adapt itself, linguistically and in other ways, to the Coptic majority. Athanasius as patriarch was notable for the support he gave to the monks.

During the fifth century the Coptic character of the Alexandrian Church was fortified by its progressive adoption of the Monophysite position, which recognised in Christ a single, divine 'nature' in contrast to the formula of 'two natures inseparably united', which was that accepted by the majority of bishops assembled at the Council of Chalcedon in 451. Though there was no formal schism for another eighty years, the difference of opinion went very deep, and essentially it was a difference between the monks of the Egyptian and Syrian deserts and the secular clergy of the Greek-speaking cities of the empire. The monks spoke Coptic or Syriac. They were deeply conscious of the prophetic and apocalyptic tradition of the Bible, and they had deliberately turned their backs upon the philosophic approach to Christian doctrine of the Greek schools. To such men the Chalcedonian definition seemed to play with words. 'In perpetual warfare against the demons on the edge of the desert, and haunted by sub-conscious fears of vengeance from the old, dispossessed national gods, the monks demanded as their protection the full armour of Christ',[1] apprehended in a single reality or 'nature'. The monks influenced patriarchal appointments, especially in Alexandria, but also in Antioch, and even in Constantinople itself. Several emperors, hoping to find an acceptable compromise, havered between the Monophysite and the Chalcedonian views. Justinian's empress, Theodora, was a fanatical supporter of the Monophysites.

And so, when Justin in 519 and Justinian in 531 and 536 at last turned to persecution, the results were cataclysmic. Driven from their official sees, the Monophysite bishops proceeded to ordain and consecrate a rival hierarchy, numbering, it was said, more than 100 000 clergy, spread between the Black Sea and the Blue Nile. Egypt became a place of refuge for the heresiarchs and the organisational centre of the movement, but by no means its only theatre of evangelisation. With the Alexandrian patriarch deposed and replaced by an imperial 'Melkite' nominee, the Monophysite leaders took

[1] W. H. C. Frend, *The Rise of the Monophysite Movement* (Cambridge, 1972), p. 141.

to the desert monasteries, and their following among the people grew steadily. The Coptic Christians developed their own characteristic art, a modest school, but one which succeeded in combining native and foreign elements into a distinctive new style of considerable originality. The Copts lacked the wealth to emulate the fine stone buildings of the Melkites in Alexandria and the other great cities. They used local materials, such as limestone and wood for their churches, and wool and linen for tapestries depicting the achievements of a galaxy of local saints. The central Monophysite doctrine apart, they offered a far from united front to the world, for local beliefs and traditional customs could colour the basic faith to an almost unlimited extent. Nevertheless, the influence of the Monophysites grew steadily in the countryside, and when the Byzantine garrisons were temporarily driven from Egypt by the Persians from 617 until 626, Monophysite bishops moved back into the towns and even captured the patriarchal see. The brief return of the Byzantines from 626 until 642 was accompanied by fresh persecutions, which left the majority Church in a state of sullen gloom, so that when the Arab armies began their invasion of Egypt in December 639, they encountered little resistance from the native Egyptians. After the withdrawal of the last Byzantine garrison from Alexandria in 642, the Coptic Church was quick to settle with the new regime. Its patriarch was recognised by the Arabs, and from this time onwards Christians throughout north-eastern Africa looked to him as metropolitan for the consecration of their bishops.

The Arab conquest of Egypt was at first essentially a change of imperial administrations. For most of the three centuries that followed, Egypt was merely one province of an Arab empire, which had its centre first at Medina, then under the Umayyad dynasty (660–750) at Damascus, and finally under the Abbasid dynasty (750–1258) at Baghdad. By the Arabs, as formerly by the Byzantines, Egypt was seen as a rich and easily controlled natural granary, which could supply corn to the growing towns of hungry Arabia and revenue for the caliphal treasury. Arab power was centred upon the garrison town of Fustat, near the later capital at Cairo. Governors came and went every two or three years. They were military men, and they seldom interfered with more than three or four of the highest civilian appointments. The provincial governors were usually Arabs, but the district governors and the village headmen were for the most part Egyptian Copts. Arabisation and Islamisation proceeded slowly, following from the immigration of fresh soldiers with successive governors and from the settlement of bedouin Arabs as peasants in the Nile valley. An important influence was that of Arabic as the language of government and administration. During the eighth century it finally superseded Greek, and before long it was impinging upon Coptic. By the tenth century literate members of the Monophysite Church normally wrote and spoke in Arabic, using Coptic only for liturgical purposes. As a result, the cultural transition for those who converted to Islam was greatly eased. The successful Egyptian of the early Islamic centuries was first an Arabic-speaker and only later a Muslim. The movement began in the towns, and spread slowly to the countryside, where Arabic displaced Coptic as the vernacular only during the later Middle Ages. Christianity itself was undermined as more and more of the literate people became Muslims, although it has continued as the religion of a substantial minority until the present day.

FIG. 35. Illuminated manuscript Gospel from thirteenth-century Egypt. Coptic text with Arabic translation in margin.

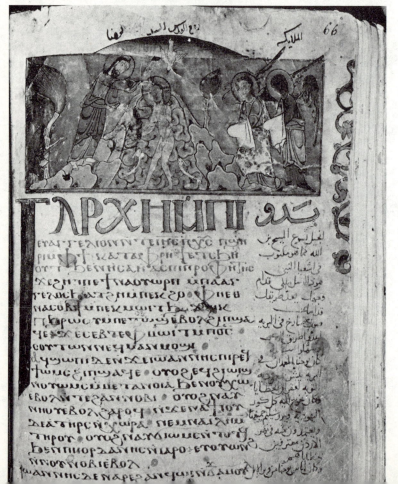

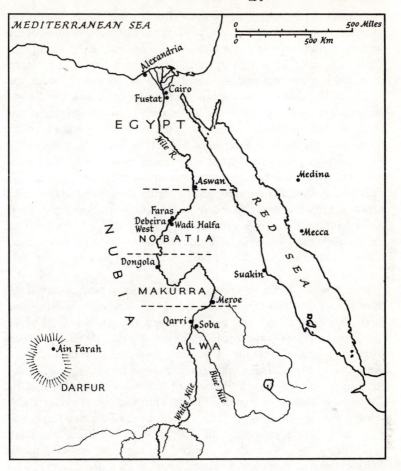

FIG. 36.   Muslim Egypt and Christian Nubia.

In Nubia the situation in the seventh century was very different. Here was no ready-made colonial framework which the Arabs could take over. Here were three kingdoms – Nobatia, Makurra and Alwa – in which the settled populations of the Nile valley, and even the Beja pastoralists of the Red Sea hills, had recently been converted to Christianity by missions, some Orthodox and some Monophysite, but both emanating from Constantinople and not from Egypt. These had been royal missions, sent by Justinian and his empress to their brother monarchs beyond the imperial frontier, whose adoption of Christianity had greatly reinforced the institutional strength of their state systems. Here Christianity had been the means of recover- 123 ing elements of literacy and culture lost during the decline of the Meroitic kingdom and the conquests by the X-Group peoples of the deserts. Militarily, these kingdoms were by no means negligible. They were ruled by a military class, which bred horses and trained them for warfare and raiding, and Nubian archers soon earned the respect of the Arabs. In 652, in the course of subjecting upper Egypt, Arab armies raided as far south as Dongola, and an agreement was reached which probably confirmed an existing arrangement between Egypt and the Nubian kingdoms. Its details were obscured in the ninth century, when Muslim jurists claimed that it provided for the supply of grain to Nubia in return for an annual tribute of 360 'heads'. This was a legal fiction, designed to justify an existing slave-trade, which would otherwise have been contrary to Islamic precepts. What really happened in the seventh century was that the Arabs saw that the conquest of Nubia would not repay the effort involved. And during the six centuries that followed they saw no reason to revise that decision.

As a result, the Sudan enjoyed during those centuries one of the most flourishing and vigorous periods in its long history. Sometime in the late seventh or early eighth century, the northernmost of the three kingdoms was absorbed by the middle one, Makurra, which from then onwards became a military power to be reckoned with, even by the Arabs. The Coptic tradition tells how in 748, when the Arab governor of Egypt imprisoned the Coptic patriarch, King Cyriacus of Makurra invaded Egypt and secured the patriarch's release. And again, in 831, after a rising of the Egyptian Copts had been brutally suppressed by the Caliph Mamoun, King Zachariah of Makurra sent his son on a splendidly equipped embassy to the Abbasid court at Baghdad; and the Caliph received the Nubians with soft words, and made it clear that he had no wish to enter upon a trial of strength with Coptic Christians in general.

Only in recent years, during the rescue operations undertaken in connection with the building of the Aswan Dam, have archaeologists begun to uncover detailed evidence of the rich cultural revival which occurred in Nubia during the two or three centuries following the Arab conquest of Egypt. Churches and cathedrals were built, and their walls were decorated in a brilliant and highly original style of mural painting. At Faras, the old capital of the northern kingdom and subsequently a diocesan city, a Polish archaeological expedition excavated the remains of a fine cathedral. When Michaelowski and his colleagues brushed the ubiquitous Nile sand from its crumbling walls, they uncovered more than a hundred gleaming frescoes of

religious and historical scenes, as well as numerous inscriptions in

Old Nubian, Coptic and Greek. The walls of one side chapel bore a list of twenty-seven bishops of the see, including the lengths of their reigns, from which it may prove possible to reconstruct a chronology for the region as a whole. Most of the dated inscriptions at Faras belong to the eleventh century, which was probably the time of greatest prosperity and artistic achievement; but the episcopal succession certainly covered a much longer period.

Alongside the churches of Nubia, there emerged a new kind of domestic architecture in sun-dried brick, frequently in two storeys. The University of Ghana's recent excavations at Debeira West were concentrated on the domestic life of the Christian Nubians. Debeira was a large village with a church and cemetery, first occupied in the seventh century, abandoned in the ninth, and then re-occupied from the eleventh century until the thirteenth. All the buildings were of sun-dried brick, with vaulted ceilings. Two storeys were usual, with a stairway leading to the roof. The village shared a common sanitary and drainage system. There was a communal oil-press and an irrigation wheel. The staple diet seems to have been *kisra*, an unleavened bread made of sorghum and dates. The bones of sheep, goats, pigs and cattle occurred plentifully in the midden heaps. Fish-bones, on the contrary, were rare. Iron, wood, stone, bone, leather and cloth were in use. Pottery was probably traded into Debeira from elsewhere, for no kilns were found on the site. The fine painted pottery of Christian Nubia, figuring birds, deer and other naturalistic designs, has been described as 'certainly the most artistic tradition existing anywhere in Africa at this period'. It has been classified into three periods – an early phase lasting from about 550 till 750, a middle phase from about 750 till 1100 and a late phase from about 1100 till 1350. Christian Nubian pottery has been found much further from the Nile valley than Meroitic pottery – in the ruins of a brick-built monastery at Ain Farah in Darfur, six hundred miles to the south-west of Dongola, and at Koro Toro in Wadai, four hundred miles to the west again.

The indigenous literature of Christian Nubia, in Greek, Coptic and Old Nubian, is nearly all ecclesiastical in character, and we have very little in the way of contemporary eye-witness reporting by outsiders. However, in the third quarter of the tenth century an Egyptian traveller, Ibn Selim al-Aswani, wrote an *Account of Nubia, Makurra, Alwa, the Bejas and the Nile*, of which the original has been lost, but of which precious fragments were copied by the fourteenth-century historian of Egypt, Makrisi. Ibn Selim's picture is, so far as it goes, entirely convincing. He describes a fifty-days' journey, mostly by boat, from Aswan to Dongola, through country 125

FIG. 37.   A painted pot from Faras, Nubia.

which was fully Christian from the second cataract southwards. Of the Dongola reach he says that 'one passed more than thirty villages in the course of two days' journeying, with pretty houses, churches and convents, with palm-groves, vineyards, gardens and meadows full of cattle and camels of a reddish hue'. From Dongola to the southern frontier of Makurra was further than from Aswan to Dongola, with the country more thickly populated and better cultivated. Alwa, according to Ibn Selim, was larger and more populated than the northern kingdom. Here, palms and vines were rarer, and the principal crop was *eleusine*, used both for bread and beer. Meat was plentiful, for there were large herds of cattle and abundant grazing. The country produced well-bred horses and Arabian red-haired camels. The king of Alwa was richer than the

126

king of Makurra, having more warriors and more horses. There was also gold in his country, and his capital town at Soba on the Blue Nile had many splendid buildings, and vast monasteries and churches filled with golden treasures. It is a tantalising glimpse, this, to which archaeology has already added a little, and to which it will one day add much more. Meanwhile, Ibn Selim's text serves a priceless purpose in helping us to place the archaeological data in a wider context, and to sense something of the organised wealth and power of the Nubian kingdoms, which enabled them to resist the infiltration of the Arabs and of Islam for so long.

In 969, just at the time of Ibn Selim's description of the Sudan, there occurred an event which changed the whole direction of Egyptian history and, ultimately, that of the Sudan also. This was the conquest of the country by the Fatimids, a dynasty claiming descent from Muhammad's daughter Fatima, which had built up a remarkable movement of sectarian (Shi'ite) opposition to the Abbasid caliphate, starting from an obscure base in eastern Algeria. The ambition of the Fatimids was no less than to replace the Abbasids, and first Tunisia and then Egypt were seen as stepping-stones to world power. After some abortive raids and much secret propaganda among the Egyptians, the Nile valley fell to the Fatimid general Jawhar and his largely Berber army. Jawhar selected the site of Cairo, and began to build there the palace city that was to outshine Baghdad, and the university mosque of al-Azhar, which was destined to be the intellectual powerhouse of the Ismaili Shi'a. The Caliph al-Mu'izz moved in, complete with the coffins of his ancestors, in 973. Under the Tulunids in the late ninth century and under the Ikshidids in the mid-tenth, Egypt had indeed seen two brief attempts by Muslim governors to establish hereditary sub-dynasties under the Abbasid caliphate. But the initiative of the Fatimids was of a different order. For the first time since the Roman conquest, the revenues of Egypt were mobilised to support an Egyptian government based on an Egyptian capital. For the first time since the fall of the Ptolemies, Egypt became the centre of an independent military and naval power. The Fatimids soon extended their rule eastwards into Palestine, Syria and Arabia. The lines of intercontinental trade, which had shifted northwards to the Persian Gulf under the Umayyads and the early Abbasids, now began to flow once more through the Red Sea and across Egypt to the Mediterranean. All the minor trade-routes leading to the Red Sea felt the benefit, especially those from Ethiopia and the Nubian kingdoms. During the eleventh century Turkish mamluks from southern Russia, but also black slave soldiers from south of the Sahara, were used to replace the Berbers in the Fatimid armies. A Persian visitor to Cairo in 1046 reported that the court of the Caliph al-Mustansir was served by thirty thousand black and white slave attendants and guarded by thirty thousand Negro soldiers. The figures were no doubt exaggerated, but they help one to appreciate the growing importance to Egypt of the lands to the south.

This importance was accentuated during the succeeding period of Fatimid decline. By the end of the eleventh century the Fatimids had ceased to exercise personal rule. Real power had passed first to a line of viziers, and then to the military bosses of the several provinces. In these circumstances the empire soon disintegrated. Syria and Palestine were conquered by Seljuk raiders. The Maghrib and Arabia transferred their nominal allegiance from Cairo to Baghdad. Egypt was now on its own. And, from 1099, its neighbours to the north were the European crusaders, who had established the kingdom of Jerusalem and other counties and principalities to the north. Cut off from supplies of Berbers and mamluks, Egypt depended increasingly upon its connections with the Red Sea, the Nile valley and the central Sudan, most obviously represented in its Negro regiments, which were now at their most numerous and disorderly. By the middle of the twelfth century the country was fast running down hill to a point at which it might well have fallen to the Crusaders. It was rescued by the Ayyubids, a dynasty of Kurdish soldiers, originally in the service of the Turkish princes of Damascus and Aleppo, who led the Muslim counterattack against the Crusader kingdoms. Invited into Egypt by one of two quarrelling factions, they stayed to rule. The great figure and real founder of the dynasty was Saladin, who became vizier in 1169, and who, on the death of the last Fatimid two years later, brought the government of Egypt back into Sunni orthodoxy by recognising the nominal suzerainty of the Abbasid caliphate.

We do not need to follow the details of Saladin's military campaigns, which led to the capture of Jerusalem and to the formation of a cluster of Ayyubid principalities in Syria. What Saladin did for Egypt was to replace the military system of the Fatimids with the much more durable system of Turkish military feudalism. The mamluk regiments were strengthened by regular importations of young Turkish slaves, who, after training as heavily armed cavalry knights, were manumitted and provided with official revenues, which they might hold for life but could not pass on to their children. The mamluks thus con-

stituted a military aristocracy of self-made men from outside Egypt, which renewed itself in every generation. The system proved so successful that in 1250 the mamluks took over the state, overthrowing the Ayyubids, and electing one of their own number as sultan for life, thus avoiding a hereditary succession. Despite the inevitable succession crises, the system worked. Real leaders were thrown up. The Ayyubids had defeated the Crusaders, but it was the mamluks who defeated the Mongols at the decisive battle of Ain Jalut in 1260. And in 1261, three years after the Mongols had destroyed the caliphate of Baghdad, the mamluk Sultan Baybars installed an Abbasid prince as nominal caliph in Cairo. In terms of political power this was an empty gesture. In terms of prestige, however, it was of the first significance. Cairo became the headquarters of orthodox Islam, the guardian of the Holy Places in Arabia, the effective centre of Arabic letters. Under the mamluks Egypt at last achieved a stable Muslim identity, which it did not wholly lose even when it was reduced into the position of an Ottoman province from the sixteenth century to the nineteenth.

It was the establishment of the mamluk sultanate in Egypt that settled the fate of the Christian kingdoms in the Sudan. It is true that Muslim settlement of the largely desert region between the first and second cataracts had started long before. Ibn Selim had described Muslims living in this region in the tenth century. Muslim tombstones inscribed in Arabic with dates of the tenth and eleventh centuries have been found in the Wadi Halfa at Meinarti and at Debeira West. But Ibn Selim is very clear that, south of the second cataract, the king of Makurra was in absolute control and that no Muslim was admitted without a passport. The Fatimids, with their need of black slaves, were only too anxious to keep the good will of the Nubians. Saladin, on the other hand, banished the Negro soldiers of the Fatimids to upper Egypt, where almost immediately they fomented a rebellion and attacked Aswan. An expedition was sent against them in 1172, and it concluded its campaign by raiding into the cataract region. But it was only with the mamluk sultans that Egypt began to raid explicitly Christian territory. Sultan Baybars (1260–77) captured the Nubian Red Sea port of Suakin, and sent three different expeditions up the Nile with the object of installing a renegade member of the Nubian royal house as his puppet ruler. He did not succeed in dethroning King David, but his armies plundered as far as Dongola and did great damage; and the story was repeated by his successor Kala'un in 1287 and 1289. Kala'un allowed himself to be bought off with an increased tribute, but not before Makurra had been badly devastated, so that, when operations were renewed by his successor, Nasir, in 1315 and 1316, the Christian king was captured without difficulty and replaced by a Muslim pretender.

The real result of the mamluk intervention, however, was not so much to extend Egyptian influence over Makurra, as, by destroying the power of Nubian resistance, to let loose a migration of nomadic, bedouin Arabs from upper Egypt into the Sudan. These soon disposed of the puppet ruler installed by Nasir, and replaced him with the Kanz ad-Dawla, the Arab chief of the cataract region. Immigrants poured south – first the Rabi'a and Juhayna Arabs of the cataracts, who now settled the Dongola reach, dispossessing and enslaving the Nubian owners; and then the camel nomads from the deserts of upper Egypt, who spread through the Nubian deserts, and on through Kordofan, Darfur, Wadai and Kanem. As they penetrated to the south, they mingled with the Negro pastoralists, becoming like them herders of cattle, until eventually the population on either side of the Nile was Arabised. The end of the southern Christian kingdom, Alwa, is known only in the vaguest outline. Cut off from the outside world, and enveloped by bedouin Arabs on both sides of the river valley, it seems nevertheless to have survived the fall of Makurra by about a century and a half – succumbing sometime in the fifteenth century to a confederation of Arab tribes from the deserts to the east of the

FIG. 38. The cathedral of Dongola, converted into a mosque by King Sayf al-Din 'Abdallah al-Nasir in 1317.

Nile, who, under the leadership of one Abdallah Jamaa, destroyed the old Christian capital at Soba and built their own headquarters at Qarri, a little to the north of modern Khartoum.

Christianity in Nubia did not long survive the Muslim conquests, although when a Portuguese embassy reached the Ethiopian court in 1520, it found there a delegation of Nubian Christians who had come to ask for priests. But its relatively sudden demise should not blind us to the brilliant and vigorous period which Monophysite Christianity enjoyed during the first seven centuries of the Muslim era. Of its direct influence upon Africa between the Nile and Lake Chad, we have perhaps still much to learn. Its indirect and negative influence was no less important. Through all these centuries Islam was denied its easiest line of access to black Africa. Muslim teachers, like Muslim traders, had therefore to cross the great deserts to the west. And Muslim pilgrims from West Africa had to make the long detour through Egypt on their way to the Holy Places. Of the relations between Monophysite Christians in Nubia and Ethiopia we know little, but we may wonder whether the medieval strength of the Ethiopian Church did not owe much to the existence of Nubian Christianity on its western frontier. Finally, to the legend of Prester John, and everything that it stood for in the nascent expansionism of Christian Europe, Nubia as well as Ethiopia certainly contributed.

We saw in Chapter 4 that Christianity came to Ethiopia as the culmination of a long period of Graeco-Roman and Byzantine influence in the Red Sea area. Zoscales, the second-century king of Axum, was described in the *Periplus* as literate in Greek; and his descendant of the fourth century, King Ezana, was converted to Christianity barely a generation after the conversion of the Emperor Constantine. For at least a century after this event Christianity was probably no more than the religion of expatriate merchants and a narrow indigenous elite. When Axum invaded Arabia in the sixth century, it was very much in concert with Byzantium. When the Axumite viceroys were driven out by the Persian Sassanids half a century later, it was because Byzantine rather than Ethiopian power had weakened. Thus, when Ethiopia was cut off from the Byzantine contact by the rise of Islam in the middle of the seventh century, it would hardly have been surprising if Christianity there had sickened and died. And yet it did nothing of the kind. At the beginning of the eighth century Muslim fleets captured the Dahlak Islands, which commanded the port of Adulis. From this time onwards the Greek merchants, who had traditionally organised the trade of Axum, were increasingly replaced by Arabian Muslims. And the pastoral, camel-owning tribes of the coastal lowlands, the Saho and the Afar, or Danakil, soon began to adopt the new faith of the bedouin Arabs from the opposite side of the narrow sea. But in the highlands Christianity lived on, and spread.

In fact, sometime during the late fifth or early sixth century, the Ethiopian Church had taken root. The new momentum of Christianity, here as in Nubia, seems to have been due to the steadily rising competition between Chalcedonians and Monophysites within the Church. Monophysitism was particularly strong among the monastic communities of Egypt and Syria, and whereas those of Egypt had a vast rural population among which to work, those of Syria were able to send missionaries far and wide. In Ethiopia the first wave of Monophysite evangelism may have been set in motion even before the emergence of a separate Monophysite hierarchy, by two groups of monks from Syria, remembered in ecclesiastical tradition as the Nine Saints and the *Sadqan*. Monastic communities were established throughout northern Tigre. The Bible and the liturgy were translated from Syriac and Greek originals into Ethiopic. The local people were attracted into the monastic schools. Cosmas Indicopleustes, who visited Adulis and Axum in the early sixth century, found 'everywhere churches of the Christians, and bishops, martyrs, monks and recluses by whom the Gospel of Christ is proclaimed'. When the Arab conquests of the seventh century put an end to the Byzantine connection, both the Church and the State of Axum stood firmly, each supporting the other.

Indeed, it is clear that the rise of Islam in the Red Sea area coincided with an important period of southward expansion by the Christian kingdom. Already in the sixth century Cosmas had mentioned a 'governor of Agau', who was responsible for the annual caravan of more than five hundred merchants which travelled south, with cattle on the hoof and with bars of salt and iron, to barter for gold in the land of the Sasu, which can only have been in the country to the south of the Blue Nile bend, either in Enarya or further west. The Agau were the indigenous, Cushitic-speaking people living to the south and west of the Semitic-speaking nucleus of the Christian kingdom, in the country between southern Tigre and Lake Tana. Probably, the sixth-century Axumite kingdom extended to the northern side of the Blue Nile bend, where the river flows south-eastwards after leaving Lake Tana. However, the sixth-century kings lived, like their predecessors, at Axum in the far north. In the seventh century a king called El Asham, who was a contemporary of the Prophet Muhammad, died and was buried in southern Tigre, and there are traditions of other royal tombs in this area. By the ninth century, traditions show the kings campaigning even further to the south, in Amhara and Shoa, and even as far as Enarya. Ecclesiastical traditions concerning the foundation of churches and monasteries show that the evangelisation of Amhara and central Shoa began at the same period.

When the expansion of the kingdom at last received a check during the late tenth century, it was at the hands not of any Muslim enemy, but of pagan insurgents from the southern borderlands. We know of these events only from the briefest references in contemporary Arabic sources, but the main counterattack seems to have come from the kingdom of Damot, with its centre just to the south and east of the Blue Nile bend. Certainly, the effects of the invasion were extremely grave. The Christian kingdom was overrun by marauding bands, which sacked the cities and burnt the churches. 133

The king was killed, and the old Axumite dynasty apparently extinguished. Christian-ruled territory was reduced to Tigre, Lasta and northern Amhara, and so remained for a full two centuries. At the beginning of this period there was probably no central authority at all. By the early twelfth century, however, a new dynasty, that of the Zagwe, had emerged in the high mountain area of Lasta. In medieval Ethiopian parlance, the Zagwe were not 'of the children

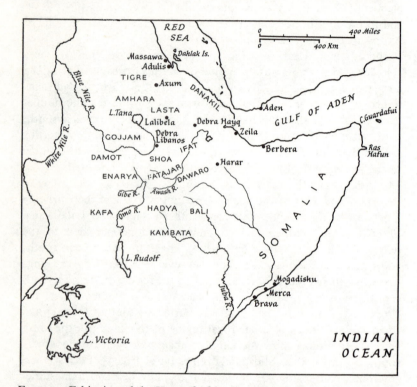

FIG. 39.   Ethiopia and the Horn of Africa in medieval times.

of Israel' – that is, they were not Semites but Cushites. They probably derived their main support from the Christianised Agau of Lasta and the country between there and Lake Tana, rather than from Tigre to the north or Amhara to the south.

The Zagwe built their capital city at or near Lalibela, near the borders of Agau and Amhara territory, and during the century and a half of their ascendancy there were constructed the eleven famous subterranean churches, excavated by hammer and chisel from the living rock. It used to be thought that these churches represented a new style of building which must have been imported into the country by foreign technicians; but in recent years scores of smaller examples have been discovered further north, in the Tigre mountains. Moreover, as Doresse and others have pointed out, the architectural style of the Lalibela churches is fully consistent with that of Christian Axum. What may have been new at Lalibela was the encircling mythology of Christian romanticism. The Zagwe dynasty maintained

FIG. 40.   The Church of St George at Lalibela, Ethiopia, hewn from solid rock.

135

excellent relations with Muslim Egypt, and the reconquest by Saladin of the Kingdom of Jerusalem from the western Crusaders in 1189 led to greatly improved conditions of pilgrimage for Ethiopian Christians, who used to march through Egypt in large companies, with drums beating and flags flying, and with regular halts for the celebration of Christian worship. Thoughts of the Holy Land dominated the imagination of the Zagwe court, and the Ethiopian historian Taddesse Tamrat has described the rock-hewn churches of Lalibela as 'a deliberate attempt to reproduce the Holy City of Jerusalem in the mountains of Wag and Lasta'. A mountain stream dividing the two main complexes of subterranean buildings was renamed the Jordan. The clink of the builders' hammers was heard by day and night, and devout rumour had it that when the monks laid down their tools at sunset, angels came and continued the work. Certainly, Lalibela has retained through more than seven centuries the reputation of a very holy place, where at the great Christian festivals pilgrims camp out in their thousands on the hillsides, while the splendid rituals of the Ethiopian Church are enacted below ground, and mostly during the hours of darkness, with the chanting of the clergy and the throbbing of the big drums marvellously magnified by the reverberations of the surrounding rock.

Although sustained by a Church which always included some literate people among its clergy, the internal written evidence for the history of Ethiopia from the ninth century until the thirteenth is sparse indeed. Scriptures and liturgies were copied at some of the main monasteries, and some biographical material about patron saints and founding fathers was recorded, of which the present generation of Ethiopian historians is beginning to make significant use. Otherwise, the written sources for this period are those which come from the outside, and are found in the works of the same Arabic writers – historians, geographers and encyclopaedists – on whom we depend for information about Egypt and North Africa, the sub-Saharan savanna lands and the coastal fringe of East Africa. What we find there is, first and foremost, information about the spread of Islam. The Christian kingdom is not ignored, but it is remoter from the authors, both in distance and in culture. They are therefore less interested in it, and it is evident that their knowledge of it had come to them at third or fourth hand.

Muslim expansion into the Horn of Africa began, as we have seen, early in the eighth century with the capture and settlement of the Dahlak Islands, where a minor but long-persisting Arab sultanate was able to give some protection to Muslim merchants trading on the mainland. Such merchants soon intermarried with the Saho and Danakil, the pastoral Eastern Cushites, whose torrid coastal plains had ample deposits of rock salt, which was the indispensable means of trading with the cultivators of the highland plateau. The camels of the pastoralists carried the salt up the 8000-foot escarpment at the back of Massawa Bay, and Muslim merchants formed a widespread and privileged community in the trading centres of the Christian kingdom. Al-Yaqubi, writing in the late ninth century, mentions 'mighty cities of the Habesha' (Abyssinians), which were visited by Arab merchants from Dahlak. But in the northern highlands at least, where Christianity had been longest established, the strength and vitality of the Church were sufficient to prevent the merchants from spreading their religion, as they did elsewhere. For example, a very different pattern developed alongside the Muslim trade from the next big Red Sea port to the south-east of Dahlak, which was situated just beyond the Bay of Tajura (the modern Jibouti), at Zeila. Here the coastal plain was much broader, and access to the interior followed an obvious route, via the salt deposits of the Danakil depression, and up the valley of the Awash, with the Shoan plateau on its northern side, and the Chercher plateau to the south. Zeila itself was, probably even at this period, a Somali town. The lower Awash valley was probably, then as now, a disputed borderland between Danakil and Somali pastoralists. The highlands on each side of the valley were occupied by a varied population, which included both Semites and Cushites, unsubjected as yet to Christian influence. Al-Yaqubi, at the end of the ninth century, mentioned Zeila as a place visited by Arab merchants from Baghdad, who presumably came there by sea from the Persian Gulf. A local Arabic chronicle claims that by the end of the same century a Muslim 'Sultanate of Shoa' had come into existence, ruled by a dynasty of the Muksumite family from Mecca. The location of this 'Shoa' is uncertain, but probably it included the middle part of the Awash valley and the foothills of the highland plateau on either side. The claim to an independent Muslim sovereignty at so early a date is dubious, but the early penetration of the Awash valley by Muslim merchant families can be accepted, and the process was no doubt strengthened by the development of Red Sea trade which followed the establishment of the Fatimid dynasty in Egypt from the late tenth century on.

The retreat of the Christian kingdom under the impact of pagan Damot occurred at the same period, and thus cleared the way for the independent development of a south-easterly trade route based on Zeila and the Awash valley. It is not until the early twelfth century, 137 however, that we have any circumstantial evidence of the conversion to Islam of sedentary Ethiopians from the edge of the plateau, and of the emergence of a Muslim state which would soon begin to challenge the southward expansion of the Christian kingdom. In 1108 the Shoa chronicle reports the conversion to Islam of a people who were probably the Argobba, a Semitic-speaking group living in the eastern foothills of the Shoan plateau and also around Harar on the southern side of the Awash valley. Again, in 1128, it reports that 'the Amhara fled from the land of the Warjih', the latter being a pastoral people, perhaps to be identified with the Danakil. Thus, at the period corresponding very closely with the resurgence of Christian Ethiopia under the Zagwe dynasty in the central and northern highlands, we see Islam establishing itself not merely among the nomads of the Somali and Danakil deserts, but among Semitic-speaking cultivators living in a strategic corner of the southern highlands, which commanded all the natural lines of communication running west and south of the Shoan plateau. During the thirteenth century the Maksumi sultanate fell apart in a series of internal succession struggles, until, in 1285, it was conquered and annexed by Ifat, a more recently founded Muslim state, ruled by an Arabian dynasty called the Walasma, which had built up its influence lower down the Awash valley in the region between Zeila and the escarpment.

On the economic side, the objective both of the Christian expansion from the north and of the Muslim expansion from the east was to control as much as possible of the rich trade with the still-pagan areas inhabited by the Western Cushitic-speaking, Sidama peoples in the southern and south-western parts of the highland region. For the Christian kingdom, this meant first and foremost the attempt to dominate Damot, and so to regain access to the gold-producing areas to the south of the Blue Nile bend. For the Muslim traders of Ifat, it meant the development of a series of trade routes fanning out to the south and west from the upper reaches of the Awash valley. One of these lines of communication ran southwards down the Rift Valley, tapping the districts of Dawaro and Bali to the east of the valley's chain of lakes, and those of Fatajar, Hadya and Kambata to their west. All this was later to become the central area of Galla occupation, but during the medieval period it seems to have been Sidama country, and the source of most of the light-skinned Ethiopian slaves who fetched the highest prices in the markets of the Red Sea and the Persian Gulf. Hadya, in particular, became well known as a source of eunuchs, who were mutilated by the traders and then nursed back to health before being sent on to the coastal markets.

Although literary references to these Rift Valley states begin only in the thirteenth and fourteenth centuries, when they were in the course of being conquered and made tributary by the Christian kingdom, the fact that their ruling elements were already by this time strongly Muslim suggests that the origin of this Islamic slave-raiding frontier must have been almost contemporary with the origins of Zeila, Ifat and the Shoan sultanate. Probably one should imagine a pattern of co-operation between immigrant Muslim traders and the most accessible Sidama chiefs, who became first the raiding agents and later the religious proselytes of the Muslims. Thus, with the advance of the raiding frontier, the territory of the Muslim states would have expanded at the expense of their pagan neighbours, and a new political configuration would have emerged. West of the slaving frontier, the remoter Sidama areas such as Enarya and Kafa traded gold and ivory and the highly valued musk combed from the fur of the civet cat. But here trade did not lead to conversion. Very likely, its organisation remained in Sidama hands. In the end, the Christian kingdom broke through from the north into direct contact with these western Sidama areas, and when it did so, it found a field still open for evangelisation.

Beyond the highland region, to the eastward, there lay the great desert plains of the Horn, stretching from the shores of the Gulf of Aden in the north to the Juba River in the south. Throughout this area the dominant people during historical times have been the Somali, with another Eastern Cushitic-speaking people, the Galla, living beyond them to the south-east. In the interpretation of Somali traditions great confusion seems to have been caused by the fact that in Somali the word *gal* means both 'pagan' and 'Galla'. Muslim Somali, questioned about the stone cairns marking ancient burials in large areas of northern Somalia, have replied that these structures were the work of the *gal*. Probably, they have usually been referring to their own pagan ancestors, but the conclusion has been widely drawn that northern Somalia was once occupied by the Galla. Again, many Somali traditions appear to describe a long process of southward expansion, at the expense of the *gal*, beginning with ancestors who arrived from Arabia. Taken at their face value, these traditions would appear to show that the Somali, though speaking an African language, arrived somehow on the southern shores of the Gulf of Aden and drove the Galla steadily southwards across the whole of present Somalia. It is today increasingly accepted that a much more satisfactory interpretation emerges if *gal* is read as 'pagan', and if the traditions of southward conquest are understood in terms of   139 religion rather than tribe. Thus it is Islam which is seen as entering by the northern coastlands, and it is Muslim Somali who triumph over pagan Somali as the faith spreads south.

It is certain that Islam must have reached the northern Somali ports of Zeila and Berbera as early as the eighth or ninth century. The first converts, however, would have been townsmen and merchants. The conversion of the pastoral Somali living between the Bay of Tajura and Cape Guardafui is traditionally associated with the migration of the founders of two of the five big clan-families into which the Somali population is organised. Sheikh Darod's arrival is usually placed in the tenth or eleventh century, Sheikh Ishak's a century or two later. It is impossible to be confident about the process of conversion, but certainly it would be naive to accept the genealogical emphasis of Somali traditions, according to which half of the Somali nation would have been physically descended from one or other of these holy men. Rather, we should perhaps envisage a pattern whereby groups of converts were received into one or other of the Muslim clan-families, much as Christian converts take the name of a patron saint. We have an illuminating glimpse of the situation around Berbera from Ibn Said in the early thirteenth century, who says that the people had mostly embraced Islam and were therefore no longer sold as slaves in the neighbouring Muslim countries. We get another glimpse of the expansion of the Muslim Somali down the Indian Ocean coast from references to the clan-family of the Hawiyya, who are located by Idrisi in the eleventh century in the neighbourhood of Ras Hafun, barely a hundred miles south of Cape Guardafui, and who are placed by Ibn Said in the hinterland of Mogadishu and Merca, nearly six hundred miles further south.

The conversion of the Hawiyya may have been at least partly due to the settlement of Muslim immigrants from the Persian Gulf and the Hadramaut in the coastal towns of the Benadir coast, notably at Mogadishu, Merca and Brava. Though traditions claim that the origins of these places go back to the seventh and eighth centuries, the earliest Muslim tombs and mosques discovered so far date rather to the twelfth and thirteenth centuries, and this is probably the period at which the local Somali began to be affected by Islam. The thirteenth century clearly saw much urban building at Mogadishu, and the emergence of a unified Muslim sultanate. In the early fourteenth century Ibn Battuta described it as a very large town, the inhabitants of which owned great flocks of camels and sheep, and were also the proprietors of an important textile industry, exporting their cloth as far afield as Egypt. The ruler in Ibn Battuta's time was of Somali origin, speaking the local dialect, but knowing Arabic. On Fridays he walked to the mosque in a solemn procession, headed by musicians playing cymbals and trumpets, and shaded by state umbrellas each surmounted by a golden bird. Unfortunately, we do not know from how far inland the trade of the Benadir coast was supplied, and in particular whether the valley of the Webi Shebelle provided a route through Galla country to Bali in the Ethiopian Rift. If it did, we should have one more reason for the Muslim orientation of south-eastern Ethiopia.

However, such, at least in outline, was the increasingly Muslim environment in which, from 1270 onwards, the new Solomonid dynasty of Christian Ethiopia had to make its way. The Solomonids, unlike the Zagwe, were Semitic-speaking Amharans. The founder, Yekuno Amlak (1270–85), appears to have been a chief, who had been imprisoned by Yitbarak, the last of the Zagwe kings, and had escaped and built up an independent power base as a warlord in the southern marches of the kingdom, in Shoa. From there he led an army to the Zagwe capital, killing Yitbarak with his own hands. The military coup d'état was completed in the northern province of Tigre, where resistance was fierce and prolonged. In material culture, the accession of the Solomonids marked a decisive break with the Axumite tradition continued by the Zagwe. Henceforward, in church-building rectangular forms gave place to round ones. Henceforward, a monastery consisted of a scatter of thatched rondavels enclosed within thorn fences, rather than of a stone-built eyrie perched upon a mountain pinnacle. Henceforward, the stone-built capital city was replaced by a tented camp arranged in concentric circles like the enclosures of other African kings, and moved regularly around the country according to the needs of defence and food supply. Nevertheless, much was done to emphasise the elements of continuity with the past. From the beginning of his career Yekuno Amlak had been careful to cultivate ecclesiastical support, especially that of the great monastic school of Lake Hayq, which had been founded about 1250 by the saintly abbot, Jesus Moa. With the aid of the southern clergy, the Solomonid coup was presented as a 'restoration' of the old dynasty of Axum. The romantic cult of the Holy Land was continued and intensified. In a new efflorescence of Ge'ez literature, the legend of Solomon and the Queen of Sheba became a part of the national mythology. Church and state reinforced each other's authority on an unprecedented scale.

Even so, Yekuno Amlak's first two successors, Yagba Siyon (1285–94) and Widim Ra'ad (1299–1314) were fully preoccupied in maintaining the unity of the kingdom within the frontiers established by the Zagwe. It was only with Amda Siyon (1314–44) that a great period 141

FIG. 41.   King Lalibela at the Church of Gabriel, Ethiopia.

of territorial expansion was inaugurated. Amda Siyon's first compaigns were designed to complete the Christian domination of the Shoan plateau, the eastern corner of which was occupied by Muslim Ifat, and the western part by pagan Damot. In a manuscript note recently discovered in the monastery of Debra Hayq, Amda Siyon records how, in the campaigning season of 1316–7,

God gave me all the people of Damot into my hands: its king, its princes, its rulers and its people, men and women without number, whom I exiled into another area. And after that God gave me all the people of Hadya, men and women without number, whom I exiled into another area.[1]

The conquest of Damot and Hadya was followed by that of Gojjam, hitherto an independent Agau-speaking kingdom situated within the bend of the Blue Nile. During the middle years of his reign the king was much preoccupied in subjugating the feudal nobility of Tigre. Later, from 1332 onwards, he came into full and successful conflict with the Muslim states of Ifat and Dawaro. These he did not attempt to annex, but left them tributary under rulers chosen by himself from the indigenous ruling families.

Thus, during the very years when the neighbouring Christian kingdoms of Nubia were beginning to founder in the face of Muslim strength, Christian Ethiopia was expanding its frontiers and adding yearly to its wealth and power. Amda Siyon's wars of conquest fed a lucrative slave trade, which passed through Dahlak and Zeila to Arabia, Egypt and the Persian Gulf. The conquests equally swelled the military power of the monarchy, since prisoners of war were regularly recruited into the regional contingents placed to guard the frontiers. Thirdly, the conquests added vastly to the extent of the royal patronage, for a large proportion of the new land was converted into fiefs (*gult*), which were used to endow administrative and military officials, monastic communities and the secular clergy. For the work of evangelisation, the key event was the foundation by the greatest of all the Ethiopian monastic leaders, Tekla Haymanot, of the community of Debra Libanos, on the borders of Shoa and Gojjam. Tekla Haymanot came from Debra Hayq to Debra Libanos in 1286, and he died there in 1313, the year before the accession of Amda Siyon. His successor Filipos was scarcely less dynamic, and there resulted a school of monasticism and theology which provided religious leaders for all the new provinces added to the kingdom by Amda Siyon. The diaspora from Debra Libanos was set in motion by an out-

[1] Taddesse Tamrat, 'The Abbots of Dabra Hayq 1248–1535', *Journal of Ethiopian Studies*, vol. VIII (1970), p. 96.

standing archbishop (*abuna*) called Yaqob, who came from Egypt to Ethiopia in 1337, and divided the southern regions among the disciples of Tekla Haymanot, so that each district soon had its monastic centre and school. The conversion of the Agau proceeded apace, and that of the Sidama peoples was begun. By the middle of the fourteenth century paganism, formerly so powerful, had ceased to be a force. The religious tension in highland Ethiopia was henceforward that between Christianity and Islam, and it centred in the provinces of Ifat, Dawaro and Bali, where the Christian kings ruled as overlords over tributary Muslim dynasties. Though conflict in this frontier region was almost continuous, the initiative remained in Christian hands throughout the fourteenth and fifteenth centuries.

13 The eastern Maghrib and the central Sudan during the early Muslim period

To the Arabs, all of North Africa beyond the boundaries of Egypt was al-Maghrib – the West. Within this Maghrib, they distinguished between a 'Near West' which stretched as far as eastern Algeria, and a 'Far West' which comprised western Algeria and Morocco. The Near West – the eastern Maghrib, as we shall call it in this chapter – had as its core the Tunisian plain, and the coastal cities from Tripoli to Bone. This had been the 'Africa' of the Romans and the Byzantines. It now became the 'Ifriqiya' of the Arabs, and no matter to what larger empire it owed theoretical allegiance, it retained a strong provincial identity, which was often combined with practically independent sovereignty. On the opposite side of the Gulf of Sirte from Ifriqiya, separated from both Tripoli in the west and Egypt in the east by four hundred miles where the desert reached the sea, lay the promontory of Cyrenaica, where the so-called Green Mountain, rising to nearly 3000 feet, brought regular winter rainfall to the surrounding region. Cyrenaica, in Islamic as in Byzantine times, fell within the political orbit of Egypt, and its coastal cities were usually reached by sea from Alexandria. The overland route from Egypt to the Maghrib cut across southern Cyrenaica, using the line of oases from Siwa to Augila, and thence bifurcating, westwards to Tripoli and south-westwards to the Fezzan. Though drier than in Roman times, the Fezzan was still spattered with oases, supporting a settled population living in dense concentrations around the diminishing water supplies. These oases were the last outposts of the Mediterranean world. Beyond them were the Tuareg nomads of the Hoggar massif, and the Tubu and other negroid tribes of Tibesti. Beyond these again lay the central part of what the Arabs called the Bilad al-Sudan – the land of the blacks.

Cyrenaica fell to the Arabs in 642, and during the next few years their raiding parties reached both Tripoli and the Fezzan. In 647–8 an Arab army penetrated the Tunisian plain and inflicted a decisive defeat on the Byzantine force that came to meet it. The Arabs, however, withdrew to Egypt with their booty, and the Byzantine garrisons were reinforced by sea after their departure. It was not, therefore, until 670 that the permanent occupation of Ifriqiya was set in hand under the great Umayyad general Oqba ibn Nafi. Oqba established his military headquarters at Qayrawan, at the northern end of the Tunisian plain. There followed a series of revolts, which were put down only at the end of the century. By this time an Arab navy was available in the Mediterranean to help the land forces in rolling up the Byzantine coastal fortresses, and the Arab conquest was sealed by the building of a second garrison town and naval base at Tunis, near the site of Carthage which they had destroyed. By the eighth century the tide of conquest had moved further west, to Morocco and Spain, but Ifriqiya remained the centre of Arab power in the Maghrib, and it was there that the twin processes of Arabisation and Islamisation assumed their classic forms.

At the heart of the whole movement were the soldiers of Arab race, the *muhajirun*, those who had truly joined the army of the faithful. With them went prayer leaders, and in their wake followed merchants and other travellers taking advantage of the new opportunities. Next there were the *mawali* – the clients. These included, first and foremost, the soldiers and retainers recruited as volunteers or by the emancipation of slaves taken as captives or given as tribute by the Berber tribes. Below these ranked the slaves and the concubines who became the objects of a flourishing import trade. Though regarded as inferior, these people too were instructed in Islam, and their descendants joined the Arabic-speaking population of the new towns. Also numbered among the *mawali*, however, were whole Berber tribal groups which had joined the conquering armies as allies, and which had made a collective submission to the Arabs and their religion at the time of doing so. Such mass conversions, often from a very vestigial Christianity, and motivated mainly by a desire for booty, had little religious meaning until they were followed up by the teaching of Muslim clerics in later generations. The actively Christian population of Ifriqiya was largely concentrated in the coastal towns, and some of it was evacuated to Sicily along with the Byzantine garrisons. But among those who remained, Christianity and the Latin language survived, though on a declining scale, through several centuries of Muslim rule. At the beginning of the eighth century there were forty Catholic bishoprics in North Africa; by the middle of the eleventh century there were only five. Christian epitaphs have been found on tombstones of the tenth century in Tripoli and of the eleventh century in Qayrawan. It was in fact only with the beginnings of the Christian reconquest in Spain and Sicily and the Balearic Islands, and with the crusade led by King Louis IX of France to the Ifriqiyan mainland, that the Muslim rulers of North

Africa faced their few remaining Christian subjects with the choice of conversion or death.

Meanwhile, Ifriqiya had long taken on the Muslim political identity which it was to keep, with only brief intervals, for more than a thousand years. The eighth century saw the breakdown of the fragile unity created by the conquest. The army and many of the Berber allies were penetrated by Kharijism, a type of Islamic nonconformity which combined a strict theological puritanism with a rejection of the historical caliphate. Starting in 740, a series of Kharijite revolts against the Umayyad governors of North Africa and Spain resulted in the emergence of independent kingdoms, or imamates, at Tahert in the eastern Atlas, at Tlemcen in western Algeria, at Sijilmasa to the south of the High Atlas in Morocco, in the Jebel Nefusa to the south of the Tunisian plain, and in other outlying places. Ifriqiya, however, remained orthodox, under the provincial governors of the Abbasids. At the end of the century the governorship became hereditary in the family of the Aghlabids, under whom Ifriqiya achieved virtual in-

FIG. 42.   The minaret of the Friday Mosque of Qayrawan, founded in 670.

dependence. The Aghlabid capital, Qayrawan, grew into a great city, the birthplace of a distinctive Maghribi architecture, which produced mosques and ramparts, reservoirs, aqueducts and palace buildings of great splendour and grace. Around the Great Mosque of Qayrawan there grew up in the ninth century a school of theology and jurisprudence comparable to any then existing in the Muslim world, and one which followed the strict, Maliki tradition of Islamic legal interpretation. In later centuries teachers from Qayrawan were to recapture the rest of the Maghrib from Kharijism to orthodoxy, and to reach out, through the Almoravids, to the western Sahara and Sudan. Finally, it was in the Ifriqiya of the Aghlabids that there emerged the Islamic variant of the monastic life – the life of communal retreat lived around a fortified place, or *ribat*, often a former Byzantine fortress, situated by the Mediterranean coast or else along an inland frontier, where the very pious could practise a regime of ascetic discipline while at the same time being trained for the *jihad*, or holy war, against the infidels of Sicily or Spain, or against the dissident Berbers of the African interior.

There was always a marked contrast between the austere religious orientation of the legal and clerical elite of Ifriqiya and the ostentatious life of pleasure lived by the rulers and their military commanders. Already by the ninth century the wealth which flowed to the capital was based largely on trade with the Sudan. The Aghlabids were rich enough in Sudanese gold to strike their own coinage and to buy their practical independence from the Abbasid caliphate with large tributes of golden dinars. For their household troops and standing army, as also for the myriad domestic servants who ministered to them in their palace city at Qayrawan, the Aghlabids relied increasingly on Negro slaves imported from the Sudan by merchant caravans, which were already operating regularly from Tripoli and Ghadames to the oases of the Fezzan, and from there southwards to the country that was to become the kingdom of Kanem. This steady stream of forced migration from the Sudan was at least as significant for the population of the eastern Maghrib as the irregular injections of Arab soldiers and settlers from the heartlands of Islam. When in the early tenth century, the Fatimids launched their bid for world power by conquering the eastern Maghrib from the Aghlabids, they did so by enlisting the support of Berbers from the eastern Atlas and welding them into a *corps d'élite* with which, some sixty years later, they were able to move on to the conquest of Egypt. But at the same time, they relied on the gold which they obtained in increased quantities through Sijilmasa, and upon the import of black slaves. When they moved on to Egypt, their Ifriqiyan governors, the Zirids, continued to build up Negro regiments and to staff their palaces with Negro slaves.

The removal of the Fatimid dynasty to Egypt in 973, however, resulted in a decline in the relative importance and wealth of Ifriqiya, which the Zirids could not check. Eastern Algeria became independent under the Hammadid dynasty, and in the middle of the eleventh century the Zirid state in Tunisia disintegrated into a series of city-states and petty lordships, some under the control of the Banu Hilal, the collective name for a number of Arab bedouin tribes who had moved into Cyrenaica and Tripolitania during the first half of the eleventh century, disturbing the existing tribes and demanding a place in the sun. They were important in bringing about the Arabisation of the Berber population of Libya and Tunisia, and in confirming the tribal horseman as a factor in warfare and politics. Meanwhile, the disintegration of Ifriqiya prepared the way for the conquest of the eastern Maghrib by the Moroccan dynasty of the Almohads, which is discussed in the next chapter. However, when the Almohad governors of Ifriqiya, the Hafsids, proceeded, like all their predecessors, to make themselves practically independent, as they were from the mid-thirteenth until the early sixteenth century, the links between the eastern Maghrib and the central Sudan became once more predominant. The Hafsids made their capital at Tunis the main entrepot between the northern and southern shores of the Mediterranean. They received there embassies from as far afield as Norway on one side and Kanem on the other. The merchants of Tunis dealt not only in the hides and wool, the horses and camels of North Africa, but in the gold of Mali, the slaves and ivory of Kanem and Bornu, the swords and coats of mail of the German cities, the glass and guns of Venice, the timber of Scandinavia. And the population of Ifriqiya, which had already been built up of so many strands of Berber and Punic, Greek and Latin, Byzantine and Vandal, continued to absorb Arab and Negro elements, which only needed the later addition of a sprinkling of Turks and a few more southern Europeans to complete the Tunisian mix.

Beyond Ifriqiya to the south lay the desert lands sparsely grazed by nomadic Berbers and bedouin Arabs, and traversed by the trade routes of the great camel caravans which moved between the Mediterranean and Negroland. The key points on these routes were the oases situated more or less along the tropic of Cancer, to the north of the great mid-Saharan massifs of the Hoggar and Tibesti. To the 149

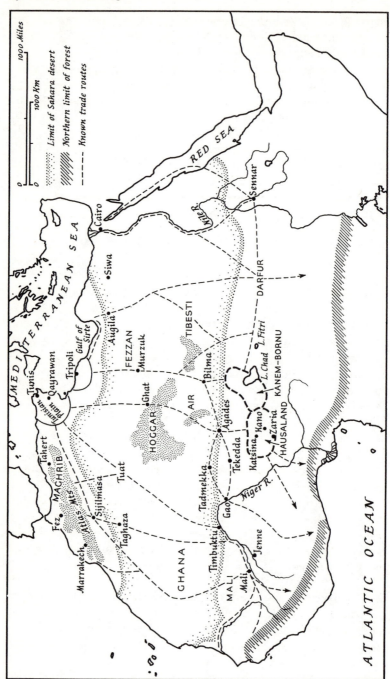

south-west of Ifriqiya was the oasis of Tuat, on the road to Timbuktu. To the south was that of Ghat, near the northern approaches of the Hoggar, over which ran the road to Aïr and Hausaland. Four hundred miles to the east of Ghat and five hundred miles due south of Tripoli, was the oasis region of the Fezzan, from which an important trade route led south to the region of Kawar, with its great salt-producing oasis of Bilma, and on from there towards Lake Chad. This was the route to Kanem and Bornu. According to the traditional history of the Arab conquests, Oqba ibn Nafi, the founder of Arab Ifriqiya, led the first Muslim expedition to Kawar while exploring the southern route to Ifriqiya in A.D. 666. Certainly by the ninth century, if not earlier, the Berber inhabitants of the Saharan oases were Kharijite Muslims of the Ibadi sect, whose religious links were with the Kharijite population of Ifriqiya and Tahert. The Arab geographer al-Yaqubi, a well-informed official in the Abbasid ministry of posts, who had visited the Maghrib in the late ninth century, knew that the town of Zawila in the Fezzan was an important centre of the Ibadi sect and also a major market for the black slaves brought from Kawar and the countries further south. 'I have been informed,' he wrote, 'that the kings of the blacks sell their own people without justification or in consequence of war.' All through the medieval period there is mounting evidence of the slave trade passing through the Fezzan both to Egypt and to Ifriqiya. So vital was the security of the road that, when the original Berber ruling family began to lose its authority in the mid-thirteenth century, the greatest of the 'kings of the blacks' sent an army across the desert to restore order and good government to the oasis region.

The earliest Negro kingdom mentioned in the works of the Arab writers is that of the black camel nomads called the Zaghawa. Al-Yaqubi, in the ninth century, mentions 'the Zaghawa who inhabit the place called Kanem', and from the tenth century we have the remarkable reference by al-Muhallabi, which we quoted in Chapter 6, to the religion of the Zaghawa being the worship of their king, who was thought to bring life and death and sickness and health.

They exalt and worship him instead of God. They imagine that he does not eat, for his food is introduced into his compound secretly, no one knowing whence it is brought. Should one of his subjects happen to meet the camel carrying his provisions, he is killed instantly on the spot. He drinks with his intimates a beverage which is concocted from millet laced with honey ... Most of his subjects are naked ... They subsist on the products of their cultivation and the stock which they own.

The Zaghawa kingdom of Kanem was no doubt one of many small states built up by horse-borne warrior pastoralists along the southern 'shore' of the Sahara during the centuries following the Arab conquest of the Maghrib. The most durable of these states, however, proved to be one founded by another group of black pastoralists, the Magumi, in the region to the north-east of Lake Chad. It may be that the Magumi state grew up alongside that of the Zaghawa and finally conquered it. At all events, by the end of the eleventh century a Magumi prince, Humai, allegedly the twelfth of his line, was the foremost ruler in Kanem, and the first to become a Muslim. Humai's successor, Dunama I, who reigned right through the first half of the twelfth century, is remembered in the traditions as a rich and powerful king, who built up the cavalry strength of his army, and who made the pilgrimage to Mecca three times. It was Dunama's grandson, Selma, who established contact with the first of the Hafsids. His great-grandson, Dunama II, who reigned through the middle of the thirteenth century, was probably the king who extended the influence of Kanem northwards to the Fezzan, establishing a provincial governorship at Traghen, between Zawila and Murzuk, which endured for about a century.

It would seem clear from the traditional accounts of both the wars and the dynastic marriages of the Magumi kings that Kanem had its origins among the desert peoples of the central Sahara rather than among the settled agriculturalists of the Sudanic belt. The Magumi *mai*s took their principal wives from the pastoral tribes of Kawar and Tibesti. The remembered wars of Dunama II were against the Tubu of Tibesti, who were, so far as one can tell, the descendants of the 'troglodyte Ethiopians' hunted by the Garamantes of the Fezzan in classical times. Seen in this light, Dunama's conquest of the Fezzan is not so extraordinary. Nevertheless it is clear that, by the thirteenth century at least, the centre of power had shifted southwards into the agricultural zone. The earliest fixed capital would seem to have been in the desert, near Bilma; it was succeeded by Njimi, quite close to the north-east corner of Lake Chad. It may be that with the desiccation of the Saharan fringes there was a tendency for pastoralists to move southward and settle down. There can be little doubt, however, that this process was intimately linked with the slave trade. The southern lands were not empty. They had to be conquered piecemeal, year by year. The main momentum of later Kanem expansion was the annual slaving campaign led by the cavalry of the *mais* against the sedentary farming peoples, known collectively as the Sao, to the south of the savanna belt. Those nearest at hand were subjected and fully assimilated: in time they came to form the mass of the Kanuri-speaking population. Those a little further away became tributary, in order to gain relief from regular raiding. Slaves, therefore, were taken from an ever-widening periphery, extending several hundred miles from the capital. And as Islam became the religion of the state, the pace of expansion increased, for the razzia was henceforward dignified with the name of *jihad*.

Despite the evident Muslim piety of many of the *mais*, the political structure which emerged in medieval Kanem retained strong traces of the pre-Islamic sacral kingship attributed by al-Muhallabi to the Zaghawa, and having many features in common with other states of the Sudanic belt. The ruler led a ritually secluded existence, surrounded by titled office-holders and palace slaves. As in so many African kingdoms, the highest positions of all were held by two women, known as the Queen Mother and the Queen Sister, each of whom had her own court and officers. The highest male dignitaries were the provincial governors theoretically responsible for the north, the east, the south and the west. In practice these seem to have been central, privy council posts: the real administration of distant provinces was entrusted to military commanders, often princes of the royal house, each of whom surrounded himself with a court and officers on the same pattern as the central one. Clearly, as in other African states, this system carried the constant danger of fragmentation following any weakening of the central control. The most serious crisis in the whole of Kanem history seems in fact to have stemmed from the huge conquests of Dunama II, when, as the king-list records, 'the sons of the ruler became separated in different regions'. A cadet branch of the dynasty, known as the Bulala, carved out an independent sovereignty on the eastern fringes of the kingdom near Lake Fitri, where they first resisted control and later turned to attack the centre. The commander established by Dunama in the Fezzan likewise threw off the imperial yoke. There was faction-fighting in the capital itself, and Dunama's two successors died by assassination. The fourteenth-century history of the dynasty is one of continuous and bitter fighting on the south-western frontiers of the old kingdom, where four successive *mais* were killed in campaigns against the Sao living to the west and south of Lake Chad.

The real significance of these wars, however, lies not in the quality of Sao resistance, but in the fact that Kanem was now again shifting its centre, this time from the north-east to the south-west of Lake Chad. The north and east of the old empire was now abandoned to the Banu Nasur of the Fezzan and the Bulala of Lake Fitri. But the drive to the south went on, and its motives were as always twofold: the inevitable southward drift of those who lived upon the margins of an expanding desert, and the dependence of the central authority on a continuing source of slaves – both for internal use in Kanem and for export in exchange for salt, cloth, horses, swords, chain-mail, books and the other luxuries necessary to attract teachers, preachers and skilled artisans from the outside world. Without a constantly expanding military frontier, Kanem could not exist. This expansion, however, took place not in concentric circles around a fixed nucleus, but from a centre which itself drifted southwards over the centuries, so that a kingdom which had its origins in mid-Sahara was by the fifteenth century centred in Bornu, in the north-east of modern Nigeria. What remained in comparison unchanging were the North African and Middle Eastern markets for black slaves. It was the persistence of this trade through more than a thousand years which made the main economic link between the eastern Maghrib and the central Sudan. The cultural link which balanced it was, of course, the steady spread of Islam and Arabic letters in Kanem and Bornu. Although during early medieval times the proportion of the population affected was doubtless very small, it would appear that by the beginning of modern times Bornu was more strongly influenced by Islam than any of the states of the western Sudan, except possibly Songhay. Kanuri Muslims went regularly on pilgrimage and stayed for education in Egypt and the Maghrib. By the end of the sixteenth century it was claimed that all the notable people were Muslims, and that the Shari'a law was applied in all the courts.

In contrast with the long period of activity on the Fezzan–Kawar route, that across Aïr to Hausaland seems to have been a late medieval development; and the current tendency among historians is to see the emergence of the Hausa peoples as a far more self-contained process than that of the Kanuri. In terms of long-distance trade, this is probably correct. However, Aïr was no less subject to climatic change than Kawar, and here again the essential development of the first half of the present millennium was the southward withdrawal of the northernmost agriculturalists – in this case the northern Hausa – and their replacement by pastoralists – in this case the Tuareg Berbers from the central Sahara. This is remembered in tradition as a long-drawn-out interaction, in which pastoralists at first settled alongside the cultivators, and only much later, when the balance of power had changed, began to drive them out. In central Hausaland, astride the modern frontier between Nigeria and Niger, the flow of displaced northern Hausa was probably one of the main factors leading to the formation of states. However, not all of the migrants were Hausa. Here, as to the west in Songhay, there are conflicting traditions of conquering bands, horse-borne and well-armed, who arrived from the north or the east. There are tales of Zaghawa moving in from Kanem. And there are traditions of a conquering hero called Bayazid, who might conceivably be connected with the followers of an Ibadi leader of that name who was driven out of southern Tunisia by the Fatimids in the mid-tenth century. It is impossible from the existing evidence to disentangle these different elements in any precise way. What is certain, however, is that early in the present millennium there were coming into existence territorial states, of which the rulers, or *sarki*s, had their citadels in walled towns, or *birni*s. A few of these towns, such as Kano and Dawura, Katsina and Zaria, have survived to the present day, and even in the absence of precise archaeological data it is possible to see roughly how they grew. In every case the walls enclosed not merely the urban centre but also a very much larger area of agricultural land. A *birni* was therefore not merely a capital but a place of refuge for the inhabitants of the surrounding countryside. A *sarki* was a territorial ruler, whose power depended on the number of his armed knights, and therefore upon the number of fiefs with which he could endow them. The feudal aristocracy lived in the town, around the *sarki*'s palace, and these were surrounded in their turn by the industrial bourgeoisie, the smiths and armourers, the tanners and the leather-workers, the weavers and the dyers, the brewers and the bakers, the musicians and the drummers, the merchants and the magicians. Beyond the walls, a circle of slave villages produced the townsmen's food. Beyond these suburbs, the Hausa peasantry farmed from their mud-walled family enclosures.

The growth of these city-states in central Hausaland does seem to have been mainly a product of competition among the Hausa themselves for the lands best provided with the subterranean water which enabled dense agricultural populations to grow up in these comparatively northerly latitudes. Certainly, no major external threat developed until the emergence of the Kanuri state in Bornu in the fifteenth century and the eastward expansion of Songhay power in the early sixteenth. Again, there is no evidence of Hausaland being involved in any of the long-distance trading networks of the early medieval period. The essential proof of this is that Islam came late to Hausaland – in the late fourteenth or even the early fifteenth 155 century – and that the first Muslims are clearly remembered as 'Wangara', that is to say, Mande-speakers from southern Mali. As we shall see in Chapter 15, these Wangara probably reached Hausaland by trade routes passing to the south of Songhay through the kola-producing areas of modern Ghana and Dahomey. Only with the opening of the roads across Aïr did Hausaland begin to trade regularly across the desert, or even as far as the salt mines of Bilma. Only then did Hausa manufactures in leather and cotton spread across North Africa to the Atlantic coast. The decisive factor here was the progress of the Aïr Tuareg towards a degree of political organisation at which they could provide security in exchange for tolls. This stage came during the early fifteenth century, when the Tuareg clans of Aïr agreed to seek a neutral ruling figure from among the Hausa of Gobir, whom they installed as Sultan of Agades. Meanwhile, the Hausa, though still pagan and isolated, had travelled far towards civilisation and material prosperity. Theirs was perhaps the best example in African history of how far development could go with only minimal outside stimulus. When Islam came at last, the Hausa were ready to absorb it, but never with the same ardour as the Kanuri, for whom it had been, almost from the first, the faith of the conquering group.

In the western Maghrib, extending from central Algeria to the Atlantic coast of Morocco, Arab conquest was less thorough and Arab settlement for a long time much sparser than in the east. Arab rule was nominally established by the Umayyad governor of Qayrawan, Musa bin Nusayr, during a great military excursion through Tlemcen to Tangier undertaken between 704 and 711, Berber tribes enlisted as allies, making a collective submission to Islam which can have been little more than nominal in its effect; and the coastal towns and settled areas were conquered and plundered with their help. A Berber convert, Tariq bin Ziyad, was installed as governor at Tangier, and in 711 he was despatched with an army of Berber levies against the crumbling kingdom of the Visigoths in southern Spain. Henceforward, Spain became the main target for Arab settlement in the 'Far West'. Arab armies followed in the wake of the Berber spearhead, and shared out the agricultural estates of the Visigothic nobility. The western Maghrib became, so far as the Arabs were concerned, a corridor, a raiding ground for slave soldiers, and a source of harsh collective tribute raised by military means. By the mid-eighth century it was seething with revolt, and it was in this political climate that anti-establishment Kharijite doctrines found a ready acceptance and led to the emergence of independent Berber states based on Tahert and Tlemcen in western Algeria and on Sijilmasa in south-eastern Morocco.

The Idrisid kingdom of Fez, based in the central plain of northwestern Morocco, had its origin in the same movement of protest. Here, in the late eighth century, Idris ibn Abdulla, an Arab of the Prophet Muhammad's family, fleeing from an unsuccessful encounter with Abbasid forces near Mecca, was recognised as *imam* by the discontented Berbers living to the north of the High Atlas. Starting from the neighbourhood of Meknes, he and his successors gradually built up a state stretching over the area from Tlemcen to the Atlantic and south from there, across the Middle Atlas, to the upper Draa. The capital city was founded at Fez between 790 and 809, and this attracted a small but concentrated nucleus of Arab settlers from Spain and Ifriqiya, under whose influence, despite the Shi'ite origin of the   157

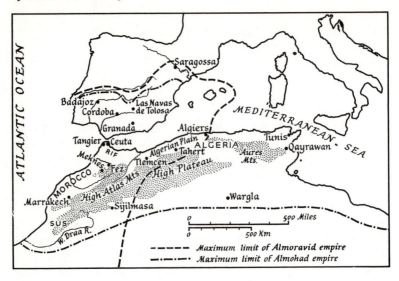

FIG. 44.   The Maghrib and Muslim Spain.

dynasty, Islamic orthodoxy and the Arabic language began to spread.
Indeed, during the ninth century, Fez under the Idrisids began to
achieve something of the lustre of Qayrawan under the Aghlabids.
But, taking the Idrisid state as a whole, Berber tribalism was never
so successfully dominated by a strong central government as it was
in Ifriqiya. On the death of Idris II in 828, the kingdom broke up
into nine tribal principalities ruled by his sons, and these fell an easy
prey to the Fatimid armies in the tenth century and to the Almoravids
in the eleventh. It was not until the Almoravids that a state was
created in southern Morocco, and even then the High Atlas remained impenetrable and largely aloof, despite a brief moment of
great significance in the twelfth century when it gave rise to the
dynasty of the Almohads. The Middle Atlas and the Rif were almost
equally secluded, as were the mountains of Kabylia and the Aures in
the eastern Maghrib.

By the end of the tenth century, the important region from Fez
to Tlemcen was in the hands of Zanata Berber leaders. This region
lay at the junction of the main east–west route across North Africa
with that running north from the oasis settlement of Sijilmasa, which
was the terminus of the main caravan route from the western Sahara
and Sudan. Sijilmasa was also in Zanata hands; but beyond, in the
desert and the Mauritanian steppe, lived the veiled Sanhaja Berbers,
158   the westerly cousins of the Tuareg, who pastured their camels and

controlled the wells and oases all the way from the Draa to the Senegal. In particular, they controlled and exploited through Negro slaves the great salt mines at Taghaza and other desert depressions where the drying up of former lakes had left deposits of rock salt. This salt was the key to the trans-Saharan trade. The Negro populations of the Sudanic belt, in most ways so self-sufficient, suffered from a grave and grievous shortage of salt, so vital to man and beasts in these warm latitudes. To obtain it, they had no choice but to trade with the pastoralists of the desert. As we pointed out in Chapters 5 and 6, there is strong presumptive evidence that this trade had originated as early as the first millennium B.C. What we do not know for certain is the date at which it became a rich trade, of international importance, as a result of the exploitation of West African gold. Except for Herodotus' possibly legendary description of the silent trade, neither the classical nor the Christian sources for North Africa make any specific mention of gold crossing the Sahara. Nevertheless, among the earliest Muslim writings there are references to it. In the traditions of the Arab conquest recorded by Ibn Abd al-Hakam in the mid-ninth century we hear of a governor of the Maghrib, 'Ubaid-Allah bin al-Habbab, who in 738 sent an expedition to 'the land of the blacks', which returned successfully, laden with slaves and gold. None of the Arab sources, however, suggests that the trade had an Arab origin. Rather, they report the increasing involvement of Muslim Zanata from the Atlas region in an already existing traffic between the Sanhaja of the Sahara and the Mande-speaking Soninke to the south of the desert. As first the Zanata and then the Sanhaja became Muslims, so acquiring wider commercial and religious connections, so no doubt both the scale and the complexity of the trade were enhanced. Although Tahert had been destroyed by the Fatimids in 909, the Ibadis of Ifriqiya, already in command of the routes through the Fezzan to the central Sudan and through the Hoggar to the Niger bend, became especially prominent along the western route also.

It is in the light of this situation that we have to consider the Almoravid movement, which on the one hand left the Sanhaja of the desert with an empire stretching from the Senegal to Saragossa, and on the other hand gave a major and lasting impulse to the spread of Islam in West Africa. The Sanhaja at the beginning of the tenth century were the undoubted masters of the western desert, but they were spread over a vast territory and they were divided into several tribes. The Lamta and the Jazula lived on the north-western side of the desert. The Masufa were towards the east, dominating the salt mines. The Lamtuna and the Joddala lived in the southern part of the desert, bordering the Negro kingdoms of Ghana and Takrur. Awdaghast, the main caravan town at the southern end of the desert route, was in country disputed between the Lamtuna and the Soninke. Islam was spreading throughout the region, but was weaker and less orthodox in the south than in the north. Around A.D. 1035 the chief of the Joddala, Yahya ibn Ibrahim, made the pilgrimage to Mecca, and as a result of his journey became aware of the shortcomings of Islam as practised in the western Sahara. On his way home, he took·the advice of theologians in Qayrawan, and was referred to a *ribat* directed by one Wajaj in southern Morocco. Here he found a Lamta teacher, Ibn Yasin, who was prepared to accompany him to his homeland in southern Mauritania. So long as Yahya lived, Ibn Yasin taught among the Joddala, though he grew increasingly unpopular on account of his rigorism. On Yahya's death he 'withdrew' with his faithful followers, perhaps to a *ribat* of his own, perhaps to that of his former master, Wajaj. When he re-emerged, it was among the Lamtuna, whose chief, Yayha ibn Umar, now became the secular leader of the movement.

The essential concern of the Almoravids (*al-murabitun*, people of the *ribat*) was with the strict observance of the external discipline of Islam – with community prayer and fasting, abstention from alcohol and unclean food, promotion of the pilgrimage and of Koranic education; but the basic premise that all these things could be promoted by force, by *jihad*, meant that the movement had to have a firm base in the ethnic politics of the region. Starting in 1042, Ibn Yasin and Yahya ibn Umar began to consolidate first the Lamtuna and then the other Sanhaja tribes into an effective political federation with a central leadership and a standing army. The alliance united, probably for the first time, tribes from the northern and the southern halves of the desert. Inevitably, it came to see as an early objective the assertion of full control over the trans-Saharan routes, including the desert ports of Sijilmasa and Awdaghast. When Sijilmasa appealed for help against its Zanata lords, Yahya ibn Umar marched north and captured the town in about 1055, and then almost at once recrossed the desert and reconquered Awdaghast, which had once been in Sanhaja territory, from the Soninke king of Ghana. Yahya was killed soon after by Joddala backsliders from the alliance, but he was succeeded by his brother, Abu Bakr, who continued the war of attrition on both sides of the desert.

That the northern sphere of operations developed into a full-scale conquest of Morocco was probably unintended by either Yahya or Abu Bakr, both of whom considered themselves men of the desert and the tented camp. However, the conquest of the Sus and the Draa could only be consolidated by establishing a base on the northern side of the High Atlas, and somewhere around 1070 Abu Bakr led an expedition through the high passes and built a fortified camp on the site of Marrakech, at the edge of the central Moroccan plain. There he left as commander of the northern army his cousin and heir-apparent, Yusuf ibn Tashfin, and also, it is said, the wife whom he had himself married while in the north, one Zaynab, a rich and am-bitious courtesan, who had refused to accompany him on his return to the desert. Zaynab understood the opportunities for a conqueror in Morocco, and soon placed both her wealth and her hand at the dis-posal of Yusuf. The Sanhaja army of the north was transformed by the recruitment of two thousand black slaves from across the Sahara and of Christian captives from Spain. Horses were bought and weapons forged, and in 1075 the new army of the Almoravids con-quered the remnants of the old kingdom of Fez, now ruled by Zanata allies of the Spanish Umayyads. Tlemcen fell likewise in 1082, and Ceuta the following year. In Spain, by this time, the Umayyad cali-phate of Cordoba had disintegrated into a score of petty principalities, which were fast losing the military initiative to the resurgent Christian kingdoms of Aragon and Castile. Calls for help soon reached Yusuf at Ceuta, and in 1083 he crossed the straits. In 1086 he won a great victory near Badajoz over Alfonso VI of Castile. By 1094 he had restored the unity of Muslim Spain.

And so, when he died in 1106, Yusuf bequeathed to his son Ali a huge empire – the Kingdom of the Two Shores – which included two-thirds of Spain, the whole of Morocco, half of Algeria and, in theory at least, the whole of Mauritania. So long as Abu Bakr lived, Yusuf accorded him a nominal primacy, sending him gifts and news of his conquests, and even striking his gold dinars in Abu Bakr's name. But after Abu Bakr's death in 1087, Yusuf claimed the succession to the whole of the Sanhaja empire. And though neither he nor his son ever again crossed the desert, there is ample evidence of the continuing importance of the Saharan trade in Almoravid times. This was the period when Ifriqiya was in eclipse, and it was easy to divert the traffic towards the west. Again, the Almoravid conquest of Spain soon demonstrated that the northern and southern shores of the Mediterranean were economically more complementary than the west and the east. Though the Sudan continued to trade across the long desert routes to Egypt, its growing links with Europe ran for two centuries primarily through Morocco. Finally, it must not be forgotten that the Almoravid movement was, not only in its origin, 161 but in its continuation, a religious movement. By their conquests and by their uncompromising support of Malikite lawyers and theologians, the Almoravids brought the western Maghrib into the mainstream of religious orthodoxy. It was an extraordinary contribution by men of the desert to the world of the cities.

In 1147 the Almoravid dynasty of Ibn Tashfin was overthrown in North Africa and Spain by the long-prepared revolution of the Almohads, which had originated some thirty years earlier with the teachings of a saintly scholar, Muhammad ibn Tumart, a Masmuda Berber from southern Morocco, who believed himself to be the divinely guided leader, or *mahdi*, of his generation. Ibn Tumart, after the usual pilgrimage to the east, spent ten years building up a small community of close followers among the mountain Berbers of the High Atlas. But he had always intended that, following the pattern set by the Prophet, the seizure of temporal power would be the sequel to spiritual reform. At the very start of his mission he had nominated his *khalifa*, or secular successor, who was a Zanata Berber from the region of Tlemcen, called Abd al-Mumin. On Ibn Tumart's death about 1128, Abd al-Mumin carried on his propaganda and extended his following right up the line of the High Atlas to the Rif. Only after seventeen years of further preparation did he move decisively against the cities of the plain. The consequences were then cataclysmic. The Sanhaja aristocracy of the Almoravid state were slaughtered, and the last representative of the dynasty executed. Abd al-Mumin became the ruler of Morocco, and soon added the eastern Maghrib to his conquests. His son and his grandson succeeded him, adding Muslim Spain, which under their patronage reached new heights of culture. At last his great-grandson, an-Nasir, suffered a crippling defeat by the Christians at Las Navas de Tolosa, which led to the final disintegration of Muslim Spain. Though the dynasty teetered on in Morocco until 1269, it was forced to abandon Ifriqiya to its Hafsid governors in 1236, and Algeria to the Abd-al-Wadids of Tlemcen in 1239. Finally, the Almohads were displaced, even in Morocco, by the Marinid dynasty of Fez.

Between them, therefore, the Almoravids and the Almohads ruled the western Maghrib for about two centuries, from the middle of the eleventh until the middle of the thirteenth century. During the whole of this period the rulers of the western Maghrib were active also in Spain. Within North Africa, the centre of gravity shifted firmly from Ifriqiya to Morocco, and the inclusion of Muslim Spain created an empire of sufficient power, prestige and wealth to draw the attention of the western Sudan to the north rather than to the east. It is with this consideration in mind that we now turn back in time, to assess the influence of the Almoravids upon the Negro peoples living to the south of the western desert.

The most important ethnic and linguistic grouping to the south of the Sanhaja were, of course, the Mande, who occupied most of the country to the west of the great bend of the Niger, and whose settlements extended from the limits of cultivation at the desert margin, right across the dry savanna and the moister woodlands, and even penetrated deep into the equatorial forest to the south. Here, as we saw in Chapter 6, comparatively dense agricultural populations must have built up in Early Iron Age times, and the prevalence of a single language grouping over a series of widely varying climatic zones is a strong argument for the early development of commercial networks for the exchange of local products between them. Political institutions among the Mande were based upon the unit called a *kafu*, a collection of villages with a total population of somewhere between 10 000 and 50 000 people, over each of which there ruled a *mansa*, a king, who exercised both secular and religious authority, and who was treated by his subjects as if he was a superhuman figure. A *mansa* did not raise his own voice: his muttered commands were repeated aloud by an intermediary, a 'linguist'. A *mansa* ate in secret. When he gave audience, people approached him crawling, and throwing dust upon their heads. Above the *kafu*, there could be an empire or confederation of *kafus* brought together by diplomacy or conquest, of which the supreme ruler would be, in the most literal sense, a 'king of kings', whose status would be symbolised by the constant attendance at his court and around his throne of the representatives, usually the children, of vassal kings. These would be treated with the utmost honour, loaded with silken robes and golden ornaments, but they were nevertheless hostages for the continued subordination of their parental houses.

The kingdom of Ghana was just such an empire of confederated *kafus*, built up in the Soninke-speaking, northern part of Mande country. According to some of the oral traditions recorded in Timbuktu nearly a thousand years later, the original dynasty was white – that is to say, Sanhaja rather than Soninke – but this is most unlikely. According to the same traditions, twenty-two kings ruled before the Muslim epoch and another twenty-two afterwards. This again is too tidy to be credited. What we can perhaps accept is that the federal empire of the Soninke antedated the Muslim connection. The earliest Arabic references are, to be sure, very brief; but the picture painted by al-Bakri of Cordoba in the middle of the eleventh century bears every sign of authenticity. Al-Bakri's main literary source is one of the tenth century, and his information is supplemented by evidence from oral witnesses who had travelled to the western Sudan right up until the eve of the Almoravid conquest. Al-Bakri leaves no room for doubt that Ghana was a pagan, Negro kingdom, which, even in his day, was only beginning to be penetrated by Islam. The capital of eleventh-century Ghana was called in Arabic *al-ghaba*, 'the grove', where the king lived, his palace apparently consisting of a series of conical huts within a palisade. Nearby were the sacred groves, where a pagan priesthood presided over the royal cults and guarded the tombs and shrines of past kings. In the king's town there was a single mosque, but most Muslims lived in a separate town, six miles away, where there were many mosques, and where most of the population were probably strangers – Zanata, Sanhaja and others engaged in the trans-Saharan trade.

The king [says al-Bakri] adorns himself with female ornaments around the neck and arms. On his head he wears gold-embroidered caps covered with turbans of finest cotton. He gives audience to the people for the redressing of grievances in a hut, around which are placed ten horses bedecked with gold caparisons. Behind him stand ten slaves carrying shields and swords mounted with gold. On his right are the sons of his vassal kings, their heads plaited with gold and wearing costly garments. On the ground around him are seated his ministers, while the governor of the city sits before him. On guard at the door are dogs of fine pedigree, wearing collars adorned with gold and silver knobs, which rarely leave his presence. The royal audience is announced by the beating of a drum ... When the people have gathered, his fellow pagans draw near upon their knees sprinkling dust upon their heads as a sign of respect, while the Muslims clap their hands as their form of greeting. Their religion is paganism and the cult of idols. When the king dies, they construct a large hut of wood over the place of burial. His body is brought on a simple bier and placed in the hut. With it they put his eating and drinking vessels, a supply of food and drink, and those who used to serve him with these things, and then the entrance is secured. They cover the hut with mats and cloth, and all the assembled people pile earth over it until it resembles a considerable hill. Then they dig a ditch around it, allowing only one means of access to the heap. They sacrifice victims to their dead, and offer them fermented drinks.[1]

The kingdom of Ghana as described by al-Bakri had succeeded in uniting, or subjecting, most of the *kafu*s between the western arm of the Niger bend and the upper waters of the Senegal. To the west of it along the lower Senegal, lay the independent Wolof- and Fulani-

[1] The translation is that of J. Spencer Trimingham, *A History of Islam in West Africa*, pp. 53–4.

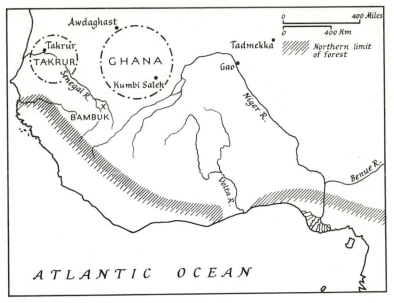

FIG. 45. The kingdom of Ghana.

speaking kingdom of Takrur, of which the ruling dynasty and at least some of the people had been converted to Islam in the early eleventh century. To the east, separated from Ghana by the stretch of desert around the northern tip of the Niger bend, was the Songhay-speaking kingdom of Gao, where, once again, the ruling dynasty had been converted to Islam in the early eleventh century, perhaps by Kharijites of the Ibadi sect, who had developed the trade route leading from southern Ifriqiya through Wargla and Tadmekka to the Niger bend. Though the most conservative in religion, Ghana was by far the largest and the most significant of the three kingdoms. In part, no doubt, this predominance was due to the wider spread of Soninke speech. In part, however, it was certainly due to Ghana's primary control over the goldfields of Bambuk, situated between the upper Senegal and Faleme rivers. The kings of Ghana did not actually rule over the mining communities, but they controlled the access to them. According to al-Bakri, they levied a duty of one gold dinar for every donkey-load of salt entering their territory from the north, and another duty of two dinars for every load leaving the country to the south. Thus, the salt bore the tax, but the tax was paid in gold, and the revenue was enough to make Ghana the wealthiest kingdom of the Sudan. On the eve of the Almoravid conquest, its frontiers were still expanding. During the first half of the eleventh century, Awda- 165 ghast, the desert port far out to the north in the Mauritanian Tagant, which had been founded under the auspices of the Sanhaja, began to pay tribute to the Soninke kings of Ghana.

Naturally, it was an early objective of the Almoravid movement to recover Awdaghast, and, as we have seen, this was achieved by Yahya ibn Umar in 1055. What followed during the long reign of Abu Bakr (1056–87) had two apparently contradictory aspects. It began with the driving out by the Sanhaja of the more northerly Soninke, in something like a racial war between Berbers and Negroes. It continued with the subjection and the forcible Islamisation of the southern Soninke centre of the Ghana kingdom. The first process was undoubtedly destructive. It involved the breaking up of farming communities and the permanent ruin of marginal agricultural land by the careless over-grazing of pastoralists. The second process may well have been beneficial. Unfortunately, the sources are too meagre to give us an adequate picture. However, it is likely that the Soninke forces suffered a severe defeat at the hands of the Almoravids sometime around 1076, and that a formal acceptance of Islam along with the payment of tribute were among the terms of peace. Probably the Almoravids never attempted to substitute their own government for the indigenous one, but merely helped the internal minority of Soninke Muslims to seize the positions of power. At all events, the written sources of the twelfth and thirteenth centuries are at one in claiming that Ghana was now a Muslim state, and that it was still the major power of the Mande-speaking region.

The archaeological record, while still far from conclusive, would seem to bear this out. The identification of the ruins at Kumbi Saleh, near the southern frontier of Mauritania with south-western Mali, with the capital of ancient Ghana is not quite certain, although it is very probable. Since 1914, five expeditions have visited the site, and extensive excavations were carried out by Mauny, Thomassy and Szumowski between 1949 and 1951. These showed the remains of a densely inhabited and partially stone-built town, which might correspond very well with the Muslim quarter described by al-Bakri. Many of the stone houses were of Mediterranean design, built in two storeys, with warehouses on the ground floor and living quarters above. Abundant spindle-whorls show the importance of weaving. The finds included quantities of fine pottery and glassware imported from the Maghrib. A radiocarbon sample taken from a site in the main street and near the great mosque showed a date around the early thirteenth century. The origins of the town may well have been much older. What is significant about the date is the indication that the capital was still flourishing between one and two centuries after the Almoravid conquest.

The same conclusion comes from the excavations carried out in recent years by Serge and Denise Robert at Tegdaoust, some three hundred miles to the north-west of Kumbi, which is the presumed site of Awdaghast. The Roberts' work has revealed a long and complex sequence of occupation, beginning with a village built in mud-brick around the eighth or ninth century. The early village is succeeded by a stone-built town, probably of the ninth century, of which the houses are grouped in several rather widely separated blocks or 'islands'. A later town was built on the ruins of this earlier one, the builders of which used the walls of older houses as foundations for their own structures and thus maintained the layout of their pre-decessors. Dried mud-brick replaced stone as the primary building material, although brick and stone were occasionally used in com-bination in pleasing architectural styles. Glass vessels and imported ceramics, including oil lamps and fine tableware, from the Maghrib and further afield are very common at this level, showing the continuance of a vigorous trade with the Maghrib until the thirteenth or even the fourteenth century.

Seen in this light, the conquest of Ghana by the Almoravids appears not as a final cataclysm, but rather as a new beginning. It may be that the political power of the Soninke was never again as extensive. It may be that its monopoly of the golden trade was less complete than before. But Ghana was still at the heart of the communi-cations bwetween West Africa and the outside world. These links were not weakened but strengthened by the establishment of a strong state

FIG. 46.   Excavations of the tenth to twelfth century at Tegdaoust, 1969.

in Morocco and Spain, itself a large consumer of gold and slaves, but also a channel for the extension of the gold trade to the countries of southern Europe. It was only when the Mali kingdom with its base in the southern woodlands established a new line of communication running up and down the western arm of the Niger bend, that the main trans-Saharan routes began to by-pass Soninke country to the east. Neither of these developments, however, occurred until the second half of the thirteenth century.

15 Mali and its neighbours c. 1250–1450

One of the consequences of the Almoravid attacks on the kingdom of Ghana seems to have been a shake-up of the population pattern throughout the Mande-speaking region. The northern Soninke, including many of those who had become Muslims, fled southwards and dispersed widely, not only among the southern Soninke, but even into Malinke country still further to the south, where they helped to spread Islam and to develop trade. Possibly as early as the twelfth century, the search for new sources of gold had led to the development of mining in the Bure region, between the upper Niger and the Tinkisso, some four hundred miles to the south-east of the older Bambuk gold fields. A Ghana weakened by conquest was in no position to extend its economic monopoly over these distant sources of supply. Therefore the political and economic benefit accrued first to the Soso, the Soninke-speaking people of southern Ghana, and secondly to the Malinke-speaking Mande in whose territory the new wealth was situated. The Soso were the first to organise a conquest state around the newly discovered resources. Originally tributary to the kings of Ghana, they broke away under the leadership of the Kante clan sometime in the twelfth century, and achieved their greatest power under a king called Samunguru Kante early in the thirteenth century. Samunguru ruled over southern Soninke and northern Malinke peoples. To the north, his army raided what remained of Ghana, even sacking its capital in 1204. To the south, he conquered the Malinke *kafu*s one by one, including that ruled by the Keita clan which was to be the nucleus of the later empire of Mali.

The oral traditions of Mali, which are probably the oldest corpus to survive in an unbroken line in any part of Africa, have as their founding hero Sundiata Keita, a crippled son of the ruling house, ostracised because of his deformity, who was miraculously cured by a blacksmith, and who thereupon took to the bush as a hunter and soldier of fortune. Accompanied by a small band of followers, he visited neighbouring countries, and so was absent from Mali when the armies of Samunguru descended upon it, laying waste its villages and exterminating the royal clan. Sundiata was summoned by the surviving forces of resistance, and returned with horsemen and foot soldiers supplied by the eastern neighbours of Soso in the southern Soninke states of Mema and Wagadu. He organised a successful alliance of the nearby Malinke *kafu*s, and won a decisive victory over the Soso forces in a great battle fought at Krina, to the north of modern Bamako. After the battle, the *mansa*s of all the participating Malinke *kafu*s assembled at the old-Keita capital at Kangaba to inaugurate a federal state, retaining their identities as local governments, but resigning their *mansa*ships to the single monarchy of Sundiata. The united Malinke armies then turned to the conquest of Soso and of its remaining tributary states to the west, notably that of the Diakhanke in Bambuk, and possibly also a kingdom of the Wolof to the south of the lower Senegal. The eastern Soninke states of Mema and Wagadu, as a reward for their initial assistance, were incorporated as allies, their rulers alone retaining the title of *mansa*. The new state of Mali now comprised the whole territory of ancient Ghana, except for the northern part which had been lost to the Sanhaja. It also included a wide stretch of Malinke country to the south, which Ghana had never ruled. It controlled the two major gold-producing areas of Bure and Bambuk. And it possessed, as Ghana had never done, the great line of water communications provided by the upper Niger and its tributaries, leading all the way from the edges of the desert through the savanna and the woodlands to the margin of the Guinea forest.

FIG. 47.   Mali and its neighbours.

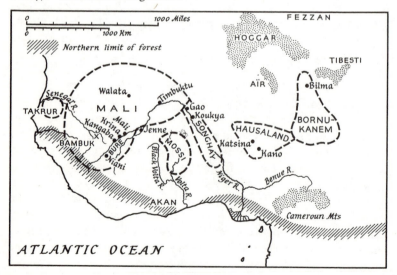

Sundiata spent his last years building a new capital for his kingdom at Niani on the Sankarani River, just within the frontiers of modern Guinea, where early archaeological surveys carried out by French administrators in the 1920s have recently been followed up in two Polish expeditions led by Filipowiak and Niane. Results are still highly tentative, but they certainly indicate that the area was once occupied by a dense agricultural population capable of supporting an urban concentration in its midst. When survey has been followed by excavation, it may be possible to answer many unresolved questions, and in particular some relating to the role of Islam in the new state. The traditional evidence portrays Sundiata essentially as an adept in pagan magic. Literary references, on the other hand, suggest that Mali had been penetrated by Islam long before the Soso conquest, and, though silent about the religion of Sundiata, leave no doubt that his son and successor, Mansa Uli, was a pious Muslim, who made the pilgrimage to Mecca, passing through Egypt during the reign of the Mamluk Sultan Baybars, that is to say, sometime between 1260 and 1277.

Mansa Uli was a conqueror like his father, and the Israeli historian Nehemia Levtzion has argued convincingly that it must have been during this reign that Mali expanded its influence to the east, encompassing the Niger bend, subjecting the ancient kingdom of Songhay with its twin capitals at Gao and Koukya, and gaining control of the desert routes leading northwards from Timbuktu to Taghaza and north-eastwards from Gao to Tadmekka and Tuat. After that of Uli, there followed three short and undistinguished reigns, during which Songhay may temporarily have regained its independence under Ali Kolen, the founder of the Sonni dynasty, which was eventually to triumph over that of Mali. Meanwhile, however, the authority of Mali was fully restored by Mansa Sakura, a usurper, who reigned with great success during the last decade of the thirteenth century, and who was eventually killed while on his homeward journey from Mecca around 1299. The throne then returned to the Keita dynasty. The two great rulers of the fourteenth century were Mansa Musa (?1312–37) and Mansa Suleyman (?1337–60), and it was during this period that Mali reached its apogee of wealth and power. When Mansa Musa went on pilgrimage in 1324, Cairo and the holy cities were staggered by his display of wealth. He travelled with a hundred camels, each reputedly loaded with three hundred pounds' weight of gold. Fifty thousand gold dinars were sent ahead as a present to the Sultan of Egypt. The value of gold in Cairo depreciated by between ten and twenty per cent as a result of his passage.

However, it was not only in the Middle East that Mali was making itself felt. Although Malians went to the Middle East on pilgrimage, and sometimes stayed there to get education, the main trading connections of the kingdom were with the states of the Maghrib and, through them, with the reviving commerce of western Europe. All three of the post-Almohad states were involved – the Marinid kingdom of Fez in Morocco, the Abd-al-Wadid kingdom of Tlemcen in western Algeria, and the Hafsid kingdom of Tunis. In all three of these states the trade with southern Europe, begun under the Almoravids and the Almohads, developed greatly during the thirteenth and fourteenth centuries, until it involved a many-sided exchange of North African wool, leather, wax, horses, dried fruit, olive oil and sugar, together with Sudanese gold, slaves, ivory, skins and feathers, and, on the other hand, European textiles, hardware, glass and timber, along with eastern silks, spices, perfumes and cowrie-shells, for which Europeans were by now the Mediterranean carriers. But the lubricating element in the whole system was the gold of Mali. It balanced an exchange which would otherwise have been heavily in Europe's favour. More than that, it was the main attraction of the African trade to European participants, whose countries were in the course of moving from the copper and silver currency systems of the early Middle Ages to systems based on gold. It was a process which had started in Spain, where the Christian kings of the north had, as early as the twelfth century, struck gold coins in imitation of those of the Almoravids. During the thirteenth century gold coinage was adopted by Marseilles, Genoa, Florence and Venice. By the early fourteenth century the practice was spreading to northern Europe. It has been calculated that throughout this period at least two-thirds of the world production of gold, on which the development of all these new currencies depended, came from the western Sudan, through territory controlled by Mali, and through one or other of the Maghrib states. It is small wonder that it was through the Maghrib that some knowledge of Mali began to leak through to the outside world. It was from the Marinid kingdom of Fez that Ibn Battuta set out on his journey through the Sudan in 1352. It was in Hafsid Tunis that the greatest of the Arab historians, Ibn Khaldun, collected most of our existing information about the dynastic history of Mali. And, as early as 1375, the Catalan map of Charles V portrayed Mansa Musa, king of Mali, seated on his throne and holding out a golden nugget towards a veiled Sanhaja who rode towards him over the desert on a camel.

Obviously, the wealth of the kings of Mali was not widely shared among their subjects, the majority of whom lived the lives of rural

FIG. 48.   Catalan map of Charles V (1375).

Key: 1 *mascarota* is ?Tangrut. 2 *tacoram*. 3 *sigilmessa* is Sijilmassa. 4 *tagaza* is Taghaza. 5 *tebelbelt* is Tabelbert. 6 *vadia* is Tuat. 7 *anzicha* is In Ziza. 8 *tacort* is Tahert. 9 *ASHARA*. 10 *vescara* is Biskra. 11 *tauser* is Tozeur. 12 *buda* is Buda. 13 *gengeu* is Gao. 14 *GINYIA* is GUINEA. 15 *sudam* is Sudan. 16 *tenbuch* is Timbuktu. 17 *ciuat de melli* is City of Mali. 18 Through this place pass the merchants who travel to the land of the Negroes of Guinea, which place they call the valley of the Draa. 19 All this region is occupied by people who veil their mouths; one only sees their eyes. They live in tents and have caravans of camels. There are also beasts called Lemp from the skins of which they make fine shields. 20 This Negro lord is called Musa Mali, Lord of the Negroes of Guinea. So abundant is the gold which is found in his country that he is the richest and most noble king in all the land.

173

people throughout the continent. The heart of Mali lay in the woodland savanna, where a rainfall of thirty to fifty inches made possible a cereal agriculture based on sorghum and dry rice. This was the central occupation of the main Mande peoples – Malinke, Soninke and Bambara. The drier, northern regions were ranching country, where Fulbe and others pastured their herds of cattle and goats. Along the Niger and its tributaries lived tribes of fisherfolk. Such were the Sorko, who formed the majority of the Songhay people, and higher up the western arm of the Niger bend, the Bozo. The mining communities of Bambuk and Bure, though part-time farmers, were hardly less specialised. And the same was true of the townsfolk, both those of the desert ports like Walata and Timbuktu and Gao, and those of the capital at Niani and the great trading city of Jenne on the Bani. Between all these groups – cultivators, pastoralists, fishermen, miners and townsmen – there was, thanks largely to the Niger waterways, an extensive exchange of produce. The millet and sorghum of the Malinke country, and the dried fish of the Niger, found their way to the cities of the Sahel, and even to the salt mines of Taghaza, far out across the desert to the north. The cities, besides handling the salt and the other imports from the outside world, were all engaged in manufacture, especially of cotton textiles, the use of which spread side by side with the religion of the Prophet. The complexities of Mali's economic system necessitated the use of currency. For large transactions, gold dust was measured by a series of standardised weights, while for everyday matters cowrie shells, imported from the Maldive Islands via Egypt and North Africa, provided a convenient if rather bulky, small-scale unit of account.

The existence of a gold and cowrie currency undoubtedly made it easier for the government of Mali to defray its expenses by taxation. Tolls there were, and tribute, both of which could be paid in cash. From these came the gold and cowries which stocked the central and provincial treasuries. Some of this revenue was paid abroad in bullion, in exchange for the horses, arms and armour which made the Mali army uniquely powerful in the sub-Saharan region. The towns, however, and also the army, required to be fed; and to this end Mali, like all the other states of the sub-Saharan belt, resorted to slave labour. Slaves captured in war, particularly from the southern borderlands of the empire, were settled in villages sited along the axes of communication by the banks of the Niger and its tributaries, and each was given a production target. In this village two hundred slaves were required to produce a thousand sacks of rice. In that village a hundred slaves were required to produce seven hundred bags of millet.

In each case the village headman, himself a slave, was held responsible and could keep any surplus. When the headman died, his wealth was seized by the state. In each province of the empire governors, often members of the royal family, were posted to ensure the collection of revenue and tribute, and so the central government was financed.

There is no doubt that, as a system of law and order, the government of Mali was strikingly successful. When Ibn Battuta crossed the desert during the reign of Mansa Suleyman, his caravan broke up at Walata, and such was the safety of the highway that he was able to travel on from there to the capital, a distance of seven or eight hundred miles, with three companions only. Though clearly irked by the manners of the Malian governor of Walata, who kept the white merchants standing in his presence and spoke to them only through a 'linguist', Ibn Battuta had to concede that

the Negroes possess some admirable qualities. They are seldom unjust, and have a greater horror of injustice than any other people. The sultan shows no mercy to anyone who is guilty of the least act of it. There is complete security in their country. Neither traveller nor any other inhabitant in it has anything to fear from robbers or men of violence. They do not confiscate the property of any white man who dies in their country, even if it be accounted wealth. On the contrary, they give it into the charge of some trustworthy person among the whites, until the rightful heir takes possession of it.

Such a state of affairs argued a long period of effective government, and also, perhaps, the steadily growing influence of Islam. As a good Muslim, there were aspects of life in Mali which Ibn Battuta found shocking – above all, the freedom given to women, who went about unveiled and chose whom they would as their companions. Worse, even at the king's court and at those of his provincial chiefs, the female slaves appeared without a stitch of clothing. Ibn Battuta was impatient with the time and respect accorded to the royal praise-singers at public functions, and he was obviously contemptuous of the grovelling practised in the royal presence. 'If anyone addresses the king and receives a reply from him, he uncovers his back and throws dust over his head, for all the world like a bather splashing himself with water. I used to wonder how it was they did not blind themselves.' So far did pagan influences survive. Nevertheless, Ibn Battuta remarked that the Malians were careful to observe the hours of prayer, assiduous in attending the mosque on Fridays, clothed always in clean white gowns, and zealous for the religious education of their children. In Niani, he visited the chief judge in his house, and found his children in chains, from which they were to be released 175 only when they had the Koran by heart. At Timbuktu, and again at Jenne, there were by this time schools of theology and law which were producing a class of literate scholars, who could serve the needs of religion and the state. The influence of these 'universities' spread very far. The Hausa cities of Kano and Katsina, a thousand miles to the east of either Timbuktu or Jenne, remember in their traditions the coming of Islam with teachers from Mali at a period around the late fourteenth or the early fifteenth century.

Certainly, the most remarkable dispersion that took place from Mali was that of the itinerant traders known collectively as Wangara. What distinguished them from other Malinke was that their business took them far beyond the bounds of Mali's temporal power, and mostly into lands to the south, which were politically much less developed. They travelled for the most part unarmed. They made their settlements away from the towns of the local people. They nursed a spirit of community which was based partly on the fact that they were Malinke abroad, but even more on the fact that they were Muslims living under pagan rule. There were literate men among them. Some made their living more by teaching than by trade. Their settlements were caravanserais, with warehouses where goods could be stored and loads redistributed. They were trading centres for local

FIG. 49.   The University Mosque of Sankore at Timbuktu.

produce. They were also centres of spiritual power. They had mosques and schools for the residents. They rendered spiritual services to the locals, praying for rain, advising on medical matters, selling talismans and charms. They survived because they were useful, and because they were seen to offer no political threat.

One of the main networks operated by Wangara traders, here usually known as Dyula, ran south from Jenne, through the country of the Lobi and the Mossi in modern Upper Volta, to that of the Akan in modern Ivory Coast and Ghana. The commercial town of Jenne had been founded, probably in the twelfth or thirteenth century, by Soninke traders, who settled among the Bozo fishermen of the Bani River. It was an easily defended site, accessible for most of the year only by water. Its commercial significance, however, was that it offered the shortest land crossing from the Niger River system to that of the Volta. An early sixteenth-century source describes how the great salt blocks carried by camel from Taghaza to Timbuktu, and thence by water to Jenne, were there divided into smaller pieces and forwarded by head-loads to the 'gold mines'. These mines can only have been those of the Lobi country in the valley of the Black Volta, and those of the Akan forest, due south from there. In all likelihood it was a trade that had begun soon after the foundation of

FIG. 50.   The Great Mosque of Jenne at dusk.

Jenne. How early it reached the Akan country may be learned for sure when the University of Ghana's excavations at Begho have made more progress. Begho is a ruined town on the margins of the savanna and the forest, on the western side of modern Ghana, which is strongly linked in the traditions of the Akan and the Mande with an early Dyula settlement which was the collecting-point for the gold of the forest. It was known to the Dutch in the early seventeenth century, but its origins were certainly medieval. It is clearly of the utmost significance that Begho lies precisely in the region where the earliest of the Akan states, that of Bono Mansu, took shape. The genealogies of the ruling dynasty would seem to place its origins in the fourteenth or fifteenth century. This is not, of course, to say that Akan dynasties were founded by Dyula Mande; still less, as some have claimed, that these events were the starting-point of Akan migrations southward from the savanna into the forest. It is simply to suggest that the production of gold and the opening of long-distance trade may have led to the appearance of more powerful chiefs among the northern Akan, and that some of the ideas and even some of the paraphernalia used by those chiefs may have first been transmitted by Mande traders to Akan village heads.

It was not only the search for gold that sent the Wangara traders radiating beyond the political frontiers of the Mali empire, to the south-east and south-west. The kola-nut, one of the few stimulants permitted by Islam and particularly refreshing when chewed in hot weather, was traded at high prices throughout the western bulge of Africa. It was a product of the equatorial forest, which occurred in different varieties all the way from modern Guinea to Nigeria. From Guinea through the Ivory Coast to modern Ghana, the long-distance traders were Wangara from Mali. On the most likely interpretation of the evidence, it was likewise Wangara who began to trade the kola of the Akan forest from there to Hausaland. The road once open, the Hausa carried it on largely by themselves, although groups of Wangara traders were established in all the main cities of Hausaland as late as the nineteenth century. Quite possibly, the 'Wangara' who brought Islam to Kano and Katsina during the reigns of late-fourteenth or early-fifteenth-century *sarki*s were clerics who accompanied the Dyula traders travelling to Hausaland from Jenne by the 'Kola road' passing across the middle of modern Ghana. Although roundabout, this may have been the only practicable route from Mali to Hausaland. The road from Gao to Aïr followed by Ibn Battuta in the early fourteenth century does not seem to have had at this period any southward extension to Hausaland. The Mossi country within the Niger bend was a turbulent area. Moreover, by the fifteenth century, Mali was losing its political control of Songhay and the Niger waterway downstream of Gao.

It was, indeed, the same with Mali as with other empires. After two centuries the will to rule subsided and the will not to be ruled increased. When the Mali empire crumbled, it did so from the east. Around 1375 Songhay, under its Sonni dynasty, ceased to pay tribute, and its fleets of armed canoes manned by the Sorko fishermen began to extend their control of the Niger waterway from Gao in the direction of Timbuktu. On land, the Tuareg moved in from Adrar of the Ifoghas, raiding Timbuktu regularly from the beginning of the fifteenth century, and finally capturing it in 1433. Meanwhile the Mossi, led by their aristocracy of armed knights, raided across the western arm of the Niger bend into Mema and Massina, one raid even reaching Walata in 1480. The Soninke *kafu*s broke away from Mali before the middle of the century. Jenne, too, seized its independence. Thus, when Songhay entered upon its period of imperial expansion with the accession of the great conqueror Sonni Ali, in 1464, it was to a large extent expansion into a vacuum. After two hundred years of great power, Mali had lost the strength of organisation needed to rule over strangers. As a federal empire of Malinke-speakers, however, stretching from the upper Niger to the lower Gambia and the Casamance, Mali continued to be of some significance throughout the fifteenth and sixteenth centuries.

16 West Africa south of Hausaland

c. 700–1400

In the southern part of West Africa, the Volta basin marks a frontier of considerable significance in medieval and early modern history. It is not primarily an ethnic frontier. Ethnically and linguistically, the Akan peoples, who live to the west of the Volta, are no more different from the Aja, the Yoruba and the Edo, who live to the east of it, than any of these peoples are from each other. All speak languages of the Kwa sub-family of Niger–Congo. All practise a pattern of cultivation suited to the humid savanna and the forest margins, which relies upon the same food plants, especially on yams and oil-palms. All share a basically common artistic tradition, and have religious and other features in common. The difference lies in the outside influences to which the two parts of the region have been subjected. Until the opening of the Atlantic in the late fifteenth century, such influences could only come from the north. 'It should be remembered,' wrote Bishop Samuel Johnson, the wise and learned historian of the Yoruba, 'that the coast tribes were of much less importance then than now. Light and civilisation came from the north . . . The centre of life and activity, of large populations and industry, was . . . in the interior.' But the interior meant different things to the east and west of the Volta. For the coastal and forest peoples from the Volta right round to the Senegal, the interior was Mandeland. For peoples east of the Volta, the interior was Hausaland and Kanem–Bornu.

To the west of the Volta, as we have seen, the nature of the Mande penetration into southern lands appears to have been basically commercial. The Dyula merchants were seeking gold, kola and slaves, in exchange for which they brought salt and also a wide variety of outside products. They happened to be Muslims, and therefore their settlements radiated Islamic influences of every kind. They were interested in the promotion of mining and in the security of trade routes, and to this extent they were no doubt concerned to bolster the political authority of the Akan rulers with whom they did business. They supplied these rulers with their information about the working of larger states further to the north. They wrote letters and carried diplomatic messages. They imported, amongst other things, ceremonial umbrellas, as used by the sultans of Egypt and

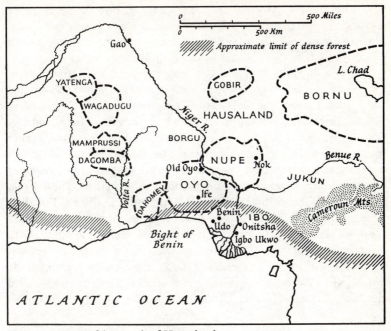

FIG. 51.   West Africa south of Hausaland.

the *mansa*s of Mali, and robes of state. East of the Volta, evidence
about the outside influences from the north has a very different
flavour. It does not seem to have been primarily commercial in intent.
Its ambience was not Muslim but pagan. And its methods seem to have
been based on conquest and settlement, and on the reorganisation of
indigenous populations by ruling minorities from outside.

The pattern of conquest is seen most clearly in the historical traditions of a line of states which stretch out westwards from the Nigerian
Middle Belt – from Jukun and Nupe in Nigeria, to Borgu in northern
Dahomey, to Dagomba and Mamprussi in northern Ghana, to the
Mossi states of Wagadugu and Yatenga in Upper Volta. All these
kingdoms trace their origins to groups of horse-borne invaders from
the east or the north-east, strong in arms though few in numbers,
who married the daughters of the local earth-priests, and whose
children grew up speaking the local languages. Some traditions suggest that the founders had been Muslims before their migration.
Others, perhaps more convincingly, paint them as conservative
pagans, who emigrated following the conversion to Islam of the ruling elements in their country of origin. Certainly, if they were once
Muslims, they failed to transmit the religion to their descendants,   181

who were either converted or re-converted during the seventeenth and eighteenth centuries, whereas, even at the western end of the line, the founders have to be dated at least to the fourteenth century, and those at the Nigerian end probably much earlier.

The Middle Belt states, as we may call them collectively, were formed amid the dense agricultural populations of the open savanna. They incorporated peoples who had previously been organised in stateless societies, such as those of the Tallensi and Konkomba of northern Ghana, and they did not completely absorb these earlier societies into their political systems. The rulers of the Middle Belt states were military men, a caste of feudal knights. They required a subject class of peasants to supply them with their food and drink, and servile castes to forge and weave and build and wait. But their numbers were limited and they did not need to carry out a systematic conquest. Indeed, as perennial raiders of slaves, it suited them to leave pockets of unadministered peoples in the boundary regions between their states. The *raison d'être* of these states was not trade but tribute. Nevertheless, in the course of time their mud-walled citadels grew into towns, harbouring traders and craftsmen. Ul-

FIG. 52.   Armoured cavalry at Niamey, Nigeria.

timately Islam was adopted, but usually in a spirit of compromise. The Middle Belt kings relentlessly pursued the rituals of pagan royalty, and balanced the power of the knightly class with growing bureaucracies of eunuchs and palace slaves.

A similar pattern of emigration and conquest seems to lie at the back of state formation in south-western Nigeria, where Yoruba and Edo-speaking autochthones were organised into states by a single set of invaders from the north or the north-east at a period comparable with that of the formation of the Middle Belt states. The legendary figure who links these southern conquests is Oduduwa, king of Ife, who is regarded as the founding ancestor of both the Benin and the Oyo dynasties. According to the Benin version, Oduduwa came from Egypt. According to the Oyo version, he came from Mecca. One story is that his father, Lamurudu, or Nimrod, was king of Mecca and had become a Muslim, while Oduduwa, the Crown Prince, relapsed into idolatry and instigated a pagan revolt. The result was a civil war, in which the Muslim party eventually triumphed, so that Oduduwa and his supporters were forced to emigrate. Some of Oduduwa's brothers went *westwards*, and settled in Gobir, the northernmost of the Hausa states, and also in 'Kukawa', that is to say, in Songhay. But Oduduwa went *eastwards*, and settled at Ife. So that, forgetting about Egypt and Mecca, and concentrating on the substance of the legend, what would seem to be at issue is the conversion to Islam of some state in the region of Hausaland, Kanem or Bornu, and the emigration of a recalcitrant pagan minority from among the princes and noble families of its capital.

As related in the traditions of Benin, Oduduwa's son, Oranmiyan, was the first of thirty-eight rulers, who can be arranged genealogically in twenty-six or twenty-seven generations. This would take us back to sometime in the thirteenth century. The dynastic genealogy of Oyo is more difficult to assess, because there was a long period during the seventeenth and eighteenth centuries when the regular system of patrilineal succession was abandoned. However, there are a few outside reference points to work on – Oyo invasions of Dahomey from the late seventeenth century on, and the overrunning of Oyo by Nupe, which can by reference to Nupe traditions be attributed to the early fifteenth century. And, behind this, there is still the memory of some ten to twelve generations of Oyo kings, so that, once again, we may say that 1300, or a little earlier, would seem to be the likely starting point. And behind this again there may lie a period of uncertain length, when the invaders were consolidating their first positions in the neighbourhood of Ife.

The traditional accounts, particularly the Yoruba ones, speak of the Oduduwa migration as if it were a great ethnic movement involving the whole of the Yoruba people. But this is plainly nonsense. Quite certainly, the invaders were a minority. Probably at the time of their arrival they spoke Kanuri or Hausa, or some other northern language. Those of them who settled in Yorubaland intermarried with the Yoruba and picked up their language, while those who settled in the direction of Benin became Edo-speaking in exactly the same way. The invaders did not, of course, settle only, or even mainly, at Benin and Oyo. These were merely the two states which emerged from a long course of development as the leading states of the region. What the invaders did was to build walled camps all along the northern fringes of the forest. The more successful camps grew into towns, and the more successful towns grew into capitals, dominating the towns around them. Both the Benin and the Oyo traditions make it clear that these kingdoms started from very modest beginnings. Oyo was for long overshadowed by Nupe. Indeed, Oranmiyan is said to have founded it only after an attempt to reconquer his 'grandfather's' kingdom in the north had been blocked by the rise of Nupe in between. Similarly at Benin, a full century after the coming of the Oduduwa dynasty, an Oba called Oguola set his subjects to dig trenches right round the city in order to keep out his enemies, especially his great enemy the ruler of Udo, another walled town some thirty miles to the west of Benin city. Clearly, Benin had not yet grown into the large state described by the Portuguese at the end of the fifteenth century.

It is against some such background picture derived from oral tradition that the findings of archaeological research in south-western Nigeria need to be assessed. This work has centred, naturally enough, in Ife, and it has involved the recovery of some sculptures in terracotta and cast brass which are acknowledged to be among the world's masterpieces. The early finds were made by collectors, starting with a scandalous episode in 1910–11, when the ethnologist Leo Frobenius, travelling on behalf of museums in Germany, ransacked the Olokun grove, inviting the citizens to join him with their hoes and offering payment by results for art objects so recovered. Nine terracotta heads were unearthed at depths between eighteen and twenty-four feet, and also a bronze head, now famous, which Frobenius tried to buy for six pounds sterling and a bottle of whisky. Frobenius left Ife convinced that he had found the remains of the lost Greek colony of Atlantis, founded in the second millennium B.C. Clearly, such work had no scientific validity, but it did serve to alert both the colonial government and the world of scholarship to the

FIG. 53.   Terracotta head of a queen of Ife, from the excavations of
1957–8 by Frank Willett.

importance of the site. Sporadic investigations were carried out in
the 1920s and 30s, and the finds were gathered in one of the most
remarkable museums in Africa. It was only after the invention of
radiocarbon dating in the 1950s, however, that archaeological work
at Ife could yield historically significant results. Only then did it
become apparent that the civilisation which had produced these mar-
vels had flourished during the early part of the present millennium –
long after any possible contact with the classical Mediterranean world,
and long before any possibility of inspiration from Renaissance
Europe – at a period essentially consistent with the findings of oral
tradition.   185

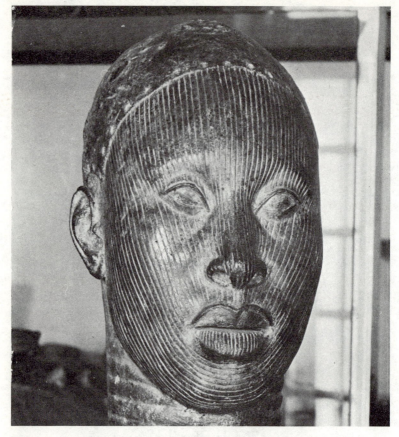

FIG. 54. Bronze head from Wunmonije Compound, Ife, showing the
finely striated face characteristic of Ife sculpture.

The modern series of excavations of Ife was initiated in 1953 by
Bernard and William Fagg and A. J. H. Goodwin, and it was carried
forward by Frank Willett, who has devoted more than ten years to
excavation and the subsequent analysis of pottery and other finds.
There are obvious difficulties in working in a city still occupied by
150 000 people, where even the sacred groves are many of them still
in active use as cult centres. It was a long time before information from
many scattered sites had built up to a point at which general conclusions could be drawn. By 1971, however, Willett was able to pro-
nounce that 'the data from the earlier deposits widely separated in Ife
appear to indicate a settlement of substantial size between the ninth
and the twelfth centuries'. The earliest dates came from charcoal

fragments deposited in burial pits sunk into the schist bedrock. Dates for layers containing terracotta sculptures and brass castings have been established in the eleventh and twelfth centuries, and these compare with a twelfth-century date for a potsherd pavement underlying a section of the town wall in the suburb of Ita Yemoo. All these dates are significantly earlier than those obtained from Benin, which begin from the twelfth or thirteenth century, at a period which is therefore fully consistent with the traditional evidence. It is the dates from Ife which have proved surprisingly early, and which show that tradition, in accounting for the primacy of Ife over Benin and Oyo by the single 'reign' of Oduduwa, has probably telescoped the events of three or four centuries into the myth of a founding hero.

The most striking feature exhibited by excavations at Ife has been the depth of deposits, extending in some places twenty-eight feet below the surface. This by itself argues lengthy occupation by a large urban population. It is clear that from the earliest times the town had an important iron industry, and also that it engaged in the manufacture of glass. Crucibles and large coloured beads of molten glass occur plentifully in the deepest levels, and in recent times, long after the industry had died out, the old burial groves in the town were used as mines for glass beads, which were traded far and wide. Brass- and bronze-casting in Ife were therefore just one branch of an extensive foundry industry, for which fuel lay to hand in the surrounding forest. The tradition of sculpture was probably an ancient one, practised by the Yoruba and Edo first in wood-carving and then in terracotta. It may well have descended from the Nok tradition practised to the north of the Benue during the first millennium B.C. However, the technique of brass-casting by the *cire perdue* method was probably introduced to Ife by the northerners who founded the city, and, so far as we know at present, it spread from there only to Benin. It is clear that copper, an essential ingredient of both brass and bronze, must have been a rare and costly import, the nearest sources of which would have been at Takedda in Air, at Hofrat en Nahas in Darfur, or, just conceivably, in the Congo Republic. At Benin, as at Ife, until the Portuguese arrived by sea with brass basins and manillas as regular articles of trade, brass-casting remained a palace art, producing sculptured heads and other cult objects for the royal shrines.

Although by the nineteenth century the whole of Yorubaland comprised about twenty city-states ruled by dynasties claiming descent from Oduduwa, there was, as we have seen, an interval of three or four hundred years between the foundation of Ife and that of Oyo, and it is very likely that the emergence of other cities was spread   187 over an even longer period. The strong indications of foreign invasion at the start of the process have therefore to be judiciously qualified by the realisation that, before it had spread very far, both the rulers and the social institutions that they operated must have become fully indigenous. The dynamic of the whole process must, in fact, have become one of agglomeration rather than of conquest. The town must have become attractive as a centre of industry and exchange, and even more as a place to live. The town wall must have offered welcome protection as well as being a means of control. The palace, no doubt, stood for temporal power exercised by the fortunate few, but it was also the centre of spiritual forces controlling the unseen world. Outside the walls, each city had its circle of client settlements, which helped to feed it in time of peace, and turned to it for refuge when enemies attacked. As the distance from the city increased, so the client settlements grew sparser. Belts of bush and forest, inhabited only by hunters, separated one city-state from another. It may be that the medieval period saw most of the urban nuclei of Yorubaland established, but it is likely that, even by the fifteenth century, the process of agglomeration had not gone very far. In contrast, only a part of Edo-speaking country was ever affected by the rule of Benin, the radius of which must have been a narrow one until the fifteenth century at least. Nevertheless, in this southerly part of West Africa, as in the sub-Saharan belt in Hausaland, there had been established the pattern of the city-state, the development of which was to distinguish this part of the continent from all others.

The largest enigma of the West African Later Iron Age occurs in Iboland – the part of Nigeria to the east of the lower Niger. The Ibo, though inhabiting the same latitudes and environment as the Yoruba and the Edo, have in general developed without urbanisation and without the centralised political institutions that went with it. The only exception to this rule lies in the most westerly part of Iboland, close to the Niger River, which came, around the late fifteenth and sixteenth century, under the political influence of Benin. In precisely this part of Iboland, about twenty-five miles south-east of Onitsha, a number of bronze objects were accidentally disinterred in 1938 at the little town of Igbo Ukwu. This led to full-scale excavations by Thurstan Shaw during the years 1959–64. In three modern compounds, named after their owners Igbo Isaiah, Igbo Richard and Igbo Jonah, Shaw uncovered a series of very rich deposits. One, Igbo Richard, was the wood-lined burial chamber of what must have been a royal personage, whose remains had been deposited in a sitting position, clothed, crowned, swathed in bead necklaces and surrounded by items of regalia, including a ceremonial staff topped with a leopard's skull in bronze. Another, Igbo Isaiah, was a muniment house, where vessels and other objects of bronze and pottery, ivory and wood, and a large collection of bead ornaments, had apparently been kept for display, until they were buried when the roof of the house collapsed. While the bronze objects in the grave had all been executed by blacksmith's work, the bronzes found in the treasure house nearby had been cast, and were consequently much more elaborate. The *pièce de résistence* was a vase, built on a stand adorned with an interlaced rope in bronze, the whole object being cast in one piece. Bronze bowls of various sizes, some in the form of calabashes, lay near the vase. The bowls, like some of the other objects in the collection, were elaborately encrusted with beetles, mantuses and other small creatures delicately worked in bronze. There were charming receptacles modelled in the form of large land snails. There was also an iron sword with a bronze scabbard. The third excavation area, Igbo Jonah, revealed a series of pits, apparently dug deliberately in order to conceal further treasures during some emergency.

FIG. 55.   Ancestral shrine in the palace of the Oba of Benin.

Had the chronological evidence of Igbo Ukwu indicated the period of the Benin ascendency in western Iboland, or a later one, these would still have been impressive finds, indicating a ramification from Benin at least as original and independent as that of Benin from Ife. But they would have presented no insuperable problem for the general context of southern Nigerian history, as known at present. But four radiocarbon datings – three of them from Igbo Jonah, and one taken from the royal stool at Igbo Richard – have yielded results around the middle of the ninth century. It is not merely that we have no warrant for institutions of kingship in Iboland at this period. These were, after all, present at Ife, and could have appeared further to the east, if only temporarily. It is also that many of the artifacts, including for example glass beads classified as Indian and Venetian, and manilla wristlets similar to those exported in large quantities to West Africa by the Portuguese, would seem to be anachronistic on a ninth-century or any other early medieval dating. Therefore Igbo Ukwu, though unquestionably one of the great Iron Age sites of Africa, and certainly one of the most expertly excavated and described, does not yet seem to have yielded results that can be considered definitive. Certainly, if future evidence should indicate a date six or seven centuries later than the present findings, Igbo Ukwu would be much more intelligible than it is at present.

Trying to view the Nigerian situation in its entirety, it is tempting to hypothesise that a common notion of the city-state pervaded Hausa, Nupe, Yoruba and Edo country, and also stretched far out to the west in what we have called the Middle Belt states. This is not necessarily to suggest that the idea originated in Hausaland and spread from there to the rest of the region. When we know more about the archaeology of Tchad, Kanem and the region immediately to the south of it may prove to have been an earlier centre of the industries and the institutions which we think of as typically Hausa. South-east of Lake Chad, in the region between the Chari and the Logone, the French archaeologist J.-P. Lebeuf has described two material cultures, Sao I and Sao II, of which the second is characterised by walled towns and has radiocarbon dates apparently going back to the middle of the first millennium A.D. Much more is still needed than Lebeuf has yet provided in the way of precisely recorded excavations and reliable carbon samples; but the possibility has to be borne in mind of an urbanising revolution spreading into Nigeria astride the Benue valley, giving rise to the medieval state of the Jukun, and extending its influence north and south from there.

17   Eastern Africa and the outside world

c. 1000—1400

The coast of eastern Africa, together with its offshore islands, has a medieval history surprisingly separate from that of the mainland interior. The coast, from the earliest recorded times, was visited and settled by people from the outside world. At the time of the *Periplus* these foreigners were mainly the seafaring Arabs of southern Arabia and the Persian Gulf. Maritime traders from western India were not far behind; and, perhaps contemporaneously, but more likely a little later, these were joined by Indonesians, whose Malayo-Polynesian language has survived until the present time on Madagascar, whose ocean-going outrigger canoes have been copied up and down the East African coast, and whose food and fruit crops — bananas and rice, coconuts and cocoa-yams — have dominated the agriculture of the coastal plain. In Madagascar we may be fairly sure that the earliest Malagasy-speakers found an uninhabited island, which was only later colonised by groups from the African mainland, who were thus linguistically assimilated by the older settlers. Elsewhere, however, on the coast and the smaller islands, the migrants from Asia mingled progressively with the native African populations, so that the difference between these and the peoples living further inland was not so much one of race or language as one of culture. The coastal people, like those of the interior, were predominantly of Negro stock. Their main language, Kiswahili, though lexically much tinctured with Arabic, was basically a Bantu language. But, unlike the peoples of the interior, the Swahili people lived in continuous contact with the world outside Africa. Maritime traders sailed to and fro, following the annual pattern of the monsoon winds, and bringing the imports — textiles and porcelain and hardware — which seldom penetrated beyond the coastal belt. With the traders came in every generation new settlers, who helped to keep alive the cultural innovations introduced by their predecessors — in plantation agriculture, in building, in town life. And finally, from the Islamic world at least, there came the preachers and the teachers, the scholars and the scribes, who kept the coastal peoples, black and brown, in some kind of contact with the developing culture surrounding a world religion. It was these contacts, more than any other, which made the East African coast a separate region, divorced from its vast hinterland.   191

For the period from the fourth century until the ninth century no contemporary eye-witness account of any part of the East African coast has come down to us; nor has archaeology as yet yielded any evidence for this period from the islands or the coastal plain. Yet we know from the Kwale-ware sites that this must have been the period when Iron Age peoples, almost certainly Bantu in speech, were spreading through the near hinterland of north-eastern Tanzania and eastern Kenya. We also know from events reported outside East Africa that during this period black people called Zanj or Zenj, thought of as living in eastern Africa to the south of the Ethiopians and the Somali, were being exported as slaves to all the countries bordering the Indian Ocean. The Umayyad and Abbasid caliphs recruited large numbers of Zenj slaves as soldiers, and, as early as 696, we hear of revolts by Zenj slave soldiers in Iraq. From the opposite end of the Indian Ocean world, there is a reference in a Chinese history of the seventh century to the fact that in 614 ambassadors from Java had presented the Emperor of China with two *Seng Chi* slaves. During the eighth and ninth centuries Chinese chronicles provide several more references to *Seng Chi* slaves reaching China from the Hindu kingdom of Sri Vijaya in Java. And there is a Chinese text of the ninth century which actually describes the geography of East Africa, and makes a clear distinction between the Somali (Barbar) pastoralists of Po-pa-li, situated on the northern part of the East African coast, who ate no cereals but lived on the milk and blood of their cattle, and on the other hand the savage blacks of Ma-lin, which is probably to be identified with Malindi on the coast of Kenya.

Without local evidence, it is very difficult to see how and from where this early medieval trade in Zenj slaves was organised. Probably, however, the sources were not far inland. To judge from remnant populations, southern Somalia and northern Kenya, especially the river deltas and the offshore islands, were at this time in Bantu occupation. It may be that the main source of Zenj slaves lay around the frontier between peoples of Eastern Cushitic and Bantu speech, where warlike Somali pastoralists were expanding southwards and subjecting the scattered colonies of north-eastern Bantu cultivators. Certainly, however, it would be a mistake to imagine that slaves were the only exports from East Africa, or that outside contact was at any time confined to the northern part of the area. The great Arab geographer al-Masudi of Baghdad, who made several voyages from the Persian Gulf to East Africa during the early tenth century, leaves no doubt that ivory was the main commodity sought by the maritime traders. Ivory was shipped to Oman, and from there to India and

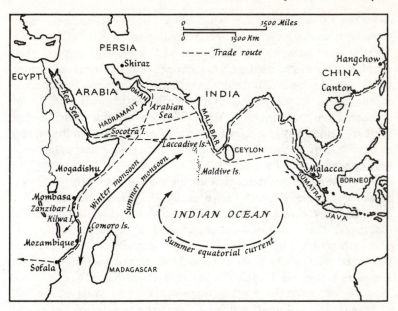

FIG. 56.   Medieval trade routes in the Indian Ocean.

China. The main staging-point mentioned by Masudi was an island called Qanbalu, 1400 miles south of Oman, which has been convincingly identified with Mkumbuu on the island of Pemba, where Arabs had settled around the middle of the eighth century and had subjected the Zenj population which they found there. From Qanbalu the ships sailed on again, as far again or further, to the land of Sofala, where lived the great king of the Zenj, whose people spent their time hunting the elephant and also digging for gold. All in all, there can be little doubt that the trading system described by Masudi stretched at least as far as the Limpopo, and that the main contacts with the people of the interior were at the southern end of the region.

The debate which has developed in recent years between archaeologists and historians of the East African coast does not, therefore, concern the date of the opening of the maritime trade, which, as we know, had extended at least as far as Cape Delgado by the time of Ptolemy. Rather, it concerns the emergence of prosperous Islamic communities at different points along the coast. Had there been no archaeological contribution to this problem, we should have been forced to rely on the earliest layers of oral tradition incorporated in the so-called 'chronicles' of the surviving coastal towns, and above all on the Kilwa Chronicle, of which some written versions were made as early as the sixteenth century. According to the Kilwa Chronicle, Muslim settlement in Somalia began with a great-grandson of the Prophet, who was harried with his followers out of Oman on account of his unorthodox Shi'ite beliefs. Another Shi'ite migration occurred in the eighth century, and in the tenth century orthodox Sunni Muslims from the town of El Ahsa on the western side of the Persian Gulf are said to have founded the towns of Mogadishu and Brava, and to have 'discovered' the trade of Sofala. Their near descendants are said to have founded Kilwa.

The findings of archaeologists during the last few years, especially those of Neville Chittick, have enriched, refined and somewhat changed these claims of traditional history, but there is no need to exaggerate their controversial significance. The ninth- and tenth-century sites have been proved to exist – not indeed at Mogadishu, but a few miles to the south at Gezira; not indeed on Pemba, but on Zanzibar at Unguja Ukuu. The oldest levels at Kilwa belong to the same period; so do those at Ungwana on the Tana estuary. Above all at Manda, in the Lamu archipelago near the frontier of Kenya and Somalia, Chittick has found and excavated a town site of forty-five acres, which sprang into sudden prosperity during the ninth century and continued so for two or three hundred years. Manda during this period may have had five thousand citizens, many of them living in houses of coral rag, cut into blocks and set in lime mortar. The site was defended from the sea by walls made of huge blocks of coral weighing up to a ton apiece and laid without mortar. The wealth of the place can be estimated from the fact that, from the time of its foundation, thirty per cent of its pottery was imported, and of this one-half consisted of glazed wares of high quality. The corresponding figure for Kilwa was five-tenths of a per cent. These wares provide the basis of the chronological evidence at present available. They are mostly early Islamic wares from Persia, with a few Chinese pieces of the same period. There are large quantities of Islamic glass, and the whole series of imported goods matches well with those found in the contemporary town site at Siraf on the Persian Gulf. Although no mosque has yet been positively identified, it must be assumed that many of the inhabitants of Manda were immigrants, that most of them were Muslims, and that the exceptional prosperity of the place was due to trade in ivory and slaves, and probably also in mangrove wood, which grows in plenty around the Lamu archipelago, and which has always been a building material of high value in the treeless lands of Arabia, Iraq and southern Persia.

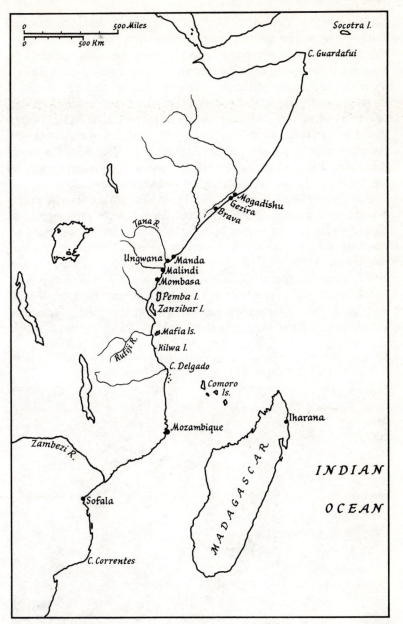

FIG. 57.   Islamic settlements on the East Coast of Africa.

It may also be, as Chittick suggests, that Manda preceded Kilwa in the role of an entrepôt market for the rich trade of Sofala – as a   195 point at which ships from the Persian Gulf turned round, after loading goods brought from further south in ships based on the African coast. However, in the tenth century both Masudi and Buzurg speak of Qanbalu (Pemba) as the main staging-point on the voyage to Sofala. Twelfth- and thirteenth-century sources stress the importance of Zanzibar, and mention Malindi and Mombasa. The thirteenth century saw the rise of Mogadishu, as well as that of Mafia and Kilwa. It would be a mistake, therefore, to think of a simple sequence of monopolistic control over the southern trade. Coastal settlements apart, the Laccadives and Maldives offered one alternative approach to the Sofala coast, the Comoros and Madagascar another.

It is against such a background that we have to see the rise of the greatest and most civilised of all the East African settlements, at Kilwa, where the facts have been established by a series of excavations carried out over seven seasons by Neville Chittick on behalf of the British Institute in Eastern Africa. Territorially, Kilwa consisted of two islands – that of Mafia, a hundred miles south of Zanzibar, and Kilwa Island, some sixty miles further on and lying less than a mile offshore. Earlier settlements had existed in both places, but around 1200 these came together under a single dynasty, which

FIG. 58.   The Great Mosque at Kilwa: an aerial view from the northern end. This structure dates to the fourteenth and fifteenth centuries.

minted a copper coinage, the first in East Africa, bearing the name of Ali bin Hasan, a name which stands first in the list of 'Shirazi' rulers reported in the most reliable version of the Kilwa chronicle. The stone-built town of Kilwa Kisiwani, including the central part of the Great Mosque, belongs to this reign, after which there followed, according to the chronicle, two generations of rulers, sons and grandsons of Ali bin Hasan, during whose reigns the prosperity of the two islands grew steadily, no doubt through their growing hold upon the Sofala trade. Then, towards the end of the thirteenth century, power was seized by a usurper, al-Hasan ibn Tulut, who founded the Mahdali dynasty, perhaps in origin from South Arabia, which survived until the coming of the Portuguese. With the new dynasty came a new style of many-domed building, exemplified in the extension of the Great Mosque at Kilwa. The Mahdalis were also responsible for the magnificent palace building of Husuni Kubwa, situated on a cliff-top at the northern end of Kilwa Island, with its fine octagonal bathing-pool overlooking the harbour, and its great reception court, its walls pitted with hundreds of niches for the oil lamps used on great occasions. Behind the palace to the south, a vast square enclosure marks the warehouse of these merchant princes, whose trade links stretched out across the ocean, and whose own

FIG. 59. A section of the bathing pool at Husuni Kubwa, Kilwa.

ships may have plied to ports in Arabia and the Persian Gulf, as well as southwards to Madagascar and Mozambique. An apartment at the northern end of Husuni Kubwa, where the main steps come up from the seashore, has an inscription referring to Sultan al-Hasan ibn Suleyman, the grandson of al-Hasan ibn Tulut. From the chronicle we know that he must have reigned from about 1320 till about 1340, and certainly it was he who was visited in 1331 by Ibn Battuta, who remembered him as a generous and humble Muslim, who sat and ate with beggars, and who honoured the holy men who came to his court from Iraq, the Hijaz and other countries. To Ibn Battuta, Kilwa was the principal town on the coast. Indeed, he remembered it as 'one of the most beautiful and well-constructed towns in the world'. Most of the inhabitants were Zenj, very black and with facial sacrifications. The sultan made frequent raids into the neighbouring countries of the pagan Zenj, as a result of which ivory and slaves were plentiful. A merchant told Ibn Battuta that it was a fortnight's journey from Kilwa to Sofala, and a month from there to the country of Yufi, presumably somewhere in western Rhodesia, whence powdered gold was carried to Sofala.

There can be no doubt that the exceptional prosperity of Kilwa from the thirteenth to the fifteenth century was due in large measure to Kilwa's exceptional involvement in the Rhodesian trade. This was achieved not only by commercial acumen and seapower, but also by some kind of political control over the Mozambique coastlands. The Kilwa chronicle refers to a rich governor of Sofala who later became Sultan of Kilwa in the thirteenth century. And when Vasco da Gama dropped anchor in Sofala in 1497, he found it still ruled by a governor from Kilwa. The site of the medieval town has not yet been located, and it is not yet possible to see clearly how this control was exercised – whether, for example, it involved merely the control of the anchorages for ocean shipping, or whether there existed some definite system of alliances with the powerful rulers of the Rhodesian plateau to keep the mainland trade routes centred upon Sofala. According to the sixteenth-century Portuguese historian Joao de Barros, to whom we owe one of the versions of the Kilwa chronicle,

The settlement which the Moors had made in this place called Sofala was not made by force of arms, nor against the will of the natives of the land, but by their wish and that of the prince who ruled at that time; because by reason of this intercourse they obtained benefits, as well as cloth and other things which they had never had before, and for which they gave gold and ivory, which was of no use to them ... In course of time, by means of the trade which the Moors had with these Kafirs, the kings of Kilwa became absolute masters of the gold trade. Chief among them was a man called Daud ... who resided there for some time and afterwards went to rule in Kilwa. From that time onwards the kings of Kilwa sent their governors to Sofala, so that everything might be transacted through their factors.[1]

Certainly, at Zimbabwe and a few other Rhodesian sites, we have the evidence, which is entirely lacking from Kilwa's own hinterland, that some of the luxury goods of China, India and the Persian Gulf were reaching this part of the African interior.

It is a question of the utmost interest how far the commercial outreach of Kilwa may have been responsible for the later medieval developments on Madagascar which had the effect of linking the island's history with that of Africa. It seems clear from the linguistic evidence that the first stage of human settlement on Madagascar was by Malayo-Polynesians, probably from Borneo. For their language to have survived, it would seem that the earliest settlers must have come direct across the ocean; and incredible though it may seem that such a migration should have taken place in simple outrigger canoes, we have the report of Buzurg that one such fleet, numbering a thousand vessels, carried out an extensive raid on the East African coast in search of ivory, tortoise-shell, leopard skins and Zenj slaves, in the year 945–6. The earliest migrants would presumably have been fishermen and tropical vegeculturalists, growing bananas and cocoa-yams, and, wherever there was the possibility of irrigation, rice. They would have begun by colonising the well-watered coastal plains on the eastern side of the island. In the drier lowlands of the west and the south, they would necessarily have been confined to scattered settlements near river mouths. For as long as possible they would have avoided the central highland region, which was covered with primeval forest. From an early stage in their settlement, these oceanic pioneers may have been joined by mixed elements from the East African mainland, who would have brought with them the African millet cereals and the domesticated animals, especially cattle, the words for which are recognisably of Bantu origin. It has to be remembered, however, that in terms of the intercontinental trade of East Africa, Madagascar had none of the commodities that were most desired. There was no gold. There were no elephants, and therefore no ivory. The population was small and scattered, and there is no record of the Malagasy being taken as slaves. Except for tortoise-shell, the commercial resources of the island were mainly in food-

[1] The translation is from G. S. P. Freeman Grenville, *The Medieval History of the Tanganyika Coast*, pp. 88–9.

stuffs, above all in rice. Madagascar was, in fact, an adjunct to the coastal trade rather than a pole of attraction in itself. Once there were urban communities on the East African coast, Madagascar could help to feed them. Once ships were sailing regularly to the Mozambique coast, some of them would call at Malagasy ports.

The archaeology of Madagascar is still very little known, but, so far as it goes, it is not inconsistent with what we have said. No site older than the present millennium has yet been identified. On the other hand, there is evidence from half a dozen widely scattered sites of fairly well-developed Iron Age communities which were in existence by the twelfth and thirteenth centuries. At Iharana, near the modern Vohémar on the north-eastern coast, one rich burial site has been excavated, which appears to be connected with the Muslim civilisation of the East African coast. The skeletons were all

FIG. 60.   An irrigated ricefield in the Madagascar highlands.

laid facing northwards, in the Muslim manner, and grave-goods included fine swords and daggers, Chinese and Persian plates and bowls, mother-of-pearl spoons, bronze mirrors, silver jewellery and necklaces of glass beads. There was the gold coin of a Fatimid caliph of the tenth century, and another gold piece of the twelfth century. At the feet of many corpses were placed three-legged steatite pots, of local manufacture, some examples of which have also been recovered by Chittick from the pre-Shirazi levels at Kilwa. The implication would seem to be that by the twelfth or early thirteenth century the agricultural settlement of Madagascar had proceeded far enough for expatriate merchant communities from the mainland coast to maintain a sophisticated existence there.

It is against this background that we have to consider the undoubted fact that, by the time when the Portuguese entered the Indian Ocean at the end of the fifteenth century, Madagascar was populated not only by Malagasy-speakers but also by Bantu communities which occupied the whole of the western part of the island and also parts of the southern interior. The simplest explanation would be that these people were the descendants of slaves captured from the Mozambique mainland by Malagasy raiders. In fact, however, there is no indication that these people were ever slaves. The coast-dwellers among them were known as Bambala – people of the mainland – and they lived in independent communities, following African social customs and religious beliefs. Those who lived in the southern interior adopted Malagasy speech, but retained African clan-names, such as Zafikazi-mambo, which suggest a connection with the ruling elements of Bantu populations north and south of the Zambezi. The suggestion put forward by the American historian Raymond Kent is that these were not slaves but deliberate colonists. If so, we are forced to consider afresh the relations between the peoples of south-central Africa and the 'Moors' of Sofala, who alone can have had the information and the ships to promote such a process of colonisation.

The problems posed by the medieval history of Madagascar are in truth as tantalising as any in Africa. But at least they serve to remind us that the coastal civilisation of East Africa was not a simple product of the southward progression of Islamic settlement from Arabia and the Persian Gulf but involves consideration of the Indian Ocean area as a whole. The luxury exports of East Africa – the ivory, the gold, the tortoise-shell – were distributed to India and China no less than to the Middle East. The imports of the coast included glass beads and textiles from India and porcelain tableware from China. Indians and Indonesians were involved in the trade from an early date: there may even have been a period during the later first millennium when Indonesian rather than Arab influences were predominant. The rise of Islam brought a revival of Arab seafaring, but for nearly five hundred years longer this was confined mainly to the western side of the Indian Ocean. A new stage, however, was reached in the thirteenth century, with the spread of Islam to central and eastern Asia, with the migration and conversion of the Mongols, with the Muslim penetration of India, with the conversion to Islam of the towns of the Malay peninsula and the islands of Sumatra and Java. By the mid-thirteenth century there were even large communities of Muslim merchants established in southern China. From this time onwards until the arrival of the Portuguese, the Indian Ocean was a Muslim preserve, and its commercial and religious bonds were mutually reinforcing. On present evidence, this was also the period during which the East African coast really became a part of this Indian Ocean Muslim world. The lesson from archaeological research is that, until the thirteenth century, Muslim communities in East Africa were relatively scattered and relatively isolated, and probably they found it difficult to preserve their faith and its accompanying culture from one generation to another. But from the thirteenth century on the situation changed greatly. The number of settlements multiplied, until virtually the whole of the coastal plain from Mogadishu to the Rufiji was included within the orbit of one or another of them. The wealthy lived in houses built of coral and standing in walled compounds, with mosques and tombs interspersed among the domestic buildings. People of ordinary means doubtless continued to live in the traditional rectangular thatched cottages of wattle and daub, dispersed among the coconut groves. But the indications are that rich and poor, slave and free, now formed one society, speaking the same Swahili language, following the same Muslim faith. The economics of the intercontinental trade do not, by themselves, begin to account for this development. A way of life had been established among the Swahili people, partly indeed through the continuing immigration of aliens, but mainly through a greatly increased level of communication with the outside world, which enabled a Muslim society to take root and keep alive even though situated on the edges of the civilised world.

18 States and trading systems of central Africa

c. 1000—1400

Our West African chapters have shown that during the first four centuries of the present millennium very extensive trading systems developed throughout the western bulge of Africa from the Mediterranean to the Bight of Benin, and that in the political field states, though not yet ubiquitous, came to embrace much of the territory, and in some cases reached imperial dimensions. Right across the savanna belt and deep into the equatorial forest, urban populations began to live in walled towns on permanent sites, with varied industries, large markets and active long-distance trade. The coastal areas of Guinea were the most backward, but even there by the end of the period merchants were coming from the interior in the service of a trading system that was to some extent intercontinental in scope. In Bantu Africa developments during the same period were certainly much slighter. Except at the East Coast settlements, urbanisation had, even by the end of the period, hardly begun. Except in the Rhodesian area, and perhaps in parts of the Congo basin, state formation was still in an early stage and on a diminutive scale. Trade, though everywhere existent in some measure, was comparatively local in its scope and seldom organised by specialists. Industry was much more limited than in West Africa. Weaving was rare. Glass-making was unknown.

So far as we can tell, the part of Bantu Africa which progressed furthest in all these directions during the first three or four centuries of the present millennium was the area between the Zambezi and the Limpopo. The reason was twofold. This region was not especially favourable from an agricultural point of view, but it had copper and gold as well as ivory, and it was accessible to the Indian Ocean trade. The coming of the Iron Age, we have seen, occurred during the first few centuries A.D. There followed a period of six or seven centuries during which agriculture and stock-raising gradually superseded the hunting and gathering way of life. Around the tenth century there seems to have been a development of rather more specialised pastoralism, which spread across central Zambia and down both sides of the Kalahari. Concurrently, in eastern Zambia and central Rhodesia, a growing population lived in larger concentrations, and engaged in more extensive exploitation of copper, gold and other natural resources than the Early Iron Age people who preceded them. This was the period at which Zimbabwe Hill was re-occupied after a long interval by its second layer of Iron Age inhabitants, but at which the main developments took place in the western part of the plateau, where there flourished the culture known as Leopard's Kopje II, characterised by walled villages, the earliest dated mining shafts, and the evidence of international contacts in the shape of glass beads typical of the Indian Ocean trade routes.

Sometime around the twelfth or thirteenth century, at a period comparable therefore with the emergence of stone-built urban settlements on the Kenya and Tanzania coast, the archaeological horizons of the second period of Zimbabwe pass, without any break in occupation, into those of the third. This period saw the introduction of radically new architectural styles, involving the construction of

FIG. 61. Zimbabwe. The valley ruins seen from the Acropolis.

much more substantial huts with larger dimensions and thicker walls. Stone began to be used for platforms and enclosures, with walling often used to join together the natural boulders of the steep Acropolis hilltop. In the valley to the south of the Acropolis there began to appear some of the earlier and more coarsely built free-standing walls of the palace structure – walls which encircled and divided from one another large round houses of clay and thatch, in much the same way as reed fences did in large dwelling complexes in other parts of Bantu Africa. The material culture of Period III at Zimbabwe, though basically continuous with Period II, shows a general enrichment in the number of metal objects and imported glass beads. It also shows one major innovation in the appearance of spindle-whorls, the sure sign of a weaving industry.

All authorities are agreed that Period III at Zimbabwe must reflect a large development in political centralisation, and the emergence of a commercial empire based on the export of gold and ivory to the Indian Ocean markets. This hypothesis is strengthened, not weakened, by the fact that Zimbabwe is situated well to the south-east of the main gold-producing area of the Rhodesian plateau. It was, in fact, a political and religious centre, not an economic one, but clearly it must have controlled the access to the gold-producing region. However, it was only in Period IV – stretching perhaps from the mid-

FIG. 62.   The great enclosure at Zimbabwe from the air. The conical tower is at the far side of the enclosure.

fourteenth to the mid-fifteenth century – that Zimbabwe reached the zenith of its wealth and power. Period IV was immediately preceded by a great fire, in which a good deal of the Period III town must have been destroyed or damaged. The rebuilding saw the introduction of a new and infinitely superior style of masonry, using dressed stones and regular coursing. It was at this stage that the palace structure in the valley took on its present shape, with its great girdle wall more than thirty feet high, and all in dressed stone, and with the solid conical tower, the purpose of which is still unknown. Once again, there was an enrichment of the material culture. It was this period that saw the arrival of nearly all the valuable foreign imports of Chinese porcelain. It was at this time that glass beads became really common. It was at this time that luxuries of African manufacture became apparent in ornaments and jewellery in gold and copper, H-shaped copper ingots like those of Sanga, and double iron gongs, which occur over the length and breadth of central Africa as a symbol of chieftainship.

Of the wealth extracted from the Rhodesian plateau at this period the ancient workings scattered thickly over the gold-bearing areas are a better witness than the royal settlement at Zimbabwe. Usually the miners worked open stopes, exploiting surface outcrops and following the reefs underground to a considerable depth. Underground mines were also dug, sometimes to a depth of twenty feet or more. Roger Summers, who collected evidence about more than three thousand of these ancient workings, made a rough estimate that between twenty and twenty-five million fine ounces of gold might have been extracted before the modern colonial period, and much of it in medieval times. Most of the wealth was produced for export. It is possible that the Shona people did not themselves prize the metal greatly. However, it is known that large quantities of golden objects were rifled from Zimbabwe before the archaeologists and the government moved in. During the early colonial period an Ancient Ruins Company was formed precisely to undertake these scandalous acts of freebooting. The two sites richest in gold which have been scientifically excavated are at Mapungubwe on the southern wall of the Limpopo valley near Beitbridge, and at Ingombe Ilede on the northern banks of the Zambezi below Kariba. At both these places quantities of golden ornaments were found in the graves of small numbers of presumably important individuals, who lived around the fourteenth and fifteenth centuries, contemporaneously with the great period of Zimbabwe. Mapungubwe, perched precariously on its cliff-top, could never have been inhabited by many people, and it has the air of a religious centre rather than a capital. Ingombe Ilede has been thought of as a trading settlement, sited at a crossing-point of land and river routes. We have no proof that either site lay within the political compass of Zimbabwe, but the possibility cannot be ruled out.

Before 1500, probably indeed by about 1450, the capital site of Zimbabwe had been abandoned. As Peter Garlake has pointed out, hardly a single import attributable to the period of Portuguese contact has ever been found there. By the time the Portuguese arrived in Sofala, the centre of political power was situated near the northern edge of the Rhodesian plateau, and, according to the traditions which they collected, it had been there for two generations, following the abandonment of a more southerly capital owing to a shortage of salt for the royal herds. The relations of the northerly kingdom with the Portuguese do not concern this volume. What does concern it is the type of polity which the Portuguese observers of the sixteenth century

FIG. 63. Distribution of Zimbabwe-type ruins in south-central Africa. Archaeological sites mentioned in the text are also shown.

described. For these accounts leave no doubt that the empire which ruled over most of east-central Africa from the Zambezi to the Limpopo and from the Kalahari to the Indian Ocean was typically African in all its institutions. The king – the Mwenemutapa, as he was called – was a typical divine king. He was supported by a Queen Sister and a Queen Mother, who completed the trio of high royalty. Besides the Queen Sister, eight other titled great wives had their own compounds within the palace complex, which housed in all some three thousand lesser wives, waiting-women and boy pages. The capital, or *zimbabwe*, consisted of the titled office-holders of the court and the representatives of the provincial chiefs and tributary kings. The main symbol of authority was the royal fire, from which burning brands were carried once a year to rekindle the chiefly fires of the subordinate rulers. This ritual followed the great New Moon ceremonies held in the month of May, when all the subordinate rulers had to assemble in the capital. For seven days the king remained secluded in communion with the spirits of his ancestors, while drums were beaten day and night: on the eighth day he emerged, and one of the assembled sub-chiefs was seized and killed as a sacrifice. Again, once a year, in September, the king and his entourage went on pilgrimage to the royal graves, and on these occasions a medium would become possessed by the spirit of the king's father, falling into an ecstasy and then imitating the speech and gestures of the late king. The Mwenemutapa would then go aside with the medium, and converse as if with his father. A Mwenemutapa, like his vassal kings, had to be physically perfect, and to commit suicide at the onset of serious illness. Except on ceremonial occasions, he was never seen in public. Within his compound he was approached crawling, and was usually concealed behind a curtain: his voice was audible, but he could not be seen. Any involuntary action of the king was imitated by his entourage. If he coughed, all coughed. If he sprained his ankle, all limped.

It is clear that, whatever the influence of the Indian Ocean trade upon the material wealth and even upon the territorial expansion of this kingdom, there was no major element in its political or religious life which could possibly be traced to the Islamic civilisation of the East Coast of Africa. The social institutions of the Mwenemutapa's kingdom, and doubtless those of the ancestral dynasty which had ruled from the stone-built Great Zimbabwe three hundred miles to the south, were pagan African institutions of the same general character as those which are known to have existed at different times all the way from Meroe to Takrur and from Ethiopia to the Transvaal.

What mainly distinguished the Rhodesian state from others in Bantu Africa is that during the last two or three centuries of the medieval period it probably grew much bigger than any other states we know of. Size, however, is not a diagnostic feature since, as we have seen, all large states grow by conquering smaller ones, and in Africa the usual method has been to leave the conquered units intact, taking tribute and hostages, but otherwise simply adding a new tier of authority, making an empire out of subordinate states. We do not therefore need to look for another large state outside Rhodesia from which migrating conquerors established a large state within Rhodesia at one fell swoop. Though we cannot reconstruct the political geography of south-central Africa in the tenth or eleventh century, we may be fairly sure that the number of units was large and their average size very small. If the Zimbabwe of Period II was a capital site at all, it was probably one of many. It is the steady growth of the installations through Periods III and IV that forms the best index of this state's expansion – this, and the very high proportion of the luxury imports, like Chinese porcelain, which found their way there, rather than to any rival centres. It is, of course, the stone structures that have given Zimbabwe its characteristic appearance and its unusual reputation. In fact, however, all this belt of Rhodesia is granite country, and the rock outcrops from the hilltops in such a way that it exfoliates in natural layers about three to seven inches thick. The process can be accelerated by first lighting fires and then pouring on cold water. As a result, stone was used for building all over the granite country. At Zimbabwe the buildings were more elaborate, but what the masons were attempting to do with their materials was still essentially the same as what other Bantu Africans did with wood, reeds and thatch. The difference was mainly in the permanence of a stone-built complex, but this was largely accidental.

The historian Donald Abraham has attempted to reconstruct the earlier periods of the Late Iron Age from a patchwork of oral traditions and retrospective documentation from the Portuguese period. Although he has so far been more than a little reticent in furnishing either exact references or verbatim texts, Abraham has asserted in several publications that the first Karanga-speaking peoples, whose descendants still live in eastern Rhodesia, settled between the Zambezi and the Limpopo around the ninth century A.D. He believes them to have sprung from the Kalanga clan which still inhabits the eastern Luba country between Lake Kisale and the south-western corner of Lake Tanganyika. According to Abraham, the newcomers fanned out over the Rhodesian plateau, coming into contact both with an earlier Iron Age population and with surviving Khoisan peoples who 209 were still practising a Late Stone Age economy. Once settled in the new territory, the Karanga employed the earlier inhabitants as cattle-herders and iron-workers. Their material culture was gradually enriched, and they began to develop shrines sacred to their ancestor cults on conspicuous hills. Their political power was based partly on their religious acumen, for the Karanga leaders acted as intermediaries between the common people and the Supreme Being, Mwari, who was shepherd of the world and of men. The living could only communicate with Mwari by way of the ancestral spirits and their mediums. This religious authority of the Karanga was combined with increasing economic control of mining activities in the rich gold and copper regions between the Zambezi and the Limpopo.

Abraham's reconstruction would seem to imply at least some drift of Later Iron Age people into central Africa from the north. And, as we have seen, archaeology would confirm that the Later Iron Age, at least in eastern Zambia, was connected with migration on a scale large enough to revolutionise pottery styles and to change potting from a male to a female occupation. There are indications that the newcomers included a substantial element of comparatively specialised pastoralists; and it is possible that the search for new grazing grounds by pastoralists practising an active milking economy was one of the strongest motives for human migration. Certainly, it is in eastern Zambia and Malawi that there existed, until the Ngoni invasions of the nineteenth century, political structures which to early Portuguese observers seemed comparable to those south of the Zambezi. Though never attaining the size or the centralisation of the empire of the Mwenemutapas, the paramount chiefs of the Nsenga, the Maravi and the Chewa were regal figures, living in capital towns called *zimbawe*s, and addressed by their subjects with the same honorific title of *mambo* as the great chiefs of the Shona. To the north of the Chewa lived the Bisa, with political institutions that were essentially similar, and with historical traditions linking them with the Luba peoples to the north again. The eighth- and ninth-century radiocarbon dates for the richly metallurgical Later Iron Age site at Sanga, in the heart of Lubaland, is consistent with the line of transmission of Later Iron Age cultures from north to south. It must be stressed that all this is still largely hypothetical, and that it is strongly resisted by some of those with their noses closest to the ground in archaeological research, who are apt to plead the cause of local evolution on every possible occasion. However, it is to be noted that, even if it is accepted that the Later Iron Age in central Africa was initiated by some degree of population movement, the scope left open both for local evolution and for simple culture contact is still very wide. We have followed the gradual growth of Great Zimbabwe from commonplace beginnings in the tenth or eleventh century to an obviously unique pre-eminence in the fourteenth and fifteenth centuries. We have noted the stimulus likely to have been exerted, without any significant population movement, by the development of the Indian Ocean trade. Migration is not claimed as the cause of all, or even of most, of the changes that took place; but to dismiss it automatically from every calculation is to be as doctrinaire as those who used to attribute all improvements to the conquests of 'superior races'.

The ethnographer Baumann published a map, which we reproduce here, of African societies with developed state systems, which he called 'neo-Sudanese' to the north of the Equator and 'Rhodesian' to the south of it. Baumann noted that the characteristics of the social

FIG. 64.   Baumann's map of Africa showing 'neo-Sudanese civilisations'.

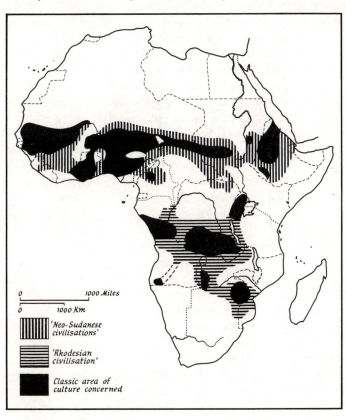

0   *1000 Miles*

0   *1000 Km*

'Neo-Sudanese civilisations'

'Rhodesian civilisation'

Classic area of culture concerned

and political institutions in the two zones were essentially similar, and the main reason why he divided them was because of the geographical discontinuity. There was a gap of three or four hundred miles between the Ethiopian and eastern Sudanic sectors of the northern zone and the interlacustrine sector of the southern zone, and on this basis Baumann was prepared to remove the connecting thread between them to a point of common origin in the Red Sea area (Erythrea) from which parallel streams of influence travelled westwards across the Sudanic belt and southwards by sea to Sofala. We now see that the weakness of such a system was in a defective chronology. Rhodesia may have provided the earliest example of an 'empire' within the southern sector, but it was not the earliest 'state'. Almost certainly, there were earlier states in the Katanga, and the connection between a hypothetical 'Erythrea' and the Katanga is more likely to have been overland than by sea.

In relation to Katanga, it is clear that copper-mining and copper-working, and the trade arising from these activities, are among the main factors to be considered. There is no doubt that the metallurgical skills revealed in the Sanga excavations are of a high order. But there is equally no doubt that amid all the evidence of copper used for jewellery and, in the form of ingots, for currency, the evidence for trade routes reaching from Katanga to the East Coast is limited to a handful of seashells and glass beads. Luba copper-miners may have been the industrial ancestors of Shona gold-miners, but the evidence does not suggest that an early trade from Katanga to, say, Manda or Kilwa, extended itself southwards into one from the Rhodesian goldfields to Sofala. On the contrary, the few imported objects recovered at Sanga reflect the extreme results of hand-to-hand barter conducted through long and tenuous exchange networks. The hoards of copper ingots found at Sanga certainly suggest that this metal had a foreign as well as a domestic value, but it is difficult to see what the Luba peoples of eastern Katanga might have imported in exchange for it, unless it was a consumer commodity such as salt. Deposits of salt are nearly as rare in Bantu Africa as in the West African forest and savanna. Lumps of salt were traded over immense distances of the interior, from such places as Ivuna and Uvinza in western Tanzania, and from Katwe in western Uganda, where saline springs left deposits that could be mined and transported. But the great deposits of salt were, of course, in the Sahara; and it may be that the possibility of early and regular canoe traffic on the inland waterways of the Congo basin has so far been too little considered. Ethnographers have frequently remarked upon the West African characteristics of the Bantu peoples who live around the southern fringe of the Congo forest –

peoples like the Kongo, the Pende, the Luba and the Songye. Here are peoples who live in rectangular houses in large semi-urban villages, laid out in streets on nearly permanent sites, with a wealth of local industries and a strong tradition of representational art, all very foreign to most of Bantu Africa. It does not seem very sensible to attribute these characteristics to the early phases of the Bantu expansion, since they are for the most part characteristics of Later Iron Age material culture, the transmission of which would be much more intelligible on the basis of regular trade communication between the regions north and south of the forest during the present millennium, and perhaps a little before.

However, one element in the cultures of central and southern Africa which we may be fairly certain did not travel through the Congo forest is the cow kept for milking. In this matter we must await the results of much more radiocarbon dating of sites containing the rouletted potteries of Kenya, Uganda, Rwanda and eastern Zaïre. These wares, it will be remembered, followed the Early Iron Age wares, and are associated, though not exclusively, with milking pastoralists. Whereas the Early Iron Age farmers chose low-lying, well-watered lands and those with deep escarpment soils, the milking pastoralists preferred the drier, more open country, much of which was still occupied by hunting and gathering peoples during the period of the Early Iron Age. The pastoralists, therefore, moved in among the surviving hunters; and at the margins they interacted with the cultivators, who welcomed the manure deposited by the cattle upon their fields and gardens. Just as the Fulani moved, century by century, across West Africa from the Senegal towards Lake Chad, so in eastern and central Africa milking pastoralists moved further and further south. In the dry centre of East Africa they were of necessity highly specialised and self-sufficient. In the marginal lands of western Uganda, Rwanda, Burundi, western Tanzania, eastern Zaïre, Zambia and Rhodesia, they interacted with the cultivators, sometimes achieving a full symbiosis in which cultivators acted as willing hosts to the pastoralists' cattle, giving goods and services in exchange for milk and manure. In many areas such a symbiosis was the hallmark of the Later Iron Age. And in these circumstances the pastoralists often assumed the dominant political role, because they were more mobile and more inured to warfare than the cultivators.

In the interlacustrine region of East Africa, the theme of interaction between incoming pastoralists and earlier established agriculturists is a standard feature of early oral tradition. All that is missing, so far, is a reliable set of dates. We have the Early Iron Age dates running through from the second century A.D. until the fifth 213 century, with one rather dubious date in the eleventh century. And we have the dates from the great pastoral site in western Uganda, running from the late fourteenth century to the early sixteenth century. But, as yet, we have nothing in between from which the beginnings of the pastoral immigration can be more accurately dated. It may be that in its origins it was early enough to have spread southwards to Zambia by the ninth or tenth century. It may be that it was so much later than this that other possible routes have to be considered. One thing, however, is certain. The pastoral invasion of Bantu Africa is not to be amalgamated with any surge in metallurgical skills, or with any more intensive exploitation of minerals: 'One does not herd cattle and blow bellows.' Pastoralists need iron only for their spearheads. Among pastoralists, smelting and smithing are despised arts practised by lesser breeds without the law. To achieve a satisfactory hypothesis for the origins of Later Iron Age Rhodesia, one has to imagine a fusion between pastoralists from the north-east and skilled metallurgists from the north-west – a fusion which may have begun to occur as far north as the Katanga.

There seems to be no real doubt that the immense series of state systems in the region between the Katanga and the coast of Angola owes its origin, like the states of eastern Zambia and Rhodesia, to developments in Lubaland. The series of state systems to the north and south of the Congo estuary has been seen by some authorities as an earlier offshoot from the same stock. The latest views, propagated by the veteran oral historian Jan Vansina, tend to place the states of the Kongo, the Vili and the Tyo in a series linking northwards to the Sudanic side of the Congo forest. At present so little is known of the areas immediately to the north of the Congo basin that we have no reliable means of measuring potential contact between West and central Africa. Recently, a French historian, Pierre Kalck, has attempted to study the early history of the Central African Republic. Among other sources, he has examined the early sixteenth century *Description of Africa* by Leo Africanus, and has identified Leo's kingdom of Gaoga with an early state centred on Darfur, and enjoying riverine trade-links via the Uele and the Ubangi with the heartlands of the Congo basin. Here again, we must await the recovery of archaeological evidence. But at least there is no longer any need to think of Baumann's 'neo-Sudanese' states as a separate series from his 'Rhodesian' ones. The possible overland links from north to south are at least as promising, and probably more so, as any theory of contacts passing directly from the Horn of Africa to the Zambezi mouth by sea.

Suggestions for further reading

These suggestions are not intended to be exhaustive, but only to be a brief guide. We hope that *Africa in the Iron Age* has acted as a catalyst to stimulate the reader's interest in various directions, to study a whole range of topics more deeply than has been possible in the brief space available to us. Most of the works mentioned have bibliographies which will carry the inquiring reader even further on his way. The first suggestions relate to the methodology of African history and to general topics which affect the whole of Africa, or large parts of it. After this, we suggest further reading on each of the main regions. We have preferred to cite books rather than articles, although a few of the latter are mentioned where they are especially important.

THE AFRICAN IRON AGE – GENERAL

For those readers who want a wider survey of African history which puts the Iron Age into context the Penguin *Short History of Africa* (5th ed., 1975) by Roland Oliver and J. D. Fage offers a brief account running from the earliest times to the present day. The Iron Age itself has received as yet little treatment from historians, although Basil Davidson's *Old Africa Rediscovered* (1959) was a good popular account of the situation as it was fifteen years ago. The methodological problems of studying the African past have been discussed by Daniel McCall in his *Africa in Time Perspective* (1964). The basic principles of archaeology have never been discussed in a specifically African context, but Brian M. Fagan, *In the Beginning* (1972) covers much African ground. Jan Vansina's *Oral Tradition* (1965) remains the authoritative treatise on traditional history in Africa. The classification of African peoples, their cultures and institutions, is covered most accessibly by G. P. Murdock, *Africa – Its Peoples and Their Culture History* (1959). This book should be used with care, but as an ethnographic compendium it is useful. A more reliable work is H. Baumann and D. Westermann, *Völkerkunde Afrikas*, which has been translated into French as *Les Peuples et les civilisations de l'Afrique* (1948). In English, C. G. Seligman's *Races of Africa* (3rd ed., 1957), despite the author's obsession with 'the Hamitic myth', is still the best short introduction to the subject. J. H. Greenberg, *The Languages of Africa* (2nd ed., 1966) is the most widely recognised work on the classification of African languages, but readers should not neglect the critical review of it by Malcolm Guthrie in the *Journal of African History*, vol. v (1964). Frank Willett's *African Art* is the standard synthesis on this important aspect of African life and history. No reader of 215

Africa in the Iron Age

this book should be without J. D. Fage, *An Atlas of African History* (1963). We should also mention the periodic lists of Iron Age radiocarbon dates which are published at regular intervals in the *Journal of African History*, and which provide an invaluable source of information on new chronological evidence for the African Iron Age. Among collections of published papers likely to interest the reader who is seeking quick access to key articles, there is Roland Oliver and J. D. Fage, *Papers in African Prehistory* (1970), which offers a selection of archaeological articles first published in the *Journal of African History*. Robert O. Collins, *Problems in African History* (1968) focuses on major historical issues, and is widely used in the United States for university courses. In French, Hubert Deschamps has edited a two-volume *Histoire générale de l'Afrique Noire* (1970–1), of which the introductory section contains background articles by leading French authorities.

STONE AGE ARCHAEOLOGY AND THE SPREAD OF FOOD PRODUCTION

Those readers who wish to extend their interests backwards into the Stone Age should turn first to J. Desmond Clark, *The Prehistory of Africa* (1970). This is an authoritative short synthesis, with a comprehensive and up-to-date bibliography. The Late Stone Age is well covered in this volume, as also in the same author's *Prehistory of Southern Africa* (1959), which contains an especially useful account of daily life in the Late Stone Age. Serious students of the origins of agriculture would be well advised to start outside Africa with a perusal of V. Gordon Childe, *Man Makes Himself* (1942). This is a work of synthesis, giving a general survey of the consequences of food production which is worth any historian's attention. Stuart Struever, *Prehistoric Agriculture* (1971) brings together a series of papers which discuss the theoretical underpinnings of Childe's work, as well as other, more recent theories on the origins of agriculture. J. Desmond Clark's chapter 'The Problem of Neolithic Culture in Sub-Saharan Africa' in W. W. Bishop and J. D. Clark (eds.), *Background to Evolution in Africa* (1967) is informative on Stone Age food producers. The Saharan rock paintings are vividly described by Henri Lhote, *The Search for the Tassili Frescoes* (1959). The origins of African food plants formed the subject of a special number of the *Journal of African History*, vol. III (1962). F. J. Simoons, 'Some Questions on the Economic Prehistory of Ethiopia' in vol. VI (1965) of the same journal is also worth consulting. W. Allan, *The African Husbandman* (1965) is fundamental reading for anyone interested in African agriculture.

THE BANTU PROBLEM

The first serious attempt to deduce the cradleland and the lines of dispersion of the Bantu from linguistic evidence was made by H. H. Johnston in the *Journal of the Royal Anthropological Institute* (1913), and the literature has proliferated since then. A recent summary was Roland Oliver, 'The Problem of the Bantu Expansion' in the *Journal of African History*, vol. VII (1966). The same journal published a comment by Merrick Posnansky, 'Bantu Genesis – Archaeological Reflections', vol. IX (1968), and also an important article by Jean Hiernaux, 'Bantu Expansion: The Evidence from Physical Anthropology', in the same volume. Linguistic controversies lie at the centre of the Bantu problem. Malcolm Guthrie's monumental, but localised, study, *Comparative Bantu* (4 vols., 1968–71) has to be reconciled with Joseph Greenberg's wide-scale classification, *The Languages of Africa* (2nd ed., 1966). A major synthesis of the evidence will be attempted by the authors of this volume in vol. 2 of the forthcoming *Cambridge History of Africa*.

AFRICA REGION BY REGION

There are gaps in our knowledge of many aspects of the African Iron Age. Archaeological research has been sparse in many regions, and the references which follow are of widely varying reliability. We cover Africa from north to south, beginning with the Nile valley.

The Nile valley

Ancient Egyptian civilisation has been described by many writers. One of the best accounts is by Cyril Aldred, *The Egyptians* (1961). E. Baumgartel, *The Cultures of Predynastic Egypt* (1947) is still a fundamental source, but should be read with Bruce Trigger, *Beyond History* (1968). The later history of Egypt dealt with in this volume is covered by Edwyn Bevan, *A History of Egypt under the Ptolemaic Dynasty* (1927) and by H. Idris Bell, *Egypt from Alexander the Great to the Arab Conquest* (1956). W. H. C. Frend, *The Rise of the Monophysite Movement* (1972) is a study of fundamental importance for the early history of Christianity in Egypt and north-east Africa.

The history of the Meroitic civilisation is summarised in A. J. Arkell, *A History of the Sudan to 1821* (1955), while the site of Meroe and related settlements are described by Peter Shinnie, *Meroe* (1967), a volume written before his latest excavations there were undertaken. Bruce Trigger has written a useful paper, 'The Myth of Meroe and the African Iron Age' in *African Historical Studies* (1969), which puts iron-working at Meroe into a wider perspective. The Meroitic script has recently been the subject of another study by Trigger, *The Meroitic Funerary Inscriptions from Arminna West* (1970).

The history of the Nile valley in Islamic times is best summarised in Stanley Lane-Poole, *A History of Egypt in the Middle Ages* (reprinted 1968) and in Chapters 14–16 of J. R. Harris, The Legacy of Egypt (2nd ed., 1971). The history of Egypt in its international aspect is covered in Bernard Lewis, 'Egypt and Syria' in the *Cambridge History of Islam*, vol. I (1970). The best study of Christian Nubia during this period is still that by Ugo Monneret de

Villard, *Storia della Nubia Cristiana* (1938), but the essential facts are well presented in J. S. Trimingham, *Islam in the Sudan*, which mainly deals with the Islamic period. Yusuf Fadl Hasan, *The Arabs and the Sudan* (1967) is the standard work on the Arab penetration and settlement. The archaeology of Christian Nubia is described by Peter and Margaret Shinnie, 'New Light on Medieval Nubia', *Journal of African History*, vol. IV (1965), which gives references to earlier literature, notably the report on Debeira West by Shinnie in *Kush*, vol. IX (1963), and that on Faras by Michaelowski, *Faras—fouilles polonaises 1961* (1962), and in *Kush*, vol. XI (1963) and XII (1964).

Ethiopia and the Horn

For the pre-Axumite and Axumite periods of Ethiopian history dealt with in this volume, the most useful recent summary is that by Jean Doresse in the first volume of his *L'empire du Prêtre Jean* (1957). Sergew Hable Sellassie, *Ancient and Medieval Ethiopian History* (Addis Ababa, 1972) provides a useful conspectus of the main sources, conservatively interpreted. For those who read Italian, C. Conti Rossini, *Storia d'Etiopia* (1928) is still the outstanding work. In English, a much more cursory treatment is to be found in A. H. M. Jones and E. Monroe, *A History of Ethiopia* (1935) and in the historical chapter of E. Ullendorff, *The Ethiopians* (2nd ed., 1972). David Buxton, *The Abyssinians* (1970) is a brief introduction to Ethiopian archaeology and history, which focuses much attention on architecture. Francis Anfray, 'Aspects de l'archéologie éthiopienne' in the *Journal of African History*, vol. IX (1968) gives some idea of the potential importance of Iron Age archaeology in Ethiopia. Otherwise, the archaeological literature is lamentably thin. Taddesse Tamrat, *Church and State in Ethiopia* (1972) is now the standard work on the later medieval period, and the introductory chapters which deal with the pre-Solomonic period are well worth consulting. Tamrat's chapter 'Ethiopia, the Red Sea and the Horn *c.* 900–1543' in the forthcoming *Cambridge History of Africa*, vol. 3 will be of great value to students. J. S. Trimingham, *Islam in Ethiopia* (1952) is of importance for the emergence of the Muslim states to the east and south of the Christian empire.

The Horn is virtually unpublished in archaeological literature, except for J. Desmond Clark's monumental *Prehistoric Cultures of the Horn of Africa* (1954), which is mainly concerned with Stone Age archaeology. The documentary sources for the Somali coast in classical and medieval times are largely the same as for East Africa, and are dealt with below. The ethnic history of the Somali people presents fundamental problems of interpretation, which can be appreciated by comparing the article by I. M. Lewis, 'The Somali Conquest of the Horn of Africa', *Journal of African History*, vol. I (1960) with that by Herbert Lewis, 'The Origins of the Galla and Somali' in the same journal, vol. VII (1966).

Among general histories of North Africa the interested reader should certainly consult first the classic *Histoire de l'Afrique du Nord* (2 vols., 1951–2) by C.-A. Julien. The first volume, which deals with the pre-Islamic period, is an outstanding work. The second volume, which deals with the Islamic period, has been revised by Roger Le Tourneau and translated into English as *History of North Africa* (1970). Jamil Abun-Nasr, *A History of the Maghrib* (1971) is a well-reflected synthesis, more cursory on the pre-Islamic period than Julien, but clearer on the Islamic period, and more aware of the Saharan frontier of North Africa. *The Phoenicians* (1962) by Donald Harden is a brief but classic work. Charles McBurney, *The Prehistory of North Africa* (1959) is a technical and somewhat outdated general synthesis, which however contains much information of value on early agriculture in the Sahara and on the Mediterranean littoral. Roman North Africa is briefly summarised in Jane Nickerson, *Short History of North Africa* (1963). Sir Mortimer Wheeler's *Rome beyond the Imperial Frontiers* (1954) has long been a starting-point for students of Rome in Africa, as have B. H. Warmington's *The North African Provinces* (1954) and *Carthage* (1960).

The pastoralists of the neolithic Sahara are well covered in Clark's *Prehistory of Africa* (1970) and by Henri Lhote, *The Search for the Tassili Frescoes* (1959). Patrick J. Munson has a very important paper, to be published in the proceedings of the 1972 Wenner Gren conference on African food crops, entitled 'Archaeological Data on the Origins of Cultivation in the South-Western Sahara and Its Implications for West Africa', which will be worth searching for. It deals with grain impressions from the Dar Tichitt sites in Mauritania. Pierre Huard, 'Introduction et diffusion du fer au Tchad', in the *Journal of African History*, vol. VII (1966), and Henri Lhote, 'Le Cheval et le chameau dans les peintures et gravures rupestres du Sahara' in *Bulletin d' IFAN* (1953) are useful for the introduction of iron and early trading in the desert. The copper industries of the western Sahara form the subject of a preliminary report by Nicole Lambert, 'Les Industries sur cuivre dans l'ouest saharien', in the *West African Journal of Archaeology*, vol. I (1971).

During the medieval period, the Sahara is better considered with the Sudan than with the Maghrib, and on the economic side the fundamental work of synthesis both for achaeological and documentary evidence is R. Mauny, *Tableau géographique de l'ouest africain au moyen age* (1961), although its layout as a work of geography presents some difficulties for historians. In English, E. W. Bovill's *Caravans of the Old Sahara* (1953), revised as *The Golden Trade of the Moors* (1968), provides an attractive introduction to the same subject. J. S. Trimingham, *A History of Islam in West Africa* (1962) is valuable for the Sahara as well as the Sudan. Denise Robert, 'Les Fouilles de Tegdaoust' in *Journal of African History*, vol. XI (1970) describes the latest work at one of the most significant medieval sites in the southern Sahara.

West Africa

Apart from Mauny's *Tableau géographique*, the only synthesis of West African archaeology is Oliver Davies, *West Africa before the Europeans* (1967), which concentrates on the Stone Age, although containing some limited information on the Iron Age and the origins of agriculture. It is somewhat controversial in some of its conclusions. The *West African Archaeological Newsletter* and its successor, the *West African Journal of Archaeology* (from 1971), have valuable articles on Iron Age archaeology. Thurstan Shaw, 'Early Crops in Africa' to be published in the proceedings of the 1972 Wenner Gren conference on African food crops, already mentioned, will be a seminal reference for the origins of agriculture in West Africa. Until then, readers should refer to J. Desmond Clark, 'The Problem of Neolithic Culture in Sub-Saharan Africa' in W. W. Bishop and J. D. Clark (eds.), *The Background to Evolution in Africa* (1967). The beginnings of the West African Iron Age are connected with the Nok culture, so far inadequately published, except for Bernard Fagg, 'Recent Work in West Africa: New Light on the Nok Culture' in *World Archaeology*, vol. 1 (1969). The artistic relationships of Nok sculpture are ably dealt with by Frank Willett, *Ife in the History of West African Sculpture* (1967). The archaeology of Benin is still not published in full, but a preliminary report is Graham Connah, 'Archaeology in Benin', *Journal of African History*, vol. XIII (1972). Thurstan Shaw, *Igbo-Ukwu* (2 vols., 1970) is one of the most complete accounts of an Iron Age site ever published.

The history of West African states has been synthesised by many authors. N. Levtzion, *Ancient Ghana and Mali* (1973) is the most useful and authoritative work covering the western Sudan, while the introductory chapters of his *Muslims and Chiefs in West Africa* (1968) describes the southward extension of commercial and religious influences from the savanna belt towards the forest. J. S. Trimingham, *A History of Islam in West Africa* (1962) is another work of great value. Much new and useful synthesis is to be found in J. F. Ade Ajayi and Michael Crowder (eds.), *A History of West Africa*, vol. 1 (1971), especially the chapter by H. F. C. Smith, 'Early States of the Central Sudan'. Yves Urvoy, *Histoire de l'empire de Bornou* (1949) and Jean Rouch, *Contribution à l'histoire des Songhay* (1953) are classic monographic studies, while M. Delafosse, *Haut-Sénégal–Niger* (1912) is still the basic quarry for the early history of the Mande peoples. H. R. Palmer's *Bornu Sahara and Sudan* (1936) is generally reckoned to be unintelligible, but his *Sudanese Memoirs* (1928) is an important collection of translations from early Arabic documents concerning Bornu and Hausaland. M. G. Smith, 'The Beginnings of Hausa Society' in J. Vansina, R. Mauny and J. Thomas (eds.), *Historians in Tropical Africa* (1964) is a useful reference. S. Johnson, *History of the Yorubas* (2nd ed., 1956) and Jacob Egharevba, *A Short History of Benin* (revised ed., 1960) are two outstanding examples of traditional history recorded by African amateur historians of the first two colonial generations. O. Houdas (ed. and tr.), *Tarikh es Sudan* (1900) and *Tarikh el Fettach* (1913) are the best-known examples of Arabic chronicles written in the western Sudan from the

220

seventeenth century onwards, which incorporate traditional material from much earlier periods.

East Africa

The history of East Africa during our period is known from literary sources only for the coastal belt. The interior is known only from archaeology, and the evidence for the Early Iron Age has mostly been accumulated only very recently. The standard works on East African history are therefore not very helpful for this period, and the interested reader must be prepared to seek fairly widely for up-to-date material. The origins of food production in eastern Africa are discussed by J. Desmond Clark in 'The Problem of Neolithic Culture' in W. W. Bishop and J. D. Clark (eds.), *Background to Evolution in Africa* (1967), while the chapter by Merrick Posnansky, 'The Iron Age in East Africa', in the same volume is one of the earlier attempts to synthesise recent work. Another is John Sutton's chapter 'The Interior of East Africa' in P. L. Shinnie (ed.), *The African Iron Age* (1971). Sonia Cole, *The Prehistory of East Africa* (2nd ed., 1964) is mainly useful for the Stone Age and, within our period, for its account of the Stone Bowl cultures of the Kenya Rift Valley. The classic paper on Dimple-based ware is that by Mary D. Leakey, L. S. B. Leakey and Archdeacon W. E. Owen, 'Dimple-based Pottery from Central Kavirondo', *Occasional Papers of the Coryndon Museum*, no. 2 (1948). Robert Soper has recently published three important papers on similar wares, 'Kwale: An Early Iron Age Site in South-Eastern Kenya' and 'Iron Age Sites in North-Eastern Tanzania', both in *Azania*, vol. II (1967); and 'Early Iron Age Pottery Types from East Africa: Comparative Analysis', *Azania*, vol. VI (1971). These papers are fully referenced, and will carry the reader into the earlier technical literature. Early salt-working sites in Tanzania are described by John Sutton and Andrew Roberts, 'Uvinza and Its Salt Industry', *Azania*, vol. III (1968) and by Brian Fagan and John Yellan, 'Ivuna' in the same volume. Engaruka is described by Hamo Sassoon, 'New Views on Engaruka', *Journal of African History*, vol. VIII (1967).

By comparison, the coast of East Africa is the subject of a rich literature, in which the best starting-point is the chapter by Gervase Mathew in Roland Oliver and Gervase Mathew (eds.), *History of East Africa* (1963). Another useful synthesis is that by Neville Chittick in B. A. Ogot and J. A. Kieran (eds.), *Zamani: A Survey of East African History* (1968). G. S. P. Freeman Grenville, *The East African Coast* (1962) is an invaluable collection of documents from Greek, Arabic, Portuguese and Swahili sources, in English translation. Two important articles by Neville Chittick are 'The Shirazi Colonisation of East Africa' in the *Journal of African History*, vol. VI (1965), and 'Discoveries in the Lamu Archipelago', *Azania*, vol. II (1967). Chittick's *Kilwa* (2 vols., 1975) embodies the results of seven seasons' work at this key site. Peter Garlake, *The Early Islamic Architecture of the East African Coast* (1966) is an exhaustive treatment of this subject. J. S. Trimingham, *Islam in East Africa* (1964) has very useful historical chapters.

221

Madagascar lies, to a great extent, outside the scope of this volume; but Hubert Deschamps, *Histoire de Madagascar* (1960) provides a magnificent short introduction to the problems of the medieval history of the island, while Raymond Kent, *Early Kingdoms in Madagascar* (1970) opens many new perspectives. Archaeology is not well served, and the reader will have to be content with Pierre Vérin's brief survey, 'Les Recherches archéologiques à Madagascar' in *Azania*, vol. 1 (1966).

Angola and Zaïre

The Iron Age archaeology of west-central Africa has so far been explored only at one or two points. The prehistory of Angola has been comparatively well served by J. Desmond Clark's comprehensive, but obscurely published, monographs. His *Distribution of Prehistoric Culture in Angola* (1966) is useful in the context of forest archaeology, while *Further Palaeoanthropological Studies in Northern Lunda* (1968) describes a scatter of Iron Age sites near Dundo and elsewhere. The Belgian physical anthropologist and archaeologist Jean Hiernaux has published many papers, especially the collection of articles jointly written with Emma Maquet, 'Cultures préhistoriques de l'âge des métaux au Ruanda-Urundi et au Kivu', *Bulletin des séances de l'Académie Royale des Sciences Coloniales* (1957–60). The Sanga site in north Katanga has been thoroughly catalogued by Jacques Nenquin, *Excavations at Sanga, 1957* (1961) and by Jean Hiernaux, Emma de Longrée and J. de Buyst, *Fouilles archéologiques dans la vallée du Haut-Lualaba: I – Sanga* (1971).

The formation of states in parts of Zaïre during the late first millennium and later is described by Jan Vansina, *Kingdoms of the Savanna* (1966), which provides an extensive bibliography for the reader interested in delving deeper. David Birmingham has worked for the most part on the later centuries of Angolan history, but the introductory chapters of *Trade and Conflict in Angola* (1966) present a valuable synthesis of the history of eastern Angola and southern Zaïre. Much controversy has surrounded the chronology of the formation of states in this area: we refer the reader to the latest contribution, by Joseph C. Miller, 'The Imbangala and the Chronology of Early Central African History' in the *Journal of African History*, vol. XIII (1972), which provides the references to earlier contributions. The question of contacts between the Congo basin and West Africa during the late first millennium and later receives some attention from Pierre Kalck, 'Pour une localisation du royaume de Gaoga', *Journal of African History*, vol. XIII (1972), which is developed at greater length in the first volume of his *Histoire centrafricaine* (1973).

Southern Africa

J. Desmond Clark, *The Prehistory of Southern Africa* (1959), although a little out of date, is still a major authority on the Stone Age cultures of southern

Africa: it provides a valuable background for the Iron Age. The Iron Age as a whole is synthesised by Brian Fagan, *Southern Africa during the Iron Age* (1965), which, however, is also becoming rather outdated. Zambian Iron Age cultures are described in Fagan, *A Short History of Zambia* (2nd ed., 1968), while the Rhodesian Iron Age has been repeatedly described by Roger Summers – 'The Southern Rhodesian Iron Age', *Journal of African History*, vol. II (1961) is a typical, fairly recent example. T. O. Ranger has edited a series of essays on central African history, *Aspects of Central African History* (1968), which cover most of the basic issues of the Iron Age. The South African Iron Age is treated in Monica Wilson and L. M. Thompson (eds.), *The Oxford History of South Africa*, vol. I (1969), Chapters 1–4. This important work should be read in conjunction with Leonard Thompson, *African Societies in Southern Africa* (1969), of which Chapters 2–5 are relevant.

Early Iron Age archaeology in Zambia has been well served by David Phillipson, whose 'The Early Iron Age in Zambia – Regional Variants and Some Tentative Conclusions' appeared in the *Journal of African History*, vol. IX (1968). He has covered the same subject for southern Africa as a whole in L. M. Thompson, *African Societies in Southern Africa*, Chapter 2. T. N. Huffman, 'The Early Iron Age and the Spread of the Bantu', *South African Archaeological Bulletin* (1970) is another technical and detailed synthesis, in which site reports are fully utilised and referenced. Later Iron Age cultures in Zambia are described by J. O. Vogel, *Kumadzulu* (1971) and by Brian Fagan, *Iron Age Cultures in Zambia – I* (1967), a monograph dealing with the Kalomo culture. *Iron Age Cultures in Zambia – II* (1969), written by Brian Fagan in collaboration with D. W. Phillipson and S. G. H. Daniels, describes the finds at Ingombe Ilede. The dating of this important site is re-evaluated by Phillipson and Fagan, 'The Date of the Ingombe Ilede Burials', *Journal of African History*, vol. X (1969). The Leopard's Kopje culture has been described by Keith Robinson, *Khami* (1959) and 'The Leopard's Kopje Culture: Its Position in the Iron Age of Southern Rhodesia', *South African Archaeological Bulletin* (1966). T. N. Huffman, 'Excavations at Leopard's Kopje Main Kraal – Preliminary Report' in the same journal (1971) amplifies earlier work. Eastern Rhodesia is described in Roger Summers, *Inyanga* (1958).

The origins of long-distance trade and its influence upon the rise of the Karanga state have been discussed by several authors. Brian Fagan, 'Early trade and raw materials in South Central Africa', *Journal of African History*, vol. X (1969) is one synthesis, while Richard Gray and David Birmingham (eds.), *Pre-colonial African Trade* (1970) has a series of essays on the subject which cover a wider geographical area. A good study of the Karanga state is Edward Alpers, 'The Mutapa and Malawi Political Systems to the Rise of the Ngoni Invasions' in T. O. Ranger, *Aspects of Central African History* (1968), which cites the more technical literature, including the difficult but fascinating work of Donald Abraham. Zimbabwe has provoked an enormous and often quite unreliable literature. Roger Summers, *A Rhodesian Mystery* (1964) is a short account of the site, which is not always reliable. Peter Garlake,

Great Zimbabwe (1973) is a comprehensive study, which is likely to remain the definitive work on the subject for many years. This volume contains extensive documentation of the technical literature.

South Africa has received very inadequate attention from Iron Age scholars. The most up-to-date general account is still that in Brian Fagan's chapter 'The Later Iron Age in South Africa' in Leonard Thompson, *African Societies in Southern Africa* (1969). This should be read in conjunction with the first volume of the *Oxford History of South Africa* cited above. The Limpopo valley sites of Mapungubwe and Bambandyanalo were originally published by Leo Fouché, *Mapungubwe* (1937) and G. A. Gardner, *Mapungubwe*, vol. II (1963). Brian Fagan, 'The Greefswald Sequence: Bambandyanalo and Mapungubwe', *Journal of African History*, vol. V (1964) puts the two sites into a wider Iron Age context. The Uitkomst and Buispoort cultures are defined rather unsatisfactorily by Revil Mason, *The Prehistory of the Transvaal* (1962): the lack of data is obvious. Stone structures in South Africa have been described by many authors. The best articles are by Timothy Maggs, and references can be found in his 'Pastoral Settlements on the Riet River', *South African Archaeological Bulletin* (1971). Unfortunately, the Early Iron Age occurrence at Castle Cavern in Swaziland, and the Palaborwa settlements in the north-eastern Transvaal, are still largely unpublished, except for Nickolaas J. van der Merwe and Robert T. K. Scully, 'The Phalaborwa Story: Archaeological and Ethnographic Investigation of a South African Iron Age Group', *World Archaeology* (1971). Three journals, *Arnoldia* (National Museums of Rhodesia), *Azania* (British Institute in Eastern Africa) and the *South African Archaeological Bulletin*, contain many articles of a technical nature on the Iron Age archaeology of eastern and southern Africa. *The South African Journal of Science* occasionally covers the same subject.

Index

Index

Index